*Experiments in*
# Electronic Devices and Circuits
*Sixth Edition*

**Theodore F. Bogart, Jr.**
University of Southern Mississippi

**James W. Brown, Sr.**
Peavey Electronics Corporation

PEARSON
Prentice Hall

Upper Saddle River, New Jersey
Columbus, Ohio

**Editor in Chief:** Stephen Helba
**Acquisitions Editor:** Dennis Williams
**Development Editor:** Kate Linsner
**Editorial Assistant:** Lara Dimmick
**Production Editor:** Stephen C. Robb
**Design Coordinator:** Diane Y. Ernsberger
**Cover Designer:** Ali Mohrman
**Cover Art:** Digital Vision
**Production Manager:** Pat Tonneman
**Marketing Manager:** Ben Leonard

This book was printed and bound by Technical Communication Services.
The cover was printed by Phoenix Color Corp.

Copyright © 2004, 2001, 1997, 1993, 1990, 1986 by Pearson Education, Inc., Upper Saddle River, New Jersey 07458. Pearson Prentice Hall. All rights reserved. Printed in the United States of America. This publication is protected by Copyright and permission should be obtained from the publisher prior to any prohibited reproduction, storage in a retrieval system, or transmission in any form or by any means, electronic, mechanical, photocopying, recording, or likewise. For information regarding permission(s), write to: Rights and Permissions Department.

**Pearson Prentice Hall™** is a trademark of Pearson Education, Inc.
**Pearson®** is a registered trademark of Pearson plc
**Prentice Hall®** is a registered trademark of Pearson Education, Inc.

10 9 8 7 6 5 4 3 2 1

ISBN 0-13-111143-4

# *Preface*

*Experiments in Electronic Devices and Circuits, Sixth Edition*, contains thirty-three laboratory experiments and three supplemental experiments dealing with many topics covered in a traditional two- or three-semester course in electronic device theory and many modern applications of those devices. Included are experiments that give students the opportunity to construct circuits and verify theoretical relationships involving diodes, bipolar and field-effect transistors, small-signal amplifiers, frequency response, differential and operational amplifiers, electronic summation, differentiation and integration, oscillators, active filters, voltage comparators, power amplifiers, power supplies, voltage regulators, four-layer and optoelectronic devices, zener diodes, UJTs, and PUTs. Some experiments focus on device characteristics and others emphasize applications. Both discrete and integrated circuit components are used. While most experiments deal with linear circuits, many important concepts from modern digital circuits are also treated, including switching circuits like inverters, building AND gates and OR gates with diodes, BJTs, MOSFETs, Schmitt triggers, the effects of capacitive loading on rise and fall times, choppers, astable multivibrators, CMOS, and A/D and D/A converters.

Each experiment is accompanied by a set of objectives, a list of materials and equipment required, a discussion of the theoretical concepts that are investigated or verified in the experiment, and a set of questions that require students to interpret the experimental data and comment on its implications. Most of the questions require students to compare experimental results with theoretical concepts, speculate on reasons for discrepancies, and learn from deductive reasoning.

SPICE is used in the form of exercises at the end of some experiments in an effort to familiarize students with its use. Students should be encouraged to use SPICE, or some other simulation tool, to verify results, help clarify any questions on circuits, or simply investigate varying quantities and their effects on circuit response.

The sequence and scope of the experiments in this book parallel the material covered in the textbook *Electronic Devices and Circuits* (Bogart, Rico, and Beasley, Sixth edition, Prentice Hall Publishing, 2003), and each experiment refers to background material in that book. However, the discussion material with each experiment and the traditional sequence in which the experiments appear should make them usable in most introductory courses, regardless of the textbook used.

The table of contents details which chapter in the textbook coincides with each experiment. Some courses will go into more or less detail, so this organization should help instructors choose which experiments should be completed for a particular course outline.

All of the experiments have been student tested and revised where necessary to improve clarity. All of the written material and the graphics were produced on an Apple® Macintosh™ computer. The authors welcome any comments or suggestions from readers about improvements to the style, scope, or clarity of any of the experiments.

We wish to express appreciation to the many students at the University of Southern Mississippi for their cooperation while performing these experiments in their laboratory courses. We also wish to thank Phyllis Brown, who helped with the editing of the manuscript, and Clay Hamilton, who designed the layout.

James W. Brown, Sr.
Theodore F. Bogart, Jr.

Apple® is a registered trademark of Apple Computer, Inc. Macintosh™ is a trademark of McIntosh Laboratory, Inc., licensed to Apple Computer, Inc.

# Contents

| (Electronic Devices and Circuits) | (Experiments in Electronic Devices and Circuits) |
|---|---|
| (Chapters 2/3) | 1 Diode Characteristics, 1 |
| | 2 Rectifiers, Filters, and Ripple, 11 |
| | 3 Zener Diodes, 19 |
| (Chapter 4) | 4 Common-Base Characteristics, 27 |
| | 5 Common-Emitter/Common-Collector Characteristics, 35 |
| | 6 The BJT Inverter, 45 |
| (Chapter 5) | 7 JFET Biasing, 49 |
| | 8 JFET Current Source and Chopper, 55 |
| | 9 MOSFET Characteristics, 61 |
| (Chapters 6/7) | 10 Common-Base Amplifier, 71 |
| | 11 Common-Emitter Amplifier, 77 |
| | 12 Common-Collector Amplifier, 83 |
| | 13 JFET Amplifiers, 89 |
| (Chapter 8) | 14 Operational Amplifier, 95 |
| | 15 Summing and Difference Amplifier, 103 |
| (Chapter 9) | 16 Lower Cutoff Frequency, 107 |
| | 17 Upper Cutoff Frequency, 115 |
| (Chapter 10) | 18 Bandwidth, Slew Rate, and Offsets, 123 |

| | | |
|---|---|---|
| (Chapter 11) | 19 | Integration and Differentiation, 131 |
| | 20 | Active Filters, 139 |
| (Chapter 12) | 21 | Comparators, 149 |
| | 22 | Oscillators, 155 |
| | 23 | Clipping and Clamping Circuits, 161 |
| (Chapter 13) | 24 | Voltage Regulators, 167 |
| (Chapter 14) | 25 | D/A and A/D Converters, 175 |
| (Chapter 15) | 26 | SCRs and TRIACs, 181 |
| | 27 | LEDs and Optocouplers, 191 |
| | 28 | UJTs and PUTs, 199 |
| (Chapter 16) | 29 | Class-A Power Amplifiers, 207 |
| | 30 | Push-Pull Amplifiers, 213 |
| (Chapter 17) | 31 | The BJT Current Mirror, 219 |
| | 32 | Differential Amplifier, 223 |
| (Chapter 18) | 33 | CMOS Logic, 229 |

Appendix A  ß Measurement, 233
Appendix B  JFET Measurements, 235
Appendix C  SPICE, 237
Appendix D  Signal Generator Divider, 239
Appendix E  Component Pin-outs, 241

# Diode Characteristics 1

## Reference

*Electronic Devices and Circuits, Sixth Edition:* Section 3-2, The Diode as a Nonlinear Device; Section 3-3, ac and dc Resistance; Section 3-4, Analysis of dc Circuits Containing Diodes; Section 2-5, Identifying Forward- and Reverse-Bias Operating Modes

## Objectives

1. To become familiar with checking diodes using volt-ohm meters.
2. To investigate the forward- and reverse-biased characteristics of diodes.
3. To learn how to determine the dc and ac resistances of a diode.
4. To demonstrate the function of diodes in basic logic circuits.

## Equipment List

1. 2-1N4004 (NTE116) silicon diodes or the equivalent
2. Variable dc power supply (0–25 Vdc)
3. Resistors: 1-470 kΩ, 1-1 kΩ
4. Two VOMs (should have sufficient voltage to bias a diode well into its forward region when set for resistance measurement).

## Discussion

A diode is a semiconductor device that conducts current much more readily in one direction than in the other. The voltage across the diode terminals determines whether or not the diode will conduct. If the anode is more positive than the cathode, the diode will conduct current and is said to be *forward-biased*. If the cathode is more positive than the anode, the diode will conduct only an extremely small leakage current and is said to be *reverse-biased*.

# EXPERIMENT 1 - DIODE CHARACTERISTICS

When forward-biased, the voltage drop across a typical silicon diode is about 0.7 V (germanium diodes drop about 0.3 V). At forward voltages below this threshold, the diode permits only a small current to flow. This threshold is known as the *knee* of the diode characteristic curve. Since the relationship between voltage across and current through the diode changes in this region, the diode's resistance changes. The following formula is used to calculate the *dynamic* or ac resistance of the diode:

$$r_D = \frac{\Delta V}{\Delta I} \text{ ohms}$$

where:
$\Delta V$ is the small change in voltage across the diode
$\Delta I$ is the corresponding change in current through the diode

The *static* or dc resistance at any point along the characteristic curve is calculated using Ohm's law:

$$R_D = \frac{V}{I} \text{ ohms}$$

where:
V is the voltage across the diode
I is the current through the diode

These relationships can be seen in the following characteristic curve diagram:

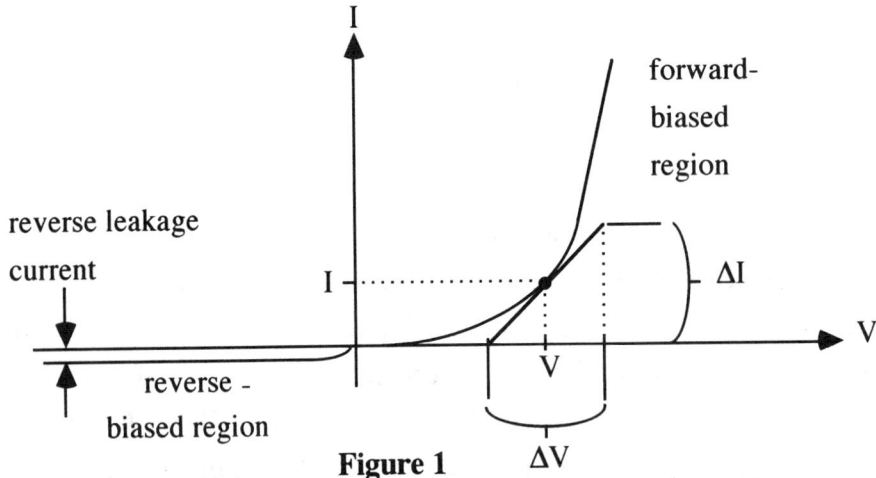

**Figure 1**

# EXPERIMENT 1 - DIODE CHARACTERISTICS

Large-signal diode circuits are those in which the current and voltage variations occur over a large range of the diode's characteristic, extending from the forward-biased region into the reverse-biased region. Thus, in large-signal circuits, diode operation is not confined to the linear region and the diode acts very much like a switch. One example of a large-signal circuit is a rectifier circuit, as in Experiment 2.

Another important application of large-signal diode circuits is that of performing digital logic functions. Digital logic *gates* are circuits that perform logical functions such as *AND* or *OR*. In the AND function, the output is *true* (a high voltage) only if both inputs are true. In the OR function the output is true if either input is true. In a typical logic circuit, an AND gate produces a 5 V output only if inputs 1 *and* 2 are both 5 V. The OR gate produces a 5 V output if either input 1 *or* input 2 is 5 V.

## Procedure

1. To determine the polarity and magnitude of the voltage at the terminals of the ohmmeter that will be used in this experiment, connect the following circuit (if only one VOM is available, substitute an oscilloscope set for DC for VOM 2):

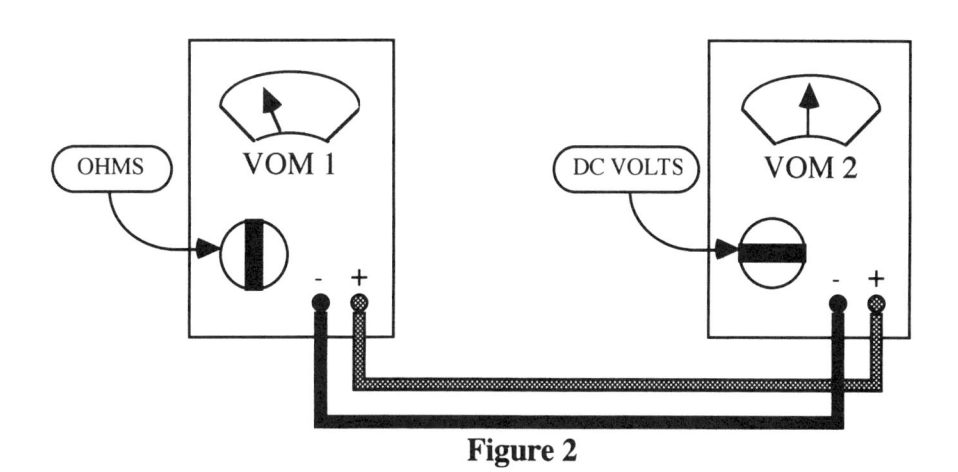

**Figure 2**

2. VOM 1 will be used to measure the resistance of a silicon diode. Use VOM 2 to determine the polarity of the voltage supplied by VOM 1 when VOM 1 is set for resistance measurement. If the voltage produced by

# EXPERIMENT 1 - DIODE CHARACTERISTICS

VOM 1 and read on VOM 2 is not at least 0.7 V, adjust the resistance scale on VOM 1 until it is. In procedure step 3, use VOM 1 with the scale setting that produces the smallest voltage greater than 0.7 V, to prevent permanent damage to the diode. The reason for determining the polarity of the voltage is that some VOMs use a negative voltage to measure resistance.

3. With the VOM 1 resistance scale set as described in procedure step 2, connect a diode between the test leads of VOM 1. Since VOMs actually measure the amount of current that flows through the resistor being measured, a large deflection means that a large current can flow (i.e. the resistance is small). If this type of deflection is observed, the diode is forward-biased. If the deflection is small, then only a small amount of current is allowed to flow (i.e. the resistance is large). If the latter condition occurs, the diode is reverse-biased. This technique can be used to determine which lead of a diode is the anode and which is the cathode.

4. Reverse the VOM connections to verify that both types of deflections can be obtained, and determine which diode terminal is the anode and which is the cathode.

5. To investigate the forward-biased characteristics of the diode, connect the following circuit:

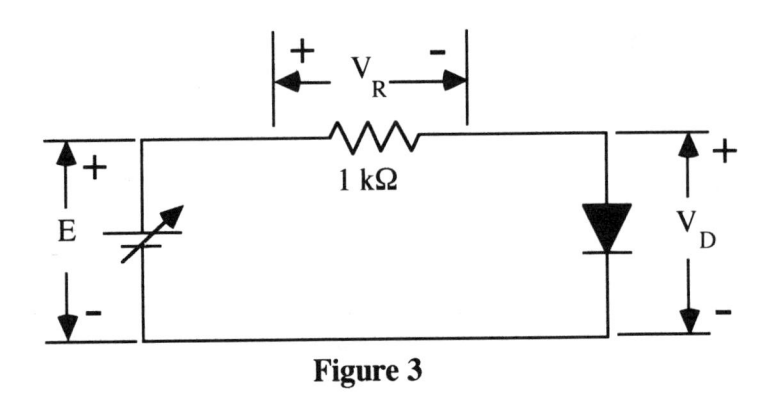

**Figure 3**

6. Adjust E so that the voltage $V_D$ across the diode increases from 0.0 V to 0.6 V, as shown in Table 1. Measure and record in Table 1 the supply voltage E and the voltage $V_R$ across the resistor for each increment of $V_D$.

7. To investigate the reverse-biased characteristics of the diode, connect the following circuit:

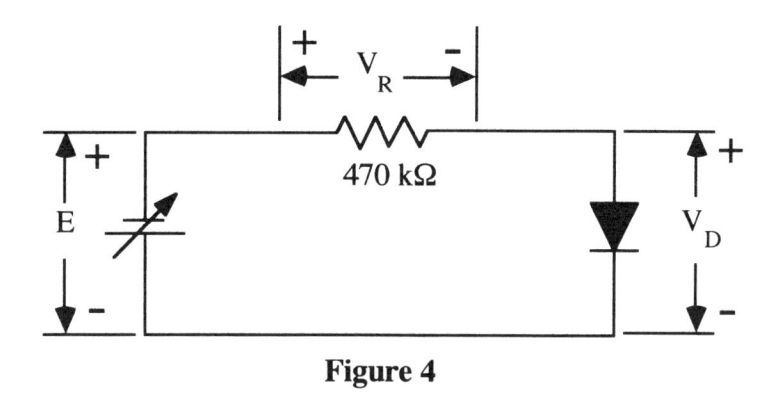

**Figure 4**

8. Adjust E so that the voltage $V_D$ across the diode decreases in decrements of 5 V from 0.0 V to –25 V, as shown in Table 2. Measure and record in Table 2 the supply voltage E for each decrement of $V_D$.

9. To investigate the use of diodes in simple digital logic gates, connect the following circuit:

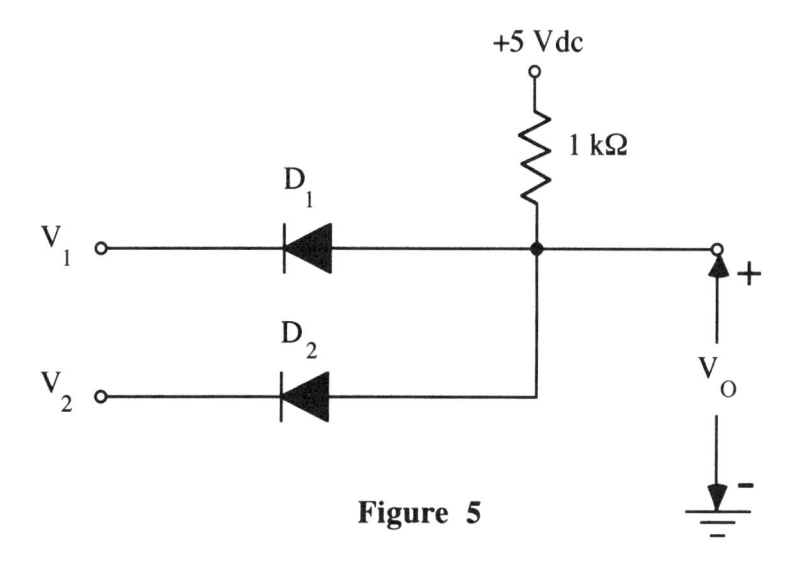

**Figure 5**

10. Measure and record the values of $V_O$ for each of the combinations of values of $V_1$ and $V_2$ in Table 3.

# EXPERIMENT 1 - DIODE CHARACTERISTICS

11. To investigate another useful logic gate, connect the following circuit:

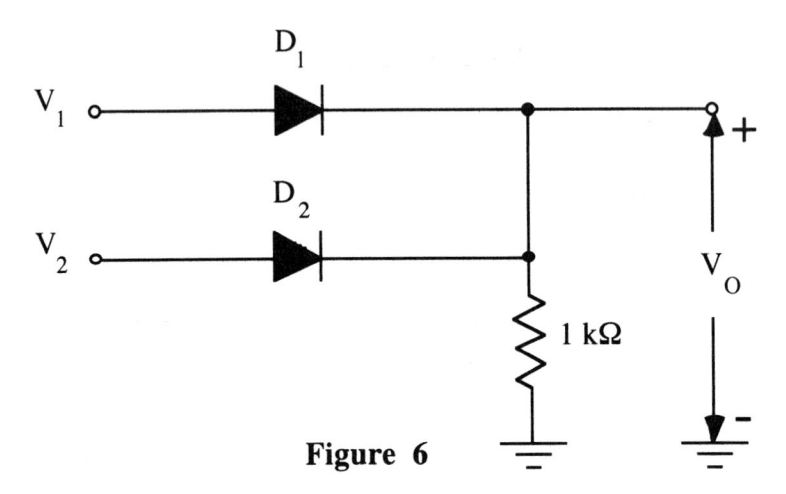

**Figure 6**

12. Measure and record the values of $V_O$ for each of the combinations of values of $V_1$ and $V_2$ in Table 4.

# EXPERIMENT 1 - DIODE CHARACTERISTICS

## QUESTIONS

1. When using a VOM to determine diode terminals as in procedure step 3, what would you conclude if you obtained:
    a. *only* high resistance measurements
    b. *only* low resistance measurements
when the diode was connected in both directions?

2. Calculate and record the current values I in Table 1; calculate the voltage $V_R$ across the resistor and current values I in Table 2.

3. Using the values obtained for I and $V_D$ in Table 1, graph the forward I-V characteristic curve of the diode. Plot I on the vertical axis and $V_D$ on the horizontal axis.

4. Determine the static resistance of the diode at 0.1 V, 0.5 V, and 0.6 V using the values obtained for I and $V_D$ from Table 1.

5. Graphically determine the dynamic resistance of the diode at 0.2 V, 0.5 V, and 0.6 V using the I-V characteristic curve obtained in question 3.

6. Using the values obtained for I and $V_D$ from Table 2, calculate the static resistance of the diode at −10 V.

7. For each set of voltages $V_1$ and $V_2$ in Tables 3 and 4, determine whether each of the diodes $D_1$ and $D_2$ is forward- or reverse-biased. Calculate $V_O$, assuming that each diode has a forward-biased voltage drop of 0.7 V. Compare the calculated values of $V_O$ with the measured values.

8. What digital logic function is performed by the circuit in Figure 5? In Figure 6?

# EXPERIMENT 1 - DIODE CHARACTERISTICS

EXPERIMENT 1 - **DIODE CHARACTERISTICS**

## Data

### TABLE 1

| $V_D$ (volts) | E (volts) | $V_R$ (volts) | $I = V_R/R$ |
|---|---|---|---|
| 0.0 | | | |
| 0.2 | | | |
| 0.4 | | | |
| 0.45 | | | |
| 0.5 | | | |
| 0.55 | | | |
| 0.6 | | | |

### TABLE 2

| $V_D$ (volts) | E (volts) | $V_R = E - V_D$ | $I = V_R/R$ |
|---|---|---|---|
| 0.0 | | | |
| -5 | | | |
| -10 | | | |
| -15 | | | |
| -20 | | | |
| -25 | | | |

### TABLE 3

| $V_1$ (volts) | $V_2$ (volts) | $V_O$ (volts) |
|---|---|---|
| 0 | 0 | |
| 0 | 5 | |
| 5 | 0 | |
| 5 | 5 | |

### TABLE 4

| $V_1$ (volts) | $V_2$ (volts) | $V_O$ (volts) |
|---|---|---|
| 0 | 0 | |
| 0 | 5 | |
| 5 | 0 | |
| 5 | 5 | |

# EXPERIMENT 1 - DIODE CHARACTERISTICS

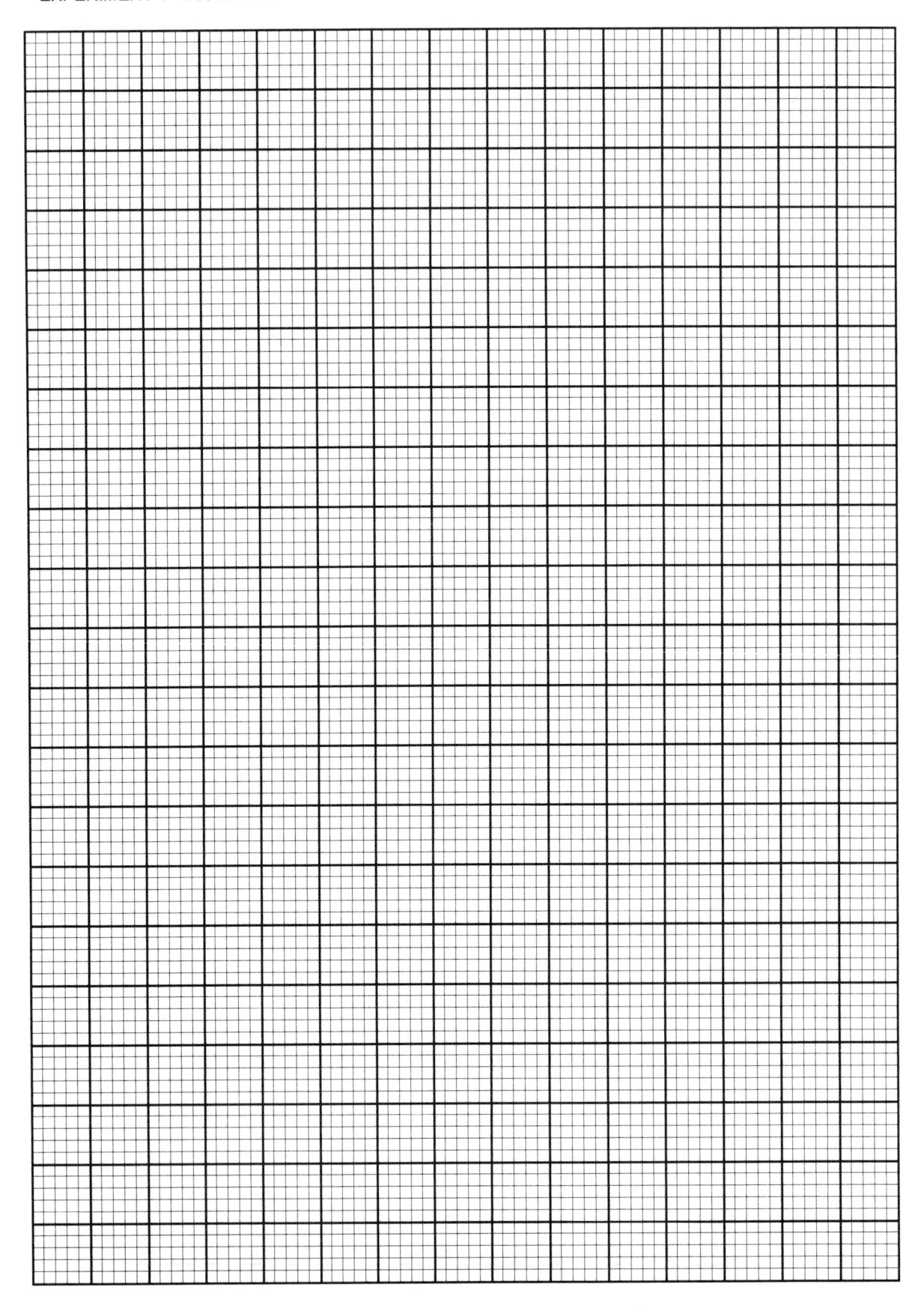

# Rectifiers, Filters, and Ripple

## Reference

*Electronic Devices and Circuits, Sixth Edition:* Section 3-5, Elementary Power Supplies

## Objectives

1. To construct half- and full-wave rectifiers.
2. To investigate the use of capacitor filters to reduce ripple.
3. To demonstrate how loading of power supplies affects ripple.
4. To demonstrate the use of RC-π filters to reduce ripple.

## Equipment List

1. 4-1N4004 (NTE 116) silicon diodes or the equivalent
2. Transformer: Triad F-192X power 24 V CT secondary (2 amp)
3. Resistors: 1-10 kΩ, 1-4.7 kΩ, 1-470 Ω
4. Capacitors: 2-220 μF (25 V), 2-47 μF (25 V)
5. Potentiometer: 50 kΩ
6. Dual-trace oscilloscope

## Discussion

A fundamental component of a dc power supply (ac to dc converter) is the *rectifier* that converts an ac input to a pulsating dc output. A half-wave rectifier allows current to flow in a load resistance during every other half-cycle of a sine wave input. A full-wave rectifier allows current to flow during every half-cycle of input, but it is designed so that current always flows in the same direction through the load resistance. Figure 1 shows half- and full-wave rectified waveforms. Figure 3 shows how a full-wave

EXPERIMENT 2 - **RECTIFIERS, FILTERS, AND RIPPLE**

rectifier can be constructed using 4 diodes (a diode *bridge*), and Figures 4 and 5 show half-wave rectifiers consisting of a single diode.

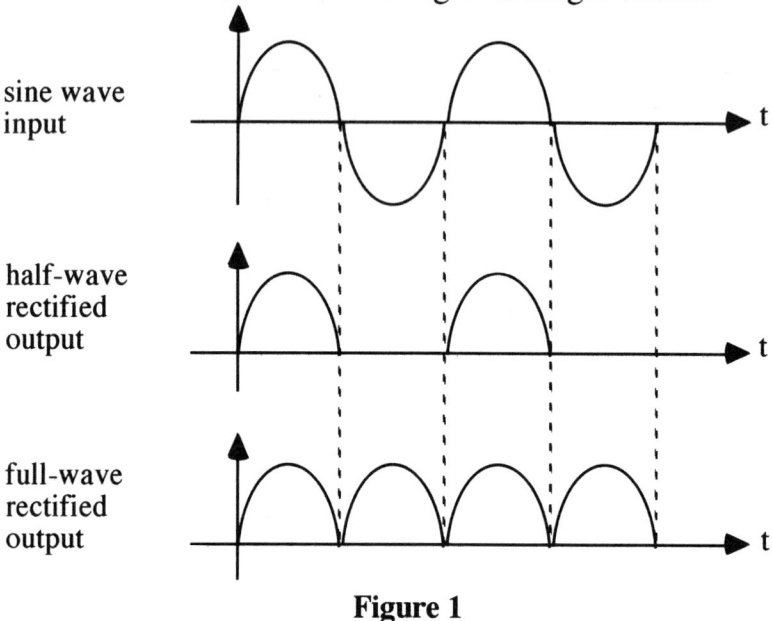

**Figure 1**

In most power-supply applications, the pulsating output of a rectifier must be *filtered* (smoothed) to reduce the voltage fluctuations. The simplest kind of filter consists of a capacitor connected directly across the rectifier, as shown in Figures 3 and 4. The RC-π filter shown in Figure 5 is also used. Filters do not eliminate voltage fluctuations entirely. Instead, a *ripple* waveform is generated as the capacitor alternately charges and discharges through the load resistance. Figure 2(a) shows a typical ripple waveform superimposed on the dc output of a filter. The smaller the $R_L C$ time constant, the greater the ripple. Figure 2(b) shows a sawtooth approximation of the ripple waveform alone. The peak-to-peak value of this sawtooth approximation can be used to estimate the rms value of the ripple:

$$V(rms) \approx \frac{V_{pp}}{2\sqrt{3}}$$

12

EXPERIMENT 2 - **RECTIFIERS, FILTERS, AND RIPPLE**

(b) Sawtooth approximation of the ripple waveform

(a) Ripple on the filtered output of a rectifier

**Figure 2**

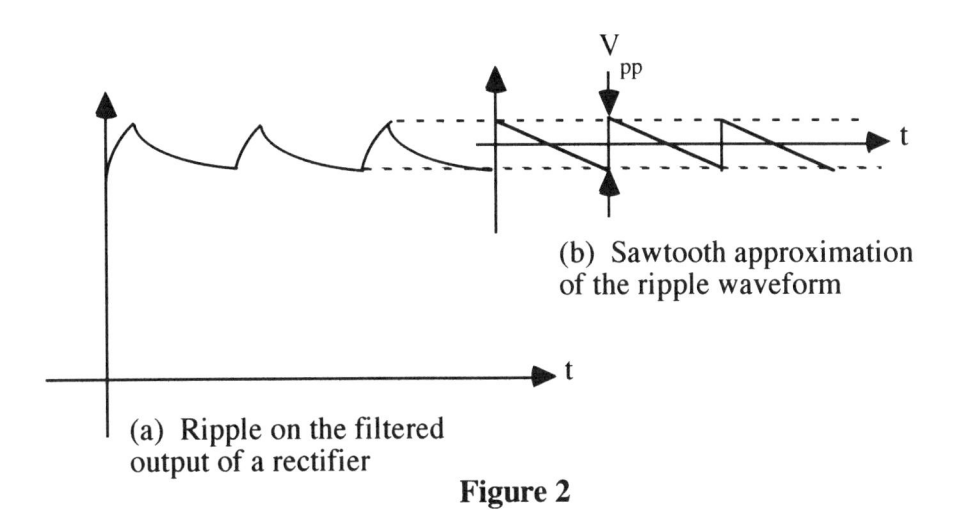

One measure of the effectiveness of a filter is the percent ripple in its output waveform:

$$\%\text{ripple} = \frac{\text{rms value of ripple waveform}}{\text{average (dc) value of entire waveform}} \times 100\%$$

A lightly loaded filter is one whose ripple is less than 6.5%. For lightly loaded capacitor filters, the following approximation can be used to estimate the percent ripple:

$$\%\text{ripple} = \frac{1}{2\sqrt{3}\, f_r R_L C} \times 100\%$$

where:
$R_L$ is the load resistance
C is the filter capacitance
$f_r$ is 60 Hz for a half-wave rectifier, 120 Hz for a full-wave rectifier (assuming the ac input to the rectifier has a frequency of 60 Hz)

The RC-$\pi$ filter shown in Figure 5 generally provides better filtering than the capacitor filter. However, because of the voltage division between $R_1$ and $R_L$, it adversely affects *voltage regulation* (to be discussed in Experiment 24) and reduces the dc value of the output.

EXPERIMENT 2 - **RECTIFIERS, FILTERS, AND RIPPLE**

## *Procedure*

1. To demonstrate the effect of filtering on the percent ripple of a power supply, connect the circuit in Figure 3. Momentarily omit the 220 µF filter capacitor. (**WARNING:** 120 V ac power is dangerous. Make all connections *before* applying power. Do not change any connections or touch any terminals with power applied. Always disconnect power before removing any component or inserting any new component. Note that the common (ground) side of the output must be isolated from the 120 V ac input.)

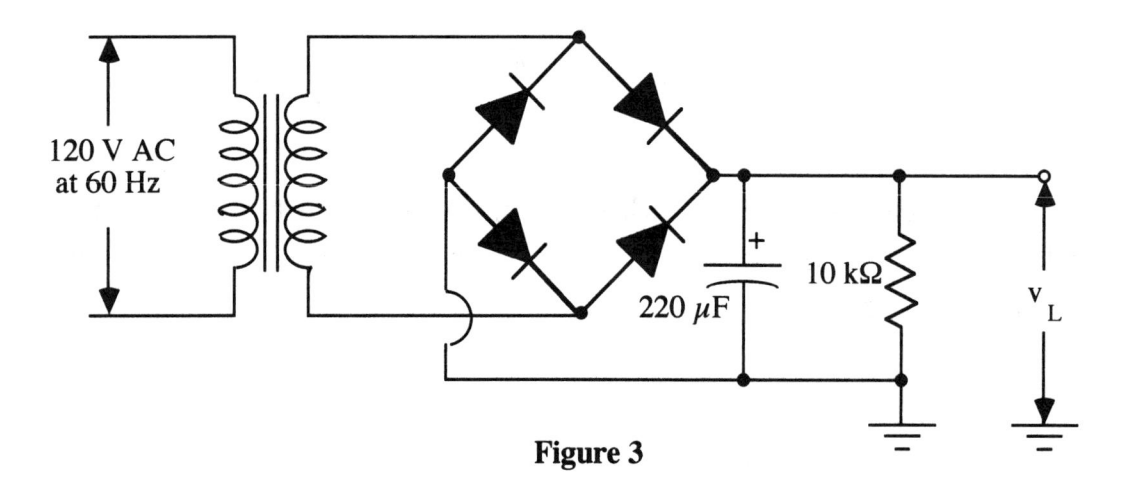

**Figure 3**

2. Using an oscilloscope with dc input coupling, observe and sketch the waveform across the 10 kΩ resistor. Then disconnect the ac power and connect the 220 µF capacitor, as shown in Figure 3. Reconnect the ac power.

3. With the oscilloscope input coupling set to ac, measure and record the peak-to-peak ripple voltage of the output $v_L$. (Adjust the vertical sensitivity of the oscilloscope so that the total deflection is large enough to make an accurate measurement.) Record this value. To measure the dc

EXPERIMENT 2 - RECTIFIERS, FILTERS, AND RIPPLE

(average) value of the output, the sensitivity must be readjusted so that the trace does not disappear when the coupling mode is changed from ac to dc. When this adjustment has been made, measure the voltage at a point on the ac-coupled waveform and at the same point on the dc-coupled waveform. The difference between these values is the dc value of the waveform.

4. Disconnect the 120 V ac power and add another 220 $\mu$F capacitor in parallel with the 220 $\mu$F capacitor in Figure 3. Reconnect power and repeat procedure step 2. (The total capacitance in the circuit is now 440 $\mu$F.)

5. To demonstrate the loading effect of small resistances on power supply ripple, connect the circuit in Figure 4. Observe the WARNING notes in step 1.

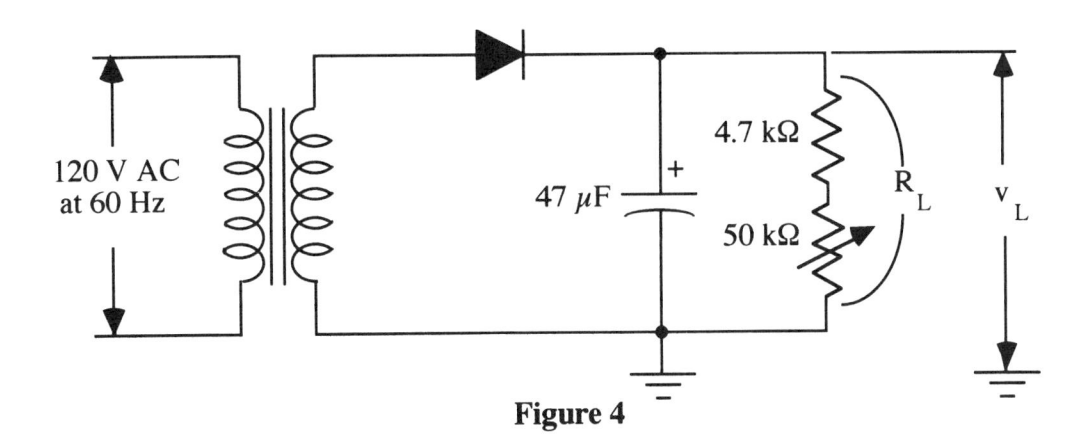

**Figure 4**

6. With the oscilloscope set for ac input coupling, vary the potentiometer and note how the magnitude of the ripple is affected.

7. Observing the WARNING notes in step 1, replace the potentiometer with a short circuit (so $R_L$ = 4.7 k$\Omega$). Using the procedure described in step 3, measure the peak-to-peak ripple voltage and the dc value of $v_L$.

8. Remove the capacitor and sketch the waveform observed across $R_L$. Observe the WARNING notes in step 1.

15

## EXPERIMENT 2 - RECTIFIERS, FILTERS, AND RIPPLE

9. To demonstrate ripple reduction by an RC-π filter, connect the circuit in Figure 5. Observe the WARNING notes in step 1.

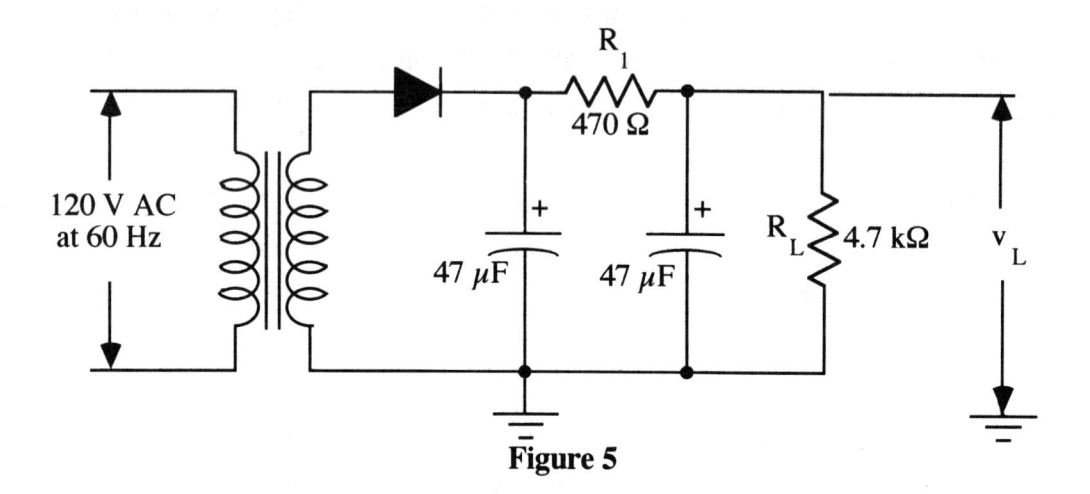

**Figure 5**

10. Using the procedure described in step 3, measure the peak-to-peak ripple and the dc value of $R_L$.

## EXPERIMENT 2 - RECTIFIERS, FILTERS, AND RIPPLE

## Questions

1. Using the measured values of ripple voltage and dc voltage obtained in procedure steps 3 and 4, calculate the percent ripple in each filter output. (Use the approximation given in the Discussion to determine the rms ripple voltage.) Are the filters lightly loaded?

2. Using the theoretical approximation for percent ripple of a lightly loaded capacitor filter, calculate the percent ripple of each of the filters constructed in procedure steps 3 and 4.

3. Describe how load resistance affects ripple, based on your observations in procedure step 6. Account for your observations, with reference to the $R_L C$ time-constant.

4. Compare the waveform observed in procedure step 8 with that observed in procedure step 2. Identify each type by name. Which waveform do you think would be more desirable, from the standpoint of ease of filtering?

5. Compare the peak-to-peak ripple measured in procedure step 10 with that obtained in procedure step 7. (Note that both circuits have the same value of $R_L$.) Also compare the dc value of the waveform obtained in procedure step 10 with that obtained in procedure step 7. How do you account for the difference in ripple values? In dc values?

## SPICE

Plot the .TRAN output of Figure 3 using a 120 VAC, 60 Hz voltage source instead of the transformer. Replot this with lower value loads to demonstrate the effect this has on ripple.

# EXPERIMENT 2 - RECTIFIERS, FILTERS, AND RIPPLE

# Zener Diodes 3

## Reference

*Electronic Devices and Circuits, Sixth Edition:* Section 3-6, Elementary Voltage Regulation

## Objectives

1. To construct the I-V characteristic of a zener diode.
2. To demonstrate the use of zener diodes as voltage regulators.
3. To measure the line regulation and output resistance of a zener diode regulator.

## Equipment List

1. 1N4736 (NTE 5071) 6.8 V (1 W) zener diode
2. Variable dc power supply (0–15 V)
3. Resistors: 1-10 kΩ, 1-8.2 kΩ, 1-6.8 kΩ, 1-4.7 kΩ, 1-2.2 kΩ, 1-1 kΩ, 1-560 Ω, 1-100 Ω
4. Digital voltmeter and dc ammeter

## Discussion

If the reverse voltage across a semiconductor diode is made sufficiently large, the diode *breaks down* and conducts heavily in the reverse direction. Breakdown does not damage a diode unless the reverse current is so large that the rated power dissipation of the diode is exceeded.

The voltage at which a diode breaks down is a function of the doping level of the semiconductor materials from which it is constructed. A zener diode is heavily doped to give it a relatively small breakdown voltage, in comparison to conventional diodes. It is designed to be operated in its reverse breakdown region, where the voltage across it remains essentially

# EXPERIMENT 3 - ZENER DIODES

constant as the (reverse) current through it is changed. This property of maintaining a constant voltage makes the zener diode useful in voltage regulator applications and as a voltage reference. Figure 1 shows a typical I-V characteristic for a zener diode, where the breakdown (zener) voltage is designated $V_Z$. Note that the forward-biased characteristic is like that of a conventional diode.

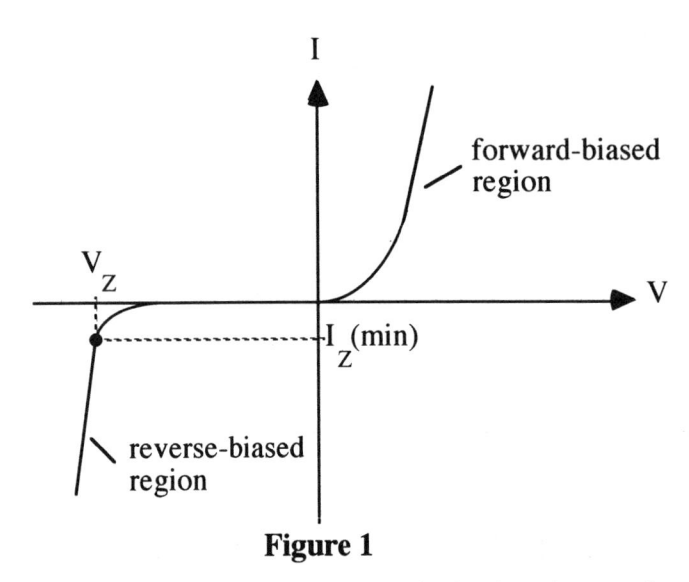

**Figure 1**

If the zener diode whose characteristic is shown in Figure 1 were *ideal*, the reverse-biased region would be perfectly vertical. In that case, $V_Z$ would remain absolutely constant as the reverse current changed to different values in the breakdown region. In other words, we would find that $\Delta V_Z/\Delta I_Z = 0$, since the change in voltage, $\Delta V_Z$, would equal zero. The impedance of a zener diode in its breakdown region is defined by:

$$Z_Z = \frac{\Delta V_Z}{\Delta I_Z}$$

The impedance of practical zener diodes is not zero but is often small enough to permit their use as voltage references—devices that maintain an essentially constant voltage when the current through them is changed.

Figure 4 shows a simple voltage regulator using a zener diode. The diode is operated in its reverse breakdown region, and the load voltage is the same as the zener voltage, $V_Z$. For the circuit to operate properly, the reverse current through the diode must be sufficiently large at all times to keep it in breakdown. The following factors must be considered in the design and use of the zener diode regulator:

1. The input voltage E (which represents a fluctuating, unregulated input) must always be large enough to supply breakdown current to the diode and to supply load current to $R_L$.
2. The load $R_L$ must not become so small and draw so much current that insufficient current is available to keep the diode in breakdown. (For example, if $R_L$ were a short circuit, no current would flow in the diode.)
3. The power dissipation in the zener diode, $P_Z = V_Z I_Z$, must not exceed the manufacturer's rated maximum. (If the load is open-circuited, *all* of the current from input E flows through the zener diode.)

Conditions 1 and 2 require large values of E and $R_L$, while condition 3 requires small values of E and $R_L$. The series limiting resistance, $R_S$, in Figure 4 is critical from the standpoint of ensuring that all conditions are met. The following inequalities impose a range on the permissible values of $R_S$:

$$R_S \leq \frac{E(min) - V_Z}{I_Z(min) + V_Z / R_L(min)}$$

$$R_S \geq \frac{E(max) - V_Z}{I_Z(max) + V_Z / R_L(max)}$$

where:
- E(min) and E(max) are the minimum and maximum values of the unregulated input
- $I_Z$(min) is the minimum reverse current required to keep the diode in breakdown (see Figure 1)
- $I_Z$(max) is the maximum reverse current that can be tolerated without exceeding the rated power dissipation of the diode:
$$I_Z(max) \leq P_Z/V_Z$$
- $R_L$(min) and $R_L$(max) are the minimum and maximum values of the load resistance

# EXPERIMENT 3 - ZENER DIODES

## Procedure

1. To determine the forward-biased characteristic of the zener diode, connect the circuit in Figure 2:

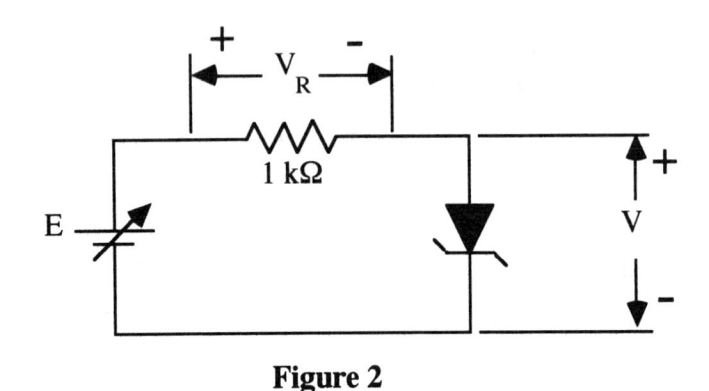

**Figure 2**

2. Adjust the applied voltage, E, so that the voltage V across the zener diode equals each value in Table 1. For each value of V, measure the voltage across the resistor (to determine the forward current through the zener diode).

3. To determine the reverse-biased characteristic of the zener diode, reverse the polarity of the power supply and replace the 1 kΩ resistor with 100 Ω, as shown in Figure 3:

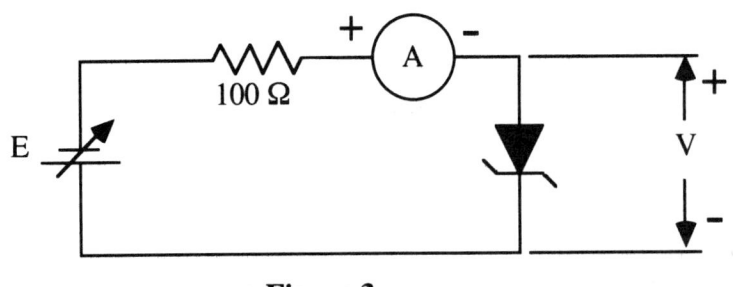

**Figure 3**

4. Adjust the applied voltage, E, so that the current through the zener diode equals each value in Table 2. For each value of $I_z$, measure the voltage V across the zener diode.

# EXPERIMENT 3 - ZENER DIODES

5. To demonstrate the use of a zener diode as a voltage regulator, connect the following circuit:

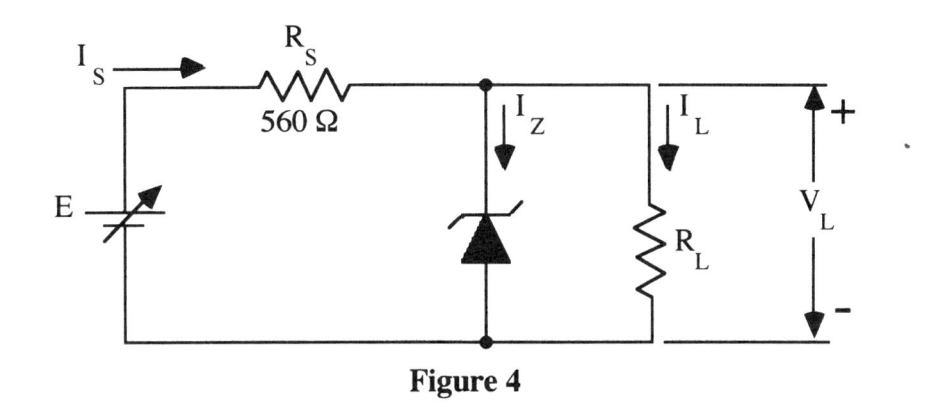

**Figure 4**

6. To determine line regulation, with $R_L$ = 10 kΩ, set E to 10 V. Measure the load voltage $V_L$. Repeat this procedure for each value of E listed in Table 3.

7. To determine the output resistance of the regulator, with E = 10 V and $R_L$ = 10 kΩ, measure the load voltage $V_L$. Repeat this procedure for each value of $R_L$ listed in Table 4.

# EXPERIMENT 3 - ZENER DIODES

## Questions

1. Using the values obtained for Tables 1 and 2, construct a graph of the characteristic curve of the zener diode.

2. Calculate the impedance, $Z_Z$, of the zener diode in the reverse breakdown region between $I_Z = 5$ mA and $I_Z = 30$ mA.

3. Using the values obtained for Table 3, calculate the line regulation, $\Delta V_L/\Delta E$, for the voltage regulator circuit of Figure 4.

4. Using the values obtained for Table 4, calculate the output resistance, $\Delta V_L/\Delta I_L$, of the voltage regulator over the range of measurements made.

5. For each value of load resistance in Table 4, calculate the power dissipated in the zener diode. Do any of the values of the power dissipation in the zener diode exceed the rated dissipation of the diode?

6. Verify that the value of $R_S$ used in Figure 4 is appropriate for the range of load resistances and input voltages at which the regulator was tested in this experiment. Use the graph drawn for question 1 to determine a value for $I_Z(min)$.

## SPICE

Use the .DC command to adjust the line voltage in Figure 4. To model the zener diode, use a diode with a BV (breakdown voltage) equal to the zener voltage. With $R_L$ set to 1 k$\Omega$, run SPICE to determine the minimum value source that will keep the zener diode in "regulation."

# EXPERIMENT 3 - ZENER DIODES

**Data**

## TABLE 1

| V(volts) | $V_R$(volts) | $I = V_R/R$ |
|---|---|---|
| 0.1 | | |
| 0.3 | | |
| 0.5 | | |
| 0.6 | | |

## TABLE 2

| I | V (volts) |
|---|---|
| 50 $\mu$A | |
| 100 $\mu$A | |
| 1 mA | |
| 5 mA | |
| 10 mA | |
| 15 mA | |
| 20 mA | |
| 30 mA | |

## TABLE 3

| E (volts) | $V_L$ (volts) |
|---|---|
| 10 V | |
| 11 V | |
| 13 V | |
| 15 V | |

## TABLE 4

| $R_L$ | $V_L$(volts) | $I_L = V_L/R_L$ | $I_S = (E-V_L)/R_S$ | $I_Z = I_S - I_L$ | $P_Z = V_L I_Z$ |
|---|---|---|---|---|---|
| 10 k$\Omega$ | | | | | |
| 8.2 k$\Omega$ | | | | | |
| 6.8 k$\Omega$ | | | | | |
| 4.7 k$\Omega$ | | | | | |
| 2.2 k$\Omega$ | | | | | |

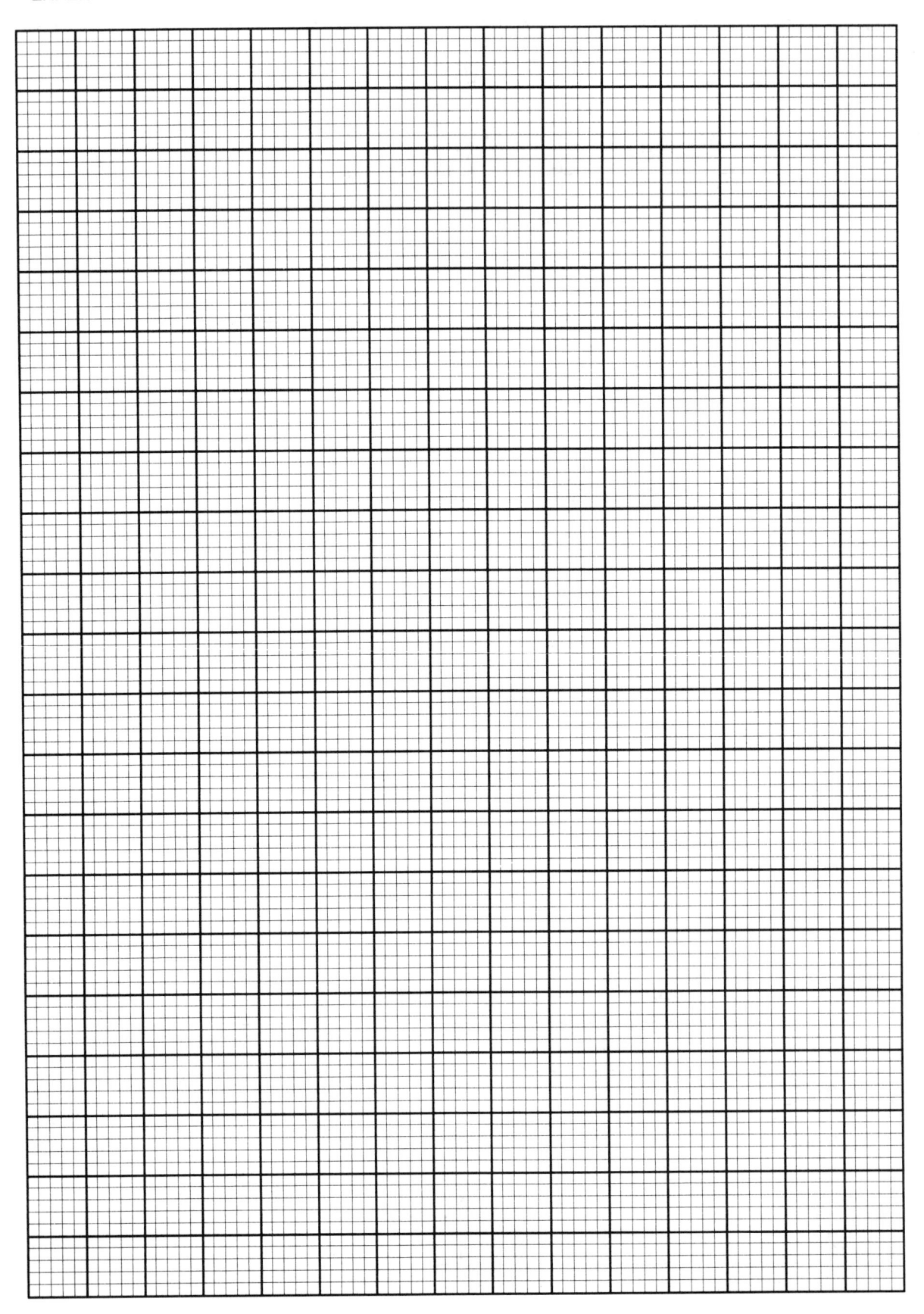

# EXPERIMENT 3 - ZENER DIODES

# Common-Base Characteristics 4

## Reference

*Electronic Devices and Circuits, Sixth Edition:* Section 4-3, Common-Base Characteristics

## Objective

To construct a set of common-base input and output characteristic curves based on laboratory measurements.

## Equipment List

1. 2N2222 silicon transistor or the equivalent
2. Two variable dc power supplies (0–40 V)
3. Resistors: 2-1 kΩ, 1-4.7 kΩ, 1-22 kΩ
4. VOM

## Discussion

In bipolar transistor amplifier circuits, one of the three transistor terminals is typically connected to ground. Later, in amplifier circuits, it will be apparent that the input signal and the output signal have this terminal in common. The three different choices of common terminals determine three different biasing configurations. Each configuration has its own particular characteristic curves for both the input circuitry and the output circuitry.

In the *common-base* configuration, the base is grounded and the input current and voltage are the emitter current $I_E$ and the base-to-emitter voltage $V_{BE}$, respectively. The output current and voltage are the collector

27

# EXPERIMENT 4 - COMMON-BASE CHARACTERISTICS

current $I_C$ and the collector-to-base voltage $V_{CB}$, respectively. The ratio of collector current to emitter current is called the *current gain*, $\alpha$ :

$$\alpha = \frac{I_C}{I_E}$$

Figure 1 shows typical *input characteristics* of a common-base transistor circuit. These characteristics display the relationship of input current $I_E$ to input voltage $V_{BE}$ for different output voltages $V_{CB}$:

**Figure 1**

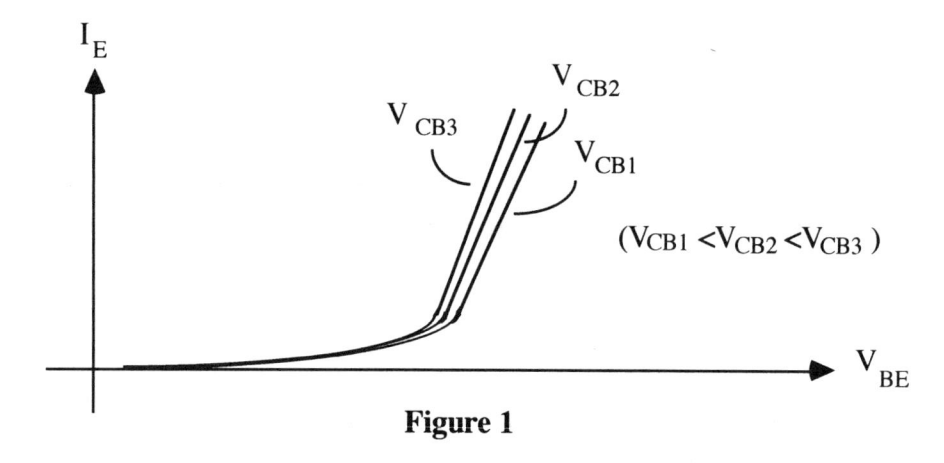

Figure 2 shows typical *output characteristics* of a common-base transistor circuit. These characteristics display the relationship of output current $I_C$ to output voltage $V_{CB}$ for various input currents $I_E$:

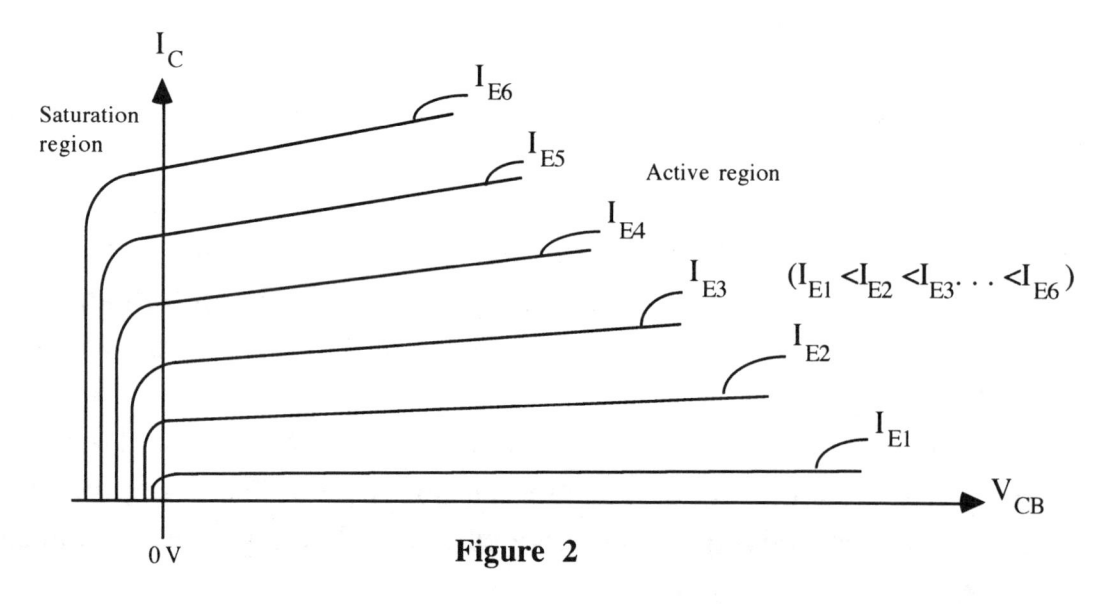

**Figure 2**

# EXPERIMENT 4 - COMMON-BASE CHARACTERISTICS

## Procedure

1. To measure the transistor's common-base input characteristics, connect the following circuit:

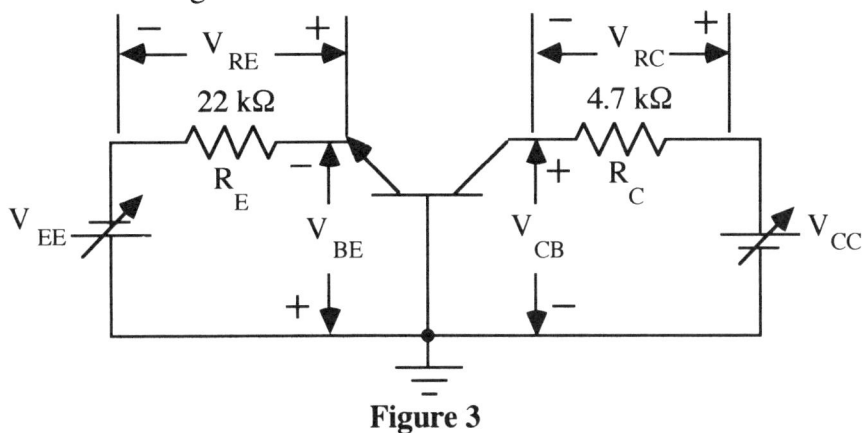

**Figure 3**

2. Adjust $V_{CC}$ to obtain $V_{CB}$ of 5 V. Then adjust $V_{EE}$ to obtain $V_{BE}$ of 0 V as shown in Table 1. $V_{CC}$ may have to be readjusted to retain the desired value for $V_{CB}$. Measure and record $V_{RE}$, which can be used to determine the emitter current $I_E$. Repeat this procedure for all values of $V_{BE}$ in the corresponding column of Table 1.

3. Repeat procedure step 2 for each of the values of $V_{CB}$ in Table 1.

4. To measure the transistor's common-base output characteristics, connect the following circuit:

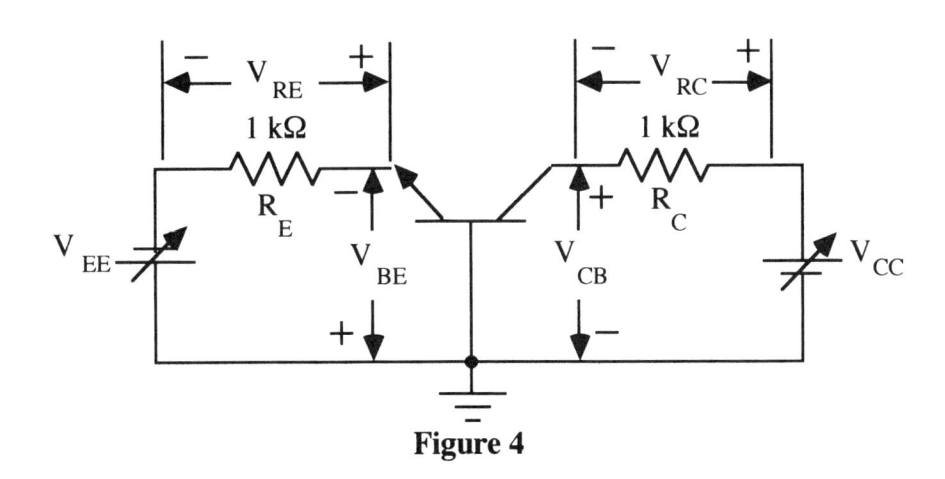

**Figure 4**

# EXPERIMENT 4 - COMMON-BASE CHARACTERISTICS

  5. Adjust $V_{EE}$ to obtain $I_E$ of 1 mA ($V_{RE}$ = 1 V). Adjust $V_{CC}$ to obtain $V_{CB}$ as shown in Table 2. The polarity of $V_{CC}$ may have to be reversed or readjusted to obtain the desired values for both $I_E$ and $V_{CB}$. Measure and record $V_{RC}$, which can be used to determine the collector current $I_C$.

  6. Repeat procedure 5 for all values of $I_E$ in Table 2.

## Questions

  1. Calculate and record the values of $I_E$ in Table 1. Using this information, plot the common-base input characteristics as shown in Figure 1.

  2. Calculate and record the values of $I_C$ in Table 2. Using this information, plot the common-base output characteristics as shown in Figure 2.

  3. Using the values of the output characteristic obtained in the third column ($I_E$ = 3 mA) of Table 2, calculate the common-base current gain $\alpha$ for each setting of $V_{CB}$. Explain why $\alpha$ is different in different regions of the characteristic.

  4. Another name for the active region of a transistor's output characteristics is the *linear region*. Explain the name linear region, in terms of $I_C$ and $I_E$, using the plot obtained from question 2.

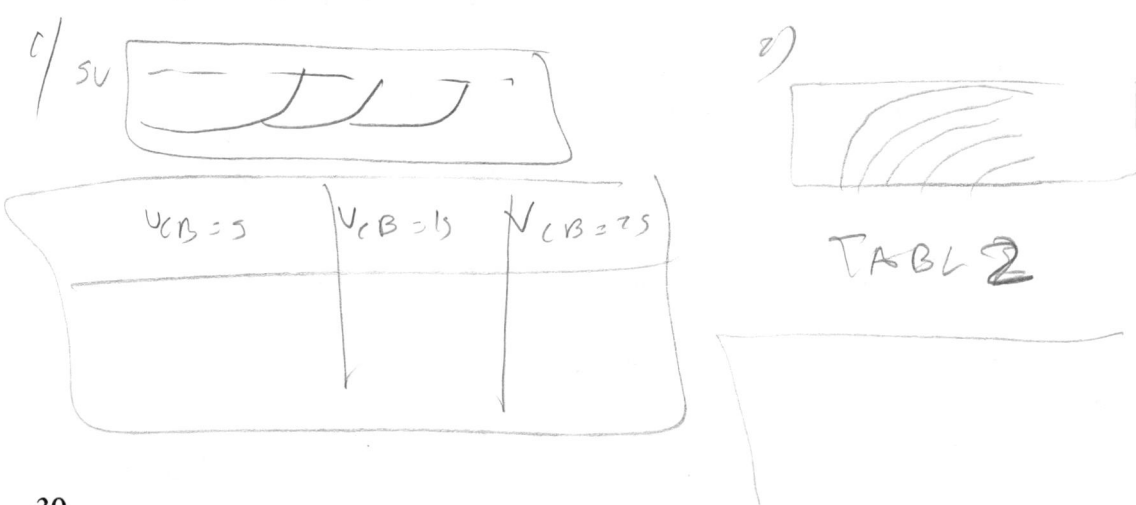

EXPERIMENT 4 - COMMON-BASE CHARACTERISTICS

## Data

3/ DATA sheet 1st page only
4/ Answer dsts on End

### TABLE 1

$R_E = 22k$

| $V_{CB} = 5$ V ||| $V_{CB} = 15$ V ||| $V_{CB} = 25$ V |||
|---|---|---|---|---|---|---|---|---|
| $V_{BE}$ | $V_{RE}$ | $I \approx V_{RE}/R_E$ | $V_{BE}$ | $V_{RE}$ | $I \approx V_{RE}/R_E$ | $V_{BE}$ | $V_{RE}$ | $I \approx V_{RE}/R_E$ |
| 0 V | 0.02m | 0 | 0 V | 0 | | 0 V | .00006 | |
| 0.2 V | 00.5m | | 0.2 V | .00002 | | 0.2 V | .00012 | |
| 0.4 V | 3.2m | | 0.4 V | .004 | | 0.4 V | .043 | |
| 0.5 V | 0.165 | | 0.5 V | 0.183 | | 0.5 V | .211 | |
| 0.55 V | 1.54 | | 0.55 V | 1.14 | | 0.55 V | 1.31 | |
| 0.6 V | 5.41 | | 0.6 V | 8.5 | | 0.6 V | 9.28 | |

### TABLE 2

$R_C = 1k$

| $V_{CB}$ | $I_E = 1$ mA || $I_E = 2$ mA || $I_E = 3$ mA || $I_E = 4$ mA || $I_E = 5$ mA ||
|---|---|---|---|---|---|---|---|---|---|---|
| | $V_{RC}$ | $I_C = V_{RC}/R_C$ | $V_{RC}$ | $I_C = V_{RC}/R_C$ | $V_{RC}$ | $I_C = V_{RC}/R_C$ | $V_{RC}$ | $I_C = V_{RC}/R_C$ | $V_{RC}$ | $I_C = V_{RC}/R_C$ |
| -.65 V | .01 | | .014 | | .056 | | .068 | | .73 | |
| -0.5 V | 0.151 | | 0.185 | | .205 | | .214 | | .223 | |
| 0.0 V | 0.613 | | .670 | | .691 | | .705 | | .716 | |
| 5 V | 0.979 | | 2 | | 2.991 | | 3.90 | | 4.85 | |
| 10 V | .980 | | 2 | | 2.991 | | 3.978 | | 4.85 | |
| 15 V | .981 | | 2 | | 3 | | 3.97 | | 4.9 | |

# EXPERIMENT 4 - COMMON-BASE CHARACTERISTICS

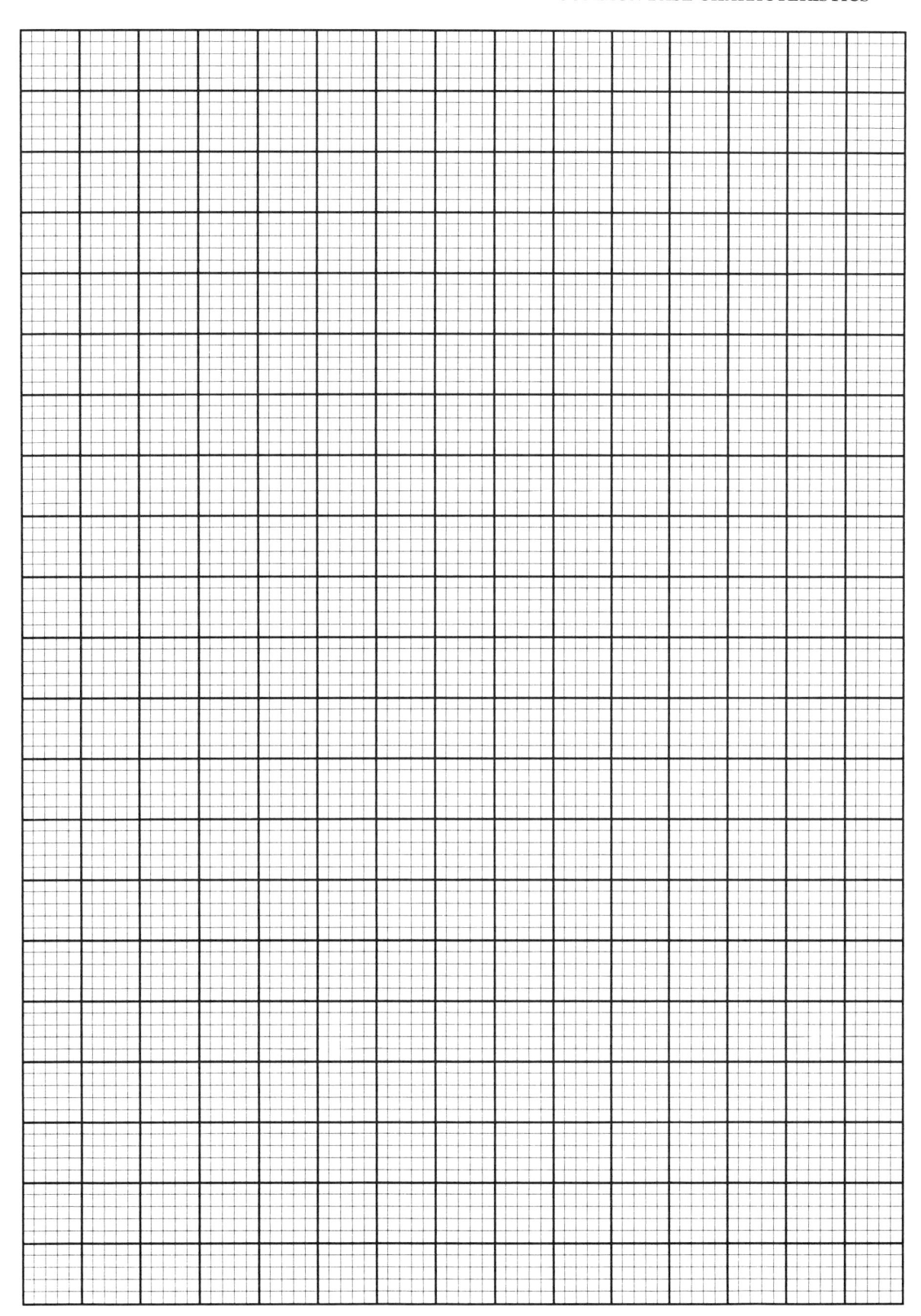

EXPERIMENT 4 - **COMMON-BASE CHARACTERISTICS**

# EXPERIMENT 4 - COMMON-BASE CHARACTERISTICS

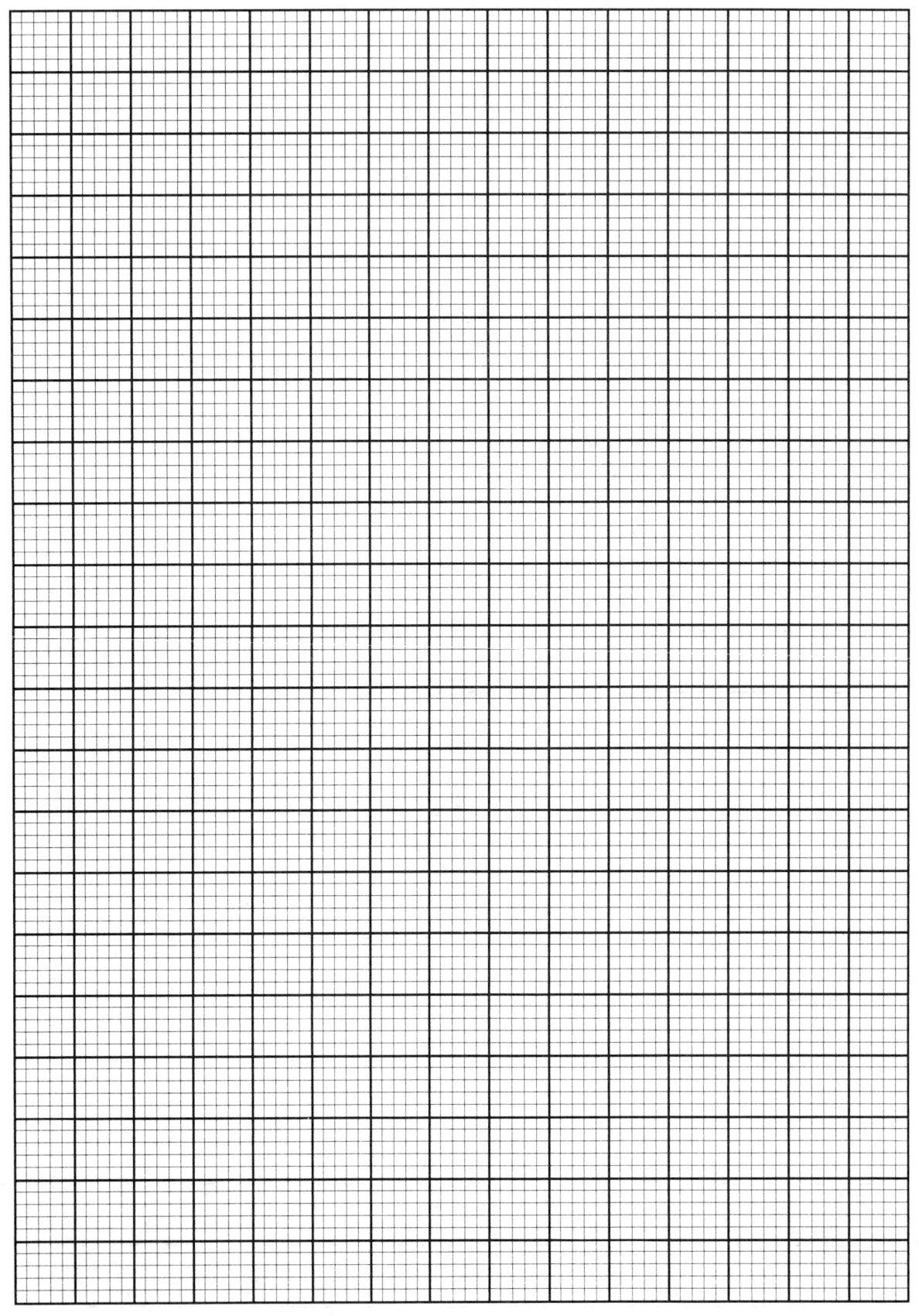

# Common-Emitter/Common-Collector Characteristics

## Reference

*Electronic Devices and Circuits, Sixth Edition:* Section 4-4, Common-Emitter Characteristics; Section 4-5, Common-Collector Characteristics

## Objectives

1. To construct input and output characteristics for the common-emitter and common-collector biasing arrangements based on laboratory measurements.
2. To determine the current gain of the common-emitter and common-collector configurations.

## Equipment List

1. 2N2222 silicon transistor or the equivalent
2. DC power supply (10 V)
3. Resistors: 1-1 kΩ, 1-100 Ω
4. Potentiometers: 1-1 MΩ, 1-10 kΩ (preferably 10-turn)
5. 2-VOMs

## Discussion

The two transistor bias methods discussed in this experiment are the common-emitter and the common-collector, or emitter follower. As discussed in Experiment 4, the common terminal is the one that will be common to input and output in an ac amplifier, i.e., ac grounded. The different bias configurations will affect the various parameters of the ac amplifier. These parameters will be discussed in a later experiment.

The transistor bias arrangement used most frequently for signal amplification is called the common-emitter configuration, in which the

## EXPERIMENT 5 - COMMON-EMITTER/COMMON-COLLECTOR CHARACTERISTICS

emitter terminal is grounded. In the common-emitter configuration, the input current and voltage are $I_B$ and $V_{BE}$, respectively. The output current and voltage are $I_C$ and $V_{CE}$, respectively. The ratio of collector current to base current is called the *current gain*, ß:

$$\beta = \frac{I_C}{I_B}$$

The relationship between ß and $\alpha$ is:

$$\beta = \frac{\alpha}{1-\alpha}$$

Figure 1 shows the input characteristics of the common-emitter biasing configuration. These characteristics display the relationship between base current and base-to-emitter voltage for a constant collector-to-emitter voltage:

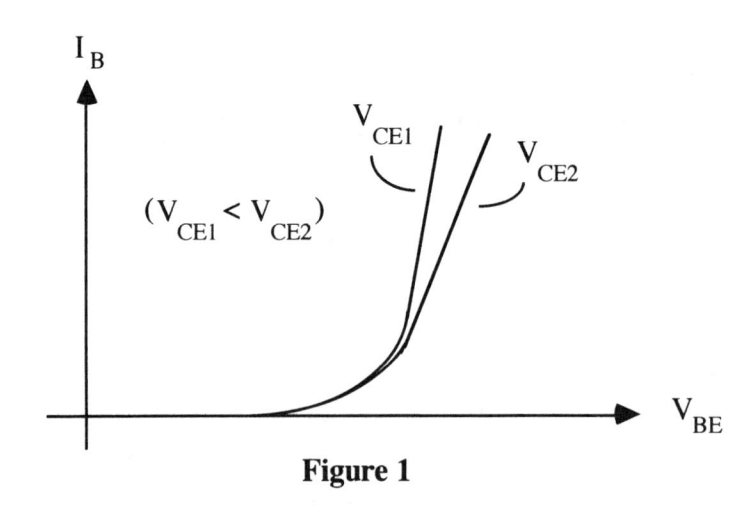

**Figure 1**

The common-collector configuration is important because it can be used for an amplifier requiring high input resistance and low output resistance—often called a buffer.

# EXPERIMENT 5 - COMMON-EMITTER/COMMON-COLLECTOR CHARACTERISTICS

Figure 2 shows the input characteristics of the common-collector biasing configuration. These characteristics display the relationship between base current and collector-to-base voltage for a constant $V_{CE}$:

**Figure 2**

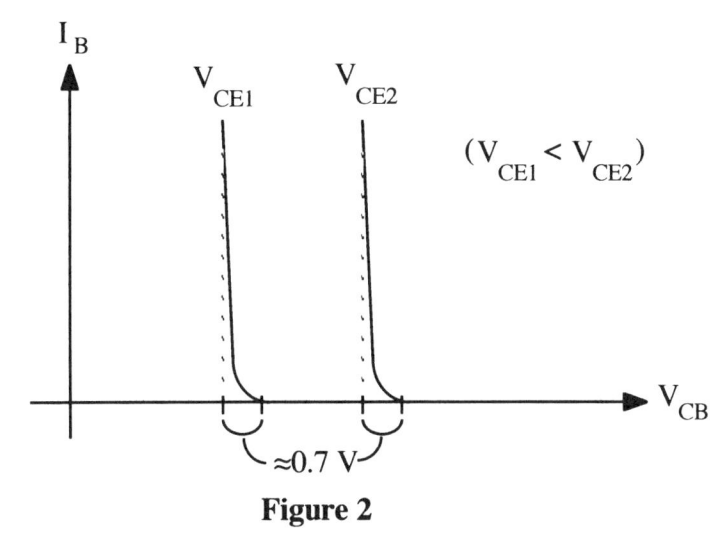

Figure 3 shows the output characteristics of the common-emitter configuration. The common-collector output characteristics are similar, except the vertical axis is $I_E$ ($I_E \approx I_C$). These characteristics display collector (or emitter) current versus collector-to-emitter voltage, for each particular amount of base current:

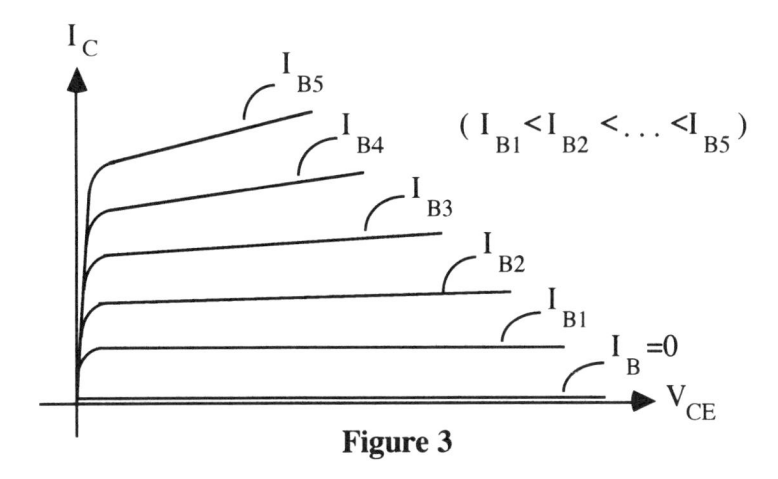

**Figure 3**

# EXPERIMENT 5 - COMMON-EMITTER/COMMON-COLLECTOR CHARACTERISTICS

## Procedure

1. To determine the input characteristics of the common-emitter configuration, connect the following circuit:

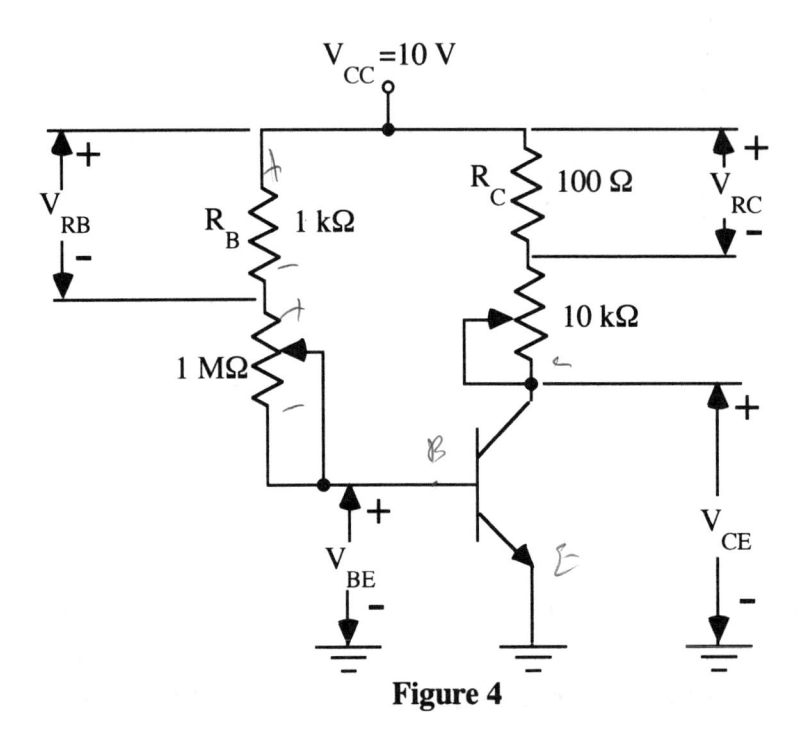

**Figure 4**

2. Adjust the 1 MΩ and 10 kΩ potentiometers to set $V_{CE}$ and $V_{BE}$, as shown in Table 1. Measure and record the voltage $V_{RB}$ across the 1 kΩ resistor, for each combination of $V_{CE}$ and $V_{BE}$ in Table 1. To set $V_{CE}$ and $V_{BE}$ for smaller values, it may be necessary to increase the values of the potentiometers by adding series resistance. It may also be necessary to use two VOMs in order to keep $V_{CE}$ constant.

3. To determine the output characteristics of the common-emitter configuration, set the 10 kΩ potentiometer in the circuit of Figure 4 to its maximum setting. This will cause $V_{CE}$ to decrease to approximately 0 V. Then adjust the 1 MΩ potentiometer to set $I_B$ to 10 μA (note that when $V_{RB}$ is 10 mV, $I_B$ is 10 μA). Next adjust the 10 kΩ potentiometer for all values of $V_{CE}$ in Table 2 making sure that $I_B$ remains constant.

# EXPERIMENT 5 - COMMON-EMITTER/COMMON-COLLECTOR CHARACTERISTICS

4. Measure and record in Table 2 the voltage $V_{RC}$ across the 100 Ω resistor for each combination of $V_{CE}$ and $I_B$ in Table 2.

5. To measure the input characteristics of the common-collector configuration, connect the following circuit:

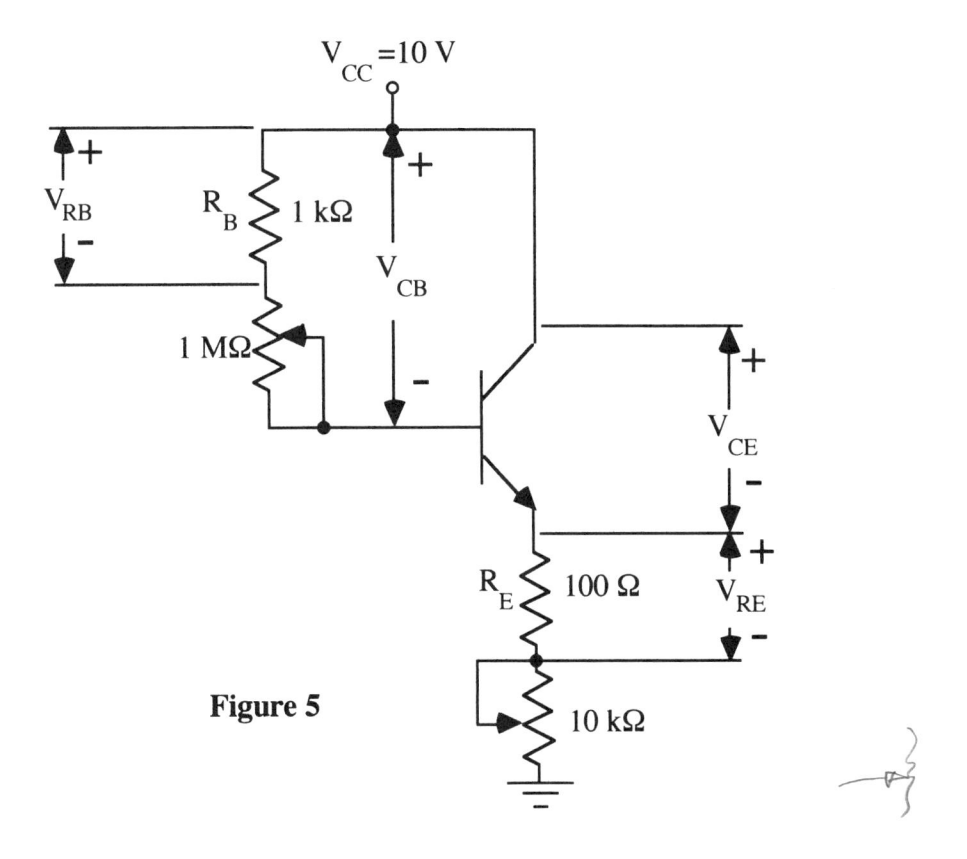

**Figure 5**

6. By carefully adjusting the 1 MΩ and 10 kΩ potentiometers, set the voltages $V_{CE}$ and $V_{CB}$ as shown in Table 3. Both $V_{CE}$ and $V_{CB}$ are very sensitive to the potentiometer settings.

7. Measure and record in Table 3 the voltage $V_{RB}$ across the 1 kΩ resistor, which can be used to calculate the current $I_B$.

# EXPERIMENT 5 - COMMON-EMITTER/COMMON-COLLECTOR CHARACTERISTICS

## Questions

1. Calculate the values of $I_B$ in Table 1, and plot the input characteristics of the common-emitter bias circuit using the values of Table 1.

2. Calculate the values of $I_C$ in Table 2, and plot the output characteristics of the common-emitter bias circuit using the values of Table 2.

3. Calculate the values of $I_B$ in Table 3, and plot the input characteristics of the common-collector bias circuit using the values of Table 3.

4. For each value of $V_{CE}$ in Table 2, calculate the value of ß for the output characteristic corresponding to $I_B = 30$ $\mu A$.

5. Calculate $\alpha$ for each of the values of ß in question 4.

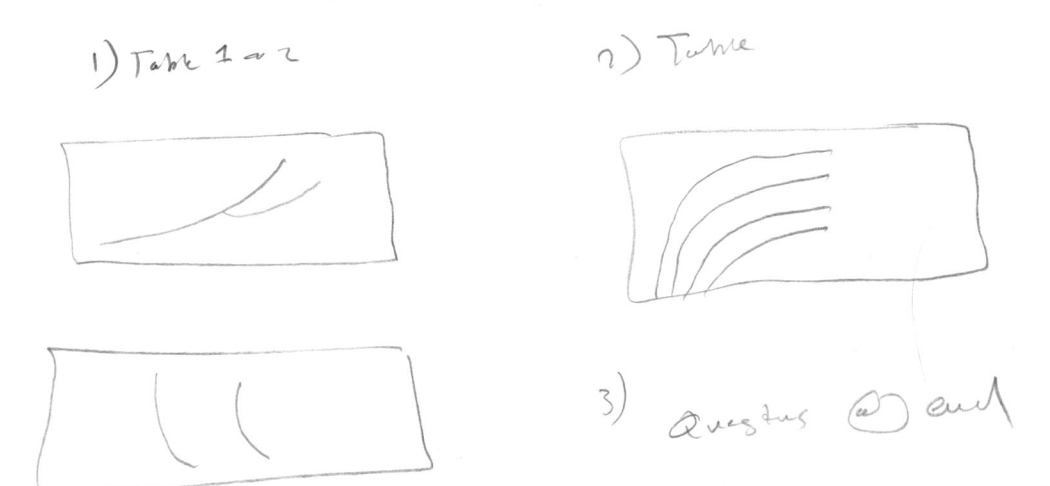

# EXPERIMENT 5 - COMMON-EMITTER/COMMON-COLLECTOR CHARACTERISTICS

## Data

### TABLE 1

| $V_{CE} = 3$ V ||| $V_{CE} = 5$ V |||
|---|---|---|---|---|---|
| $V_{BE}$ | $V_{RB}$ | $I \approx V_{RB}/R_B$ | $V_{BE}$ | $V_{RB}$ | $I \approx V_{RB}/R_B$ |
| 0.63 V |  |  | 0.63 V |  |  |
| 0.64 V | 27 mV |  | 0.64 V | 89 mV |  |
| 0.65 V | 116 mV |  | 0.65 V | 0.121 V |  |
| 0.66 V | 0.172 V |  | 0.66 V | 0.181 V |  |

### TABLE 2

| $V_{CE}$ | $I_B = 10\ \mu A$ || $I_B = 20\ \mu A$ || $I_B = 30\ \mu A$ || $I_B = 40\ \mu A$ || $I_B = 50\ \mu A$ ||
|---|---|---|---|---|---|---|---|---|---|---|
|  | $V_{RC}$ | $I_C = V_{RC}/R_C$ | $V_{RC}$ | $I_C = V_{RC}/R_C$ | $V_{RC}$ | $I_C = V_{RC}/R_C$ | $V_{RC}$ | $I_C = V_{RC}/R_C$ | $V_{RC}$ | $I_C = V_{RC}/R_C$ |
| 0.2 V | .118 |  |  |  |  |  |  |  |  |  |
| 0.4 V | .152 |  |  |  |  |  |  |  |  |  |
| 0.8 V | .153 |  |  |  |  |  |  |  |  |  |
| 1 V | .153 |  |  |  |  |  |  |  |  |  |
| 3 V |  |  |  |  |  |  |  |  |  |  |
| 5 V |  |  |  |  |  |  |  |  |  |  |

### TABLE 3

| $V_{CE} = 3$ V ||| $V_{CE} = 5$ V ||| $V_{CE} = 7$ V |||
|---|---|---|---|---|---|---|---|---|
| $V_{CB}$ | $V_{RB}$ | $I_B \approx V_{RB}/R_B$ | $V_{CB}$ | $V_{RB}$ | $I_B \approx V_{RB}/R_B$ | $V_{CB}$ | $V_{RB}$ | $I_B \approx V_{RB}/R_B$ |
| 2.4 V |  |  | 4.4 V |  |  | 6.4 V |  |  |
| 2.38 V |  |  | 4.38 V |  |  | 6.39 V |  |  |
| 2.36 V |  |  | 4.36 V |  |  | 6.38 V |  |  |
| 2.34 V |  |  | 4.34 V |  |  | 6.36 V |  |  |

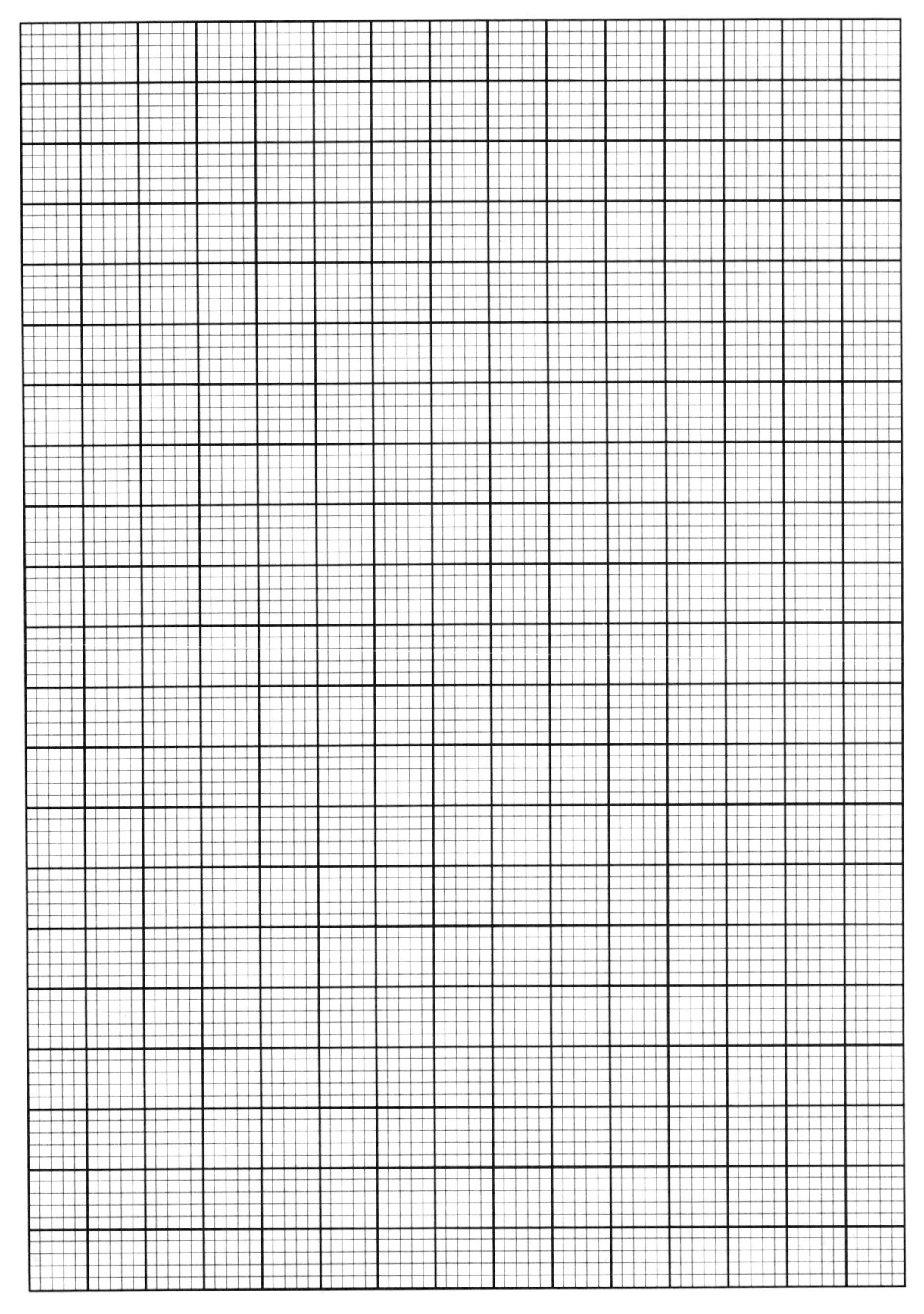

# EXPERIMENT 5 - COMMON-EMITTER/COMMON-COLLECTOR CHARACTERISTICS

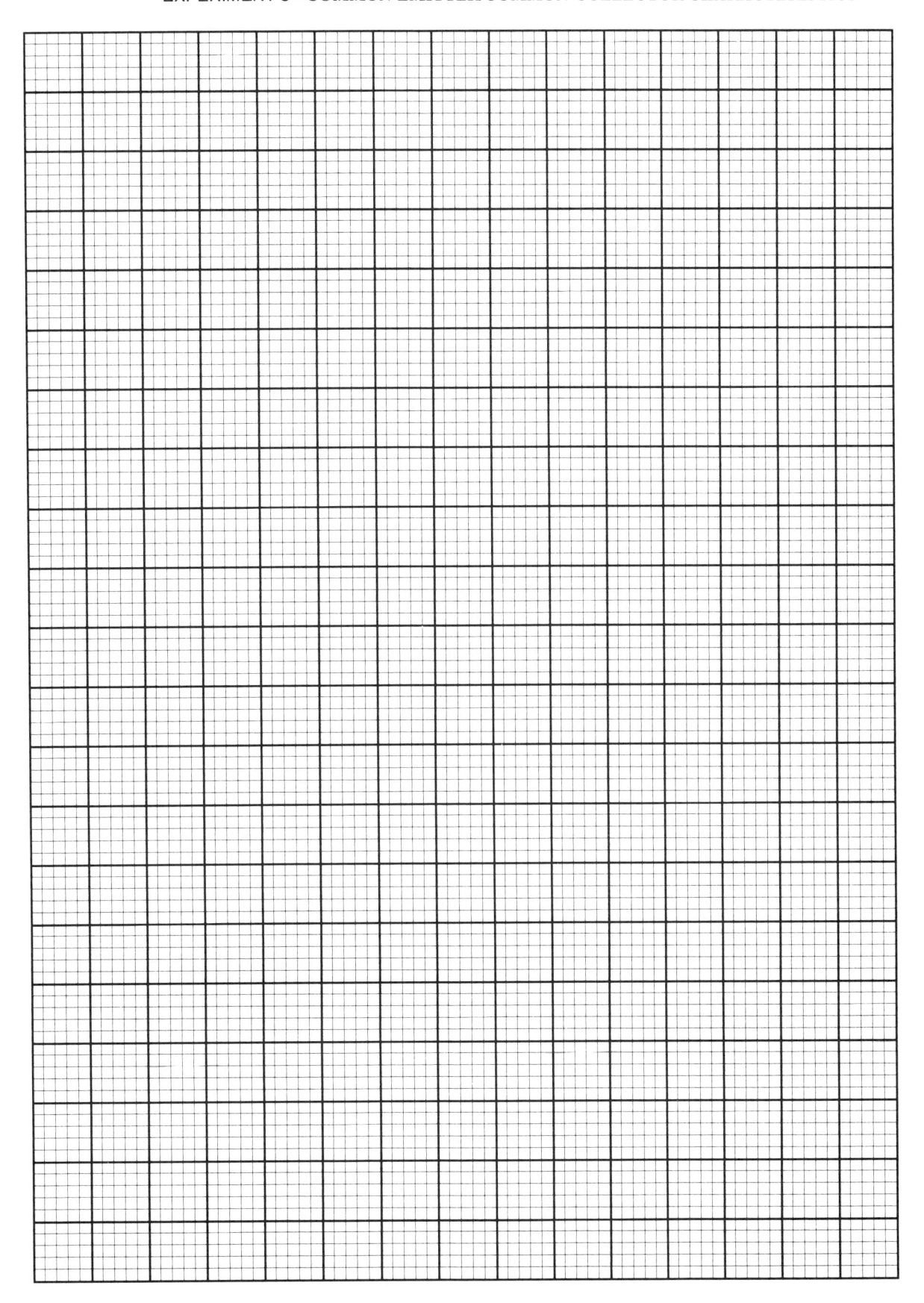

# EXPERIMENT 5 - COMMON-EMITTER/COMMON-COLLECTOR CHARACTERISTICS

**EXPERIMENT 5 - COMMON-EMITTER/COMMON-COLLECTOR CHARACTERISTICS**

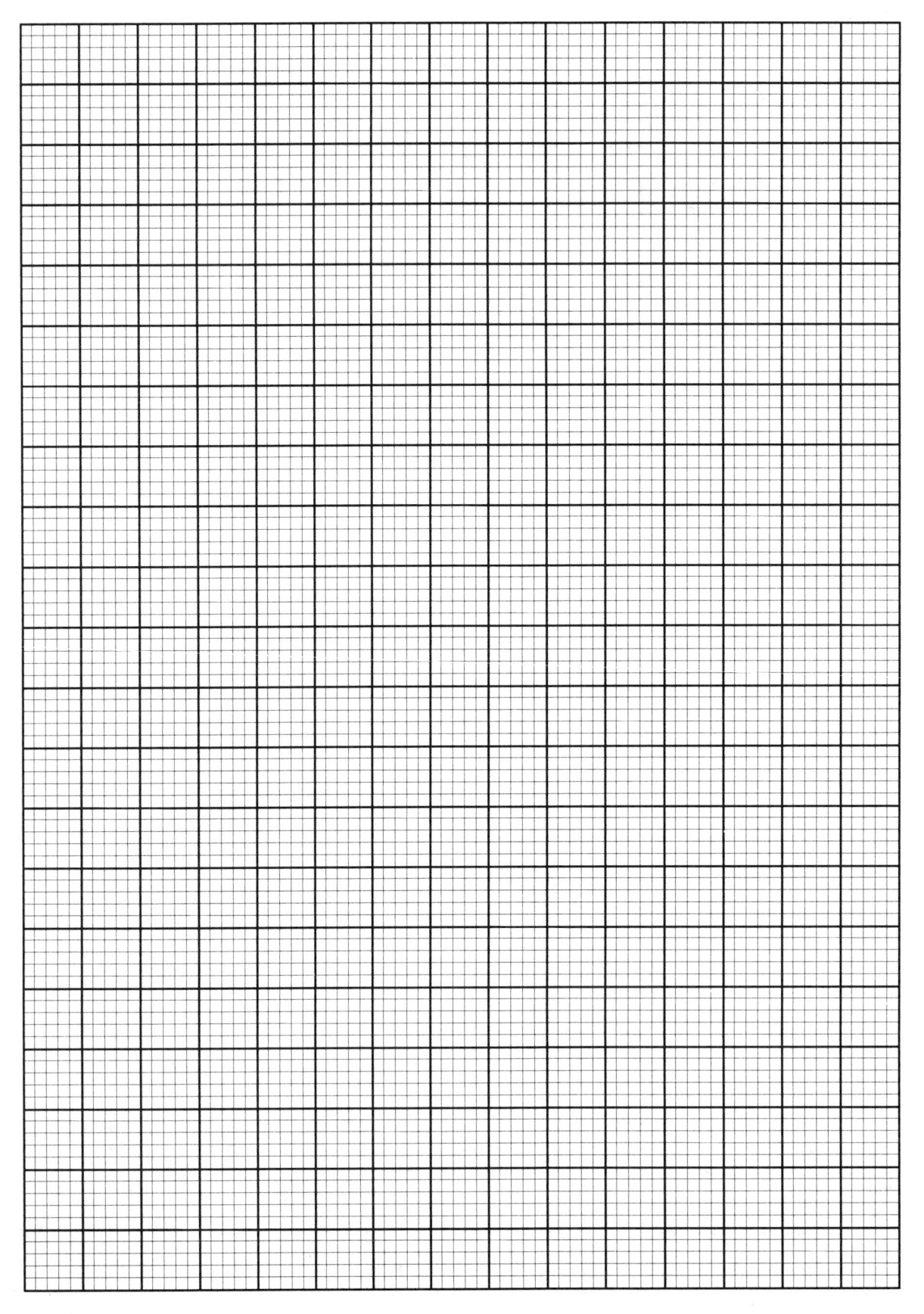

# The BJT Inverter 6

## Reference

*Electronic Devices and Circuits, Sixth Edition:* Section 4-8, The BJT Inverter (Transistor Switch)

## Objective

To demonstrate the use of a BJT as an inverter.

## Equipment List

1. 2N2222 silicon transistor or the equivalent
2. Variable dc power supply (0–5 V)
3. Analog signal generator (10 Vp-p triangle at 500 Hz, 10 Vp-p square at 1 kHz and at 100 kHz)
4. Resistors: 1-10 kΩ, 1-470 Ω
5. Dual-trace oscilloscope
6. VOM

## Discussion

Another important digital logic application is the use of a bipolar junction transistor as an *inverter*. The logical inverter's output is the opposite logical state from the input. The two possible logical states are the binary digits 0 (low voltage) and 1 (high voltage). Therefore, if the input to the inverter is a logical 0, the output will be a logical 1, and vice versa.

# EXPERIMENT 6 - THE BJT INVERTER

In electrical terms, this is analogous to the BJT common-emitter circuit when a dc voltage is applied to the base. If this dc voltage is high enough to fully saturate the transistor, i.e., if enough base current is applied, then the collector current will be large enough so that the output voltage from the collector to ground will be 0 V. If the base voltage is lower than 0.7 V, the base-emitter junction will not be forward-biased and therefore the transistor will remain cut off. When the transistor is cut off, the collector voltage equals $V_{CC}$.

The following diagram shows the digital symbol for the inverter and plots of a pulse input and the resulting output:

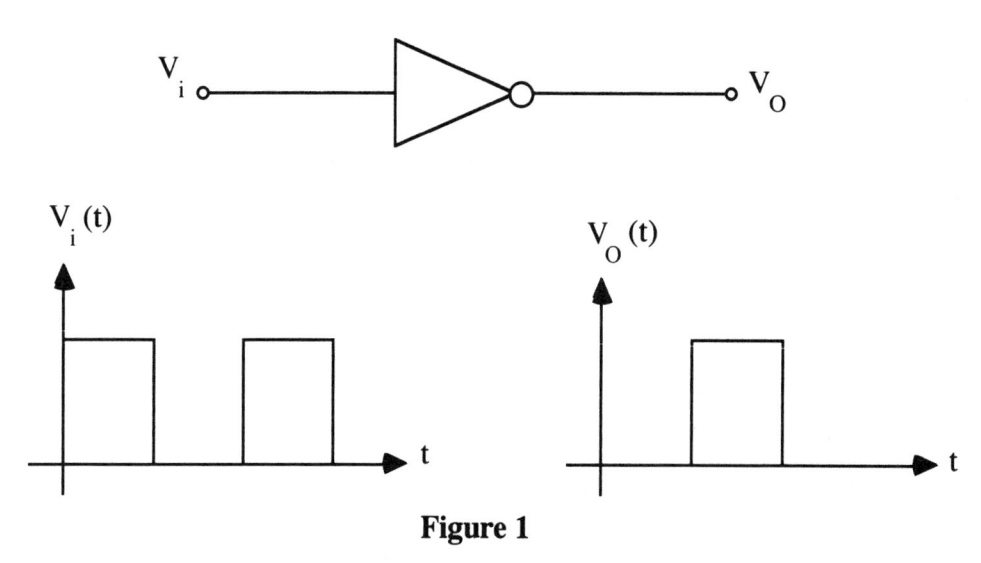

**Figure 1**

To design a BJT inverter, it is necessary to know the ß of the transistor. Notice that the inverter in Figure 2 is in the common-emitter configuration. For a particular input voltage $V_i$ and base resistor $R_B$, the base current can be calculated and multiplied by ß, giving the resulting collector current. To ensure proper operation, the transistor must be saturated when this collector current flows. Therefore, the collector resistor $R_C$ must drop all of $V_{CC}$ when the calculated collector current flows. The following inequality gives the minimum value of $R_C$ necessary to ensure saturation:

$$R_C \geq \frac{(V_{CC})(R_B)}{\beta(V_{HI} - 0.7 \text{ V})}$$

EXPERIMENT 6 - THE BJT INVERTER

## Procedure

1. Complete the procedures of Appendix A to measure the ß of the transistor.

2. To demonstrate the use of a BJT as an inverter, connect the following circuit:

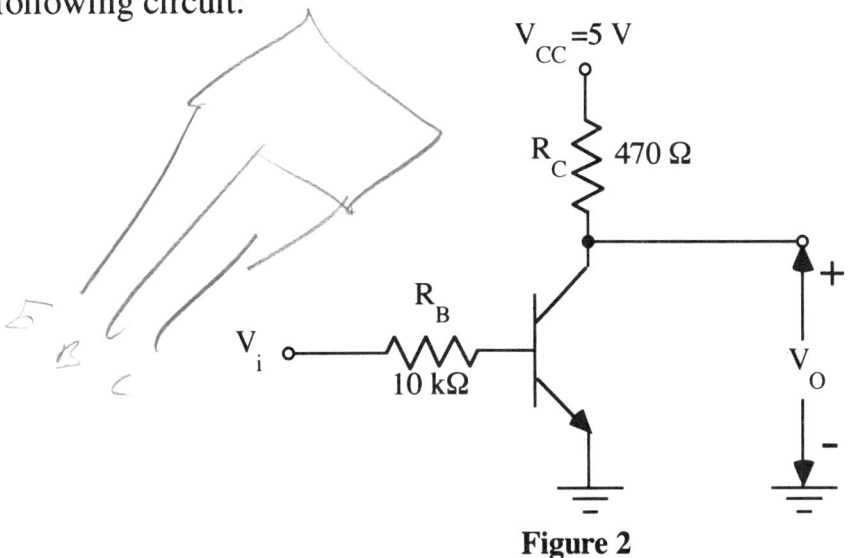

**Figure 2**

3. With $V_i = 0$ V, measure and record the output voltage $V_O$. Repeat this procedure with $V_i = V_{HI} = 5$ Vdc.

4. Apply a 10 Vp-p, 500 Hz triangle signal to the input $V_i$ of the circuit in Figure 2. Using a dual-trace oscilloscope set to dc input coupling, observe and sketch the input and output voltages $V_i$ and $V_O$ simultaneously. Be sure to note the input voltage levels for which the output changes from one level to another.

5. Replace the triangle signal with a square wave that alternates between +10 V and –10 V at 1 kHz. Sketch the input and output voltages $V_i$ and $V_O$ simultaneously, making certain to note the switching levels.

6. Repeat procedure step 5 at a frequency of 100 kHz.

# EXPERIMENT 6 - THE BJT INVERTER

## Questions

1. Using the measurements from Appendix A, calculate the ß for the transistor.

2. Using the results of question 1, analyze the circuit of Figure 2 to determine if it should perform the inversion operation. Compare calculated voltage levels with actual measured values obtained in procedure step 3.

3. What would be the expected results of cascading two BJT inverters like those in Figure 2 (i.e., connecting the output of one inverter to the input of another)? Sketch the output of the second inverter and the input to the first if the input is a 5 Vpk, 500 Hz triangle wave.

4. Using the circuit of Figure 2 as a guide, design a BJT inverter for which the input voltage is 10 V or 0 V, the supply voltage is 10 V, $R_B$ is 47 k$\Omega$, and the ß of the transistor is 100. Sketch the designed circuit.

## SPICE

Use the .TRAN control statement to plot the output voltage in the circuit of Figure 2 for 0.2 msec with a 10 Vp-p at 10 kHz square wave input and the following loads:
  a) no-load
  b) 470 $\Omega$ resistor
  c) 1 k$\Omega$ resistor and 0.2 $\mu$F capacitor in parallel

# JFET Biasing 7

## Reference

*Electronic Devices and Circuits, Sixth Edition:* Section 5-2, Junction Field-Effect Transistors; Section 5-3, JFET Biasing

## Objectives

1. To investigate the JFET self-bias configuration.
2. To investigate the JFET voltage-divider bias configuration.
3. To calculate JFET dc quiescent voltages and currents for each bias configuration.

## Equipment List

1. 2N5459 silicon N-channel JFET or the equivalent
2. DC power supply (15 V)
3. Resistors: 1-220 kΩ, 1-10 kΩ, 1-4.7 kΩ, 1-1.5 kΩ, 1-1 kΩ
4. VOM

## Discussion

Unlike bipolar junction transistors, field-effect transistors are called *unipolar* devices because only one type of charge carrier (electrons or holes) is involved in its operation. The N-channel JFET transistor conducts from drain-to-source when the voltage from gate-to-source is negative. When the voltage from gate-to-source is 0 V, the gate-to-drain junction is reverse-biased and no current can flow through the resulting depletion region.

## EXPERIMENT 7 - JFET BIASING

The interesting thing to notice about the JFET transistor is that, unlike BJTs, the output current $I_D$ is controlled by the value of input voltage $V_{GS}$. Recall that for common-emitter BJT circuits the output current $I_C$ is controlled by the corresponding input *current* $I_B$. This difference makes the JFET operate much like a vacuum tube.

Figure 1 shows the relationship between output current $I_D$ and input voltage $V_{GS}$ for a self-biased JFET like that in Figure 3. To calculate the quiescent current and voltage, one must first know the maximum values for both $I_D$ and $V_{GS}$. If $V_{GS} = 0$ V, $I_D$ is a maximum and is known as $I_{DSS}$, or the *drain saturation current*. If $V_{GS}$ is increased (made more negative), a point is reached where the current $I_D$ is 0 A. The value of $V_{GS}$ where this occurs is called the *pinch-off* voltage, $V_P$.

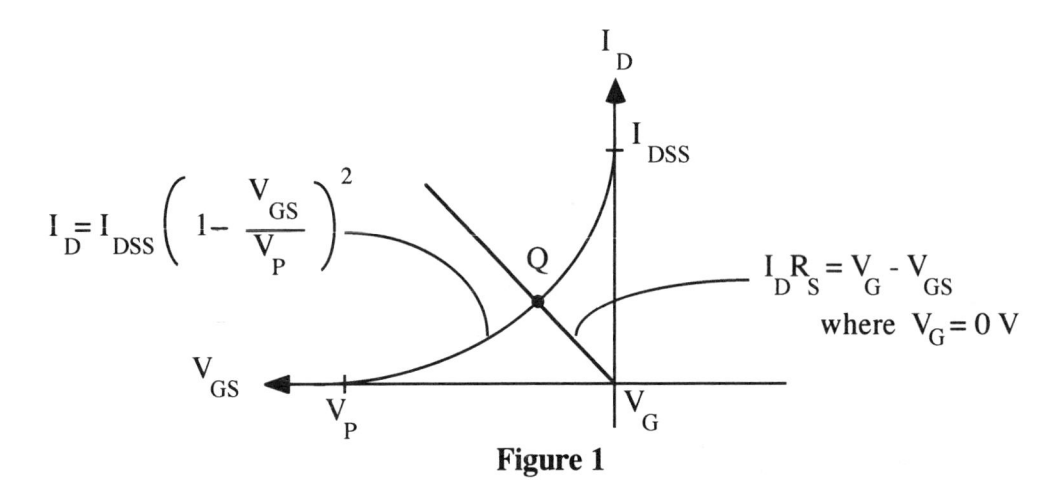

$$I_D = I_{DSS}\left(1 - \frac{V_{GS}}{V_P}\right)^2$$

$$I_D R_S = V_G - V_{GS} \quad \text{where } V_G = 0 \text{ V}$$

**Figure 1**

To calculate the quiescent voltage and current, one must solve the equations in Figure 1 simultaneously. The leftmost equation is the transfer equation for the transistor. The rightmost equation is the load line for the self-biased JFET.

Figure 2 shows the transfer equation and load line for the voltage-divider–biased JFET in Figure 4. With the voltage-divider bias configuration, changes in $V_P$ or $I_{DSS}$ will not change $I_D$ as much as is the case with the self-bias configuration.

EXPERIMENT 7 - JFET BIASING

$$I_D = I_{DSS}\left(1 - \frac{V_{GS}}{V_P}\right)^2$$

$$I_D R_S = V_G - V_{GS}$$
where $V_G \neq 0$ V

**Figure 2**

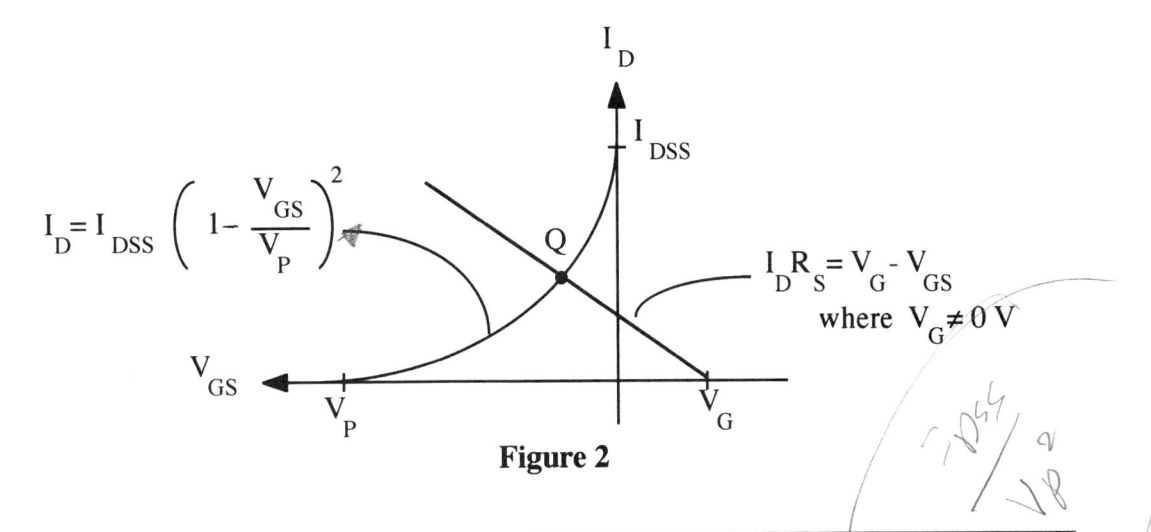

## Procedure

1. To determine the values of $I_{DSS}$ and $V_P$ for the JFET, complete the procedures in Appendix B.

2. To investigate the JFET self-bias configuration, connect the following circuit:

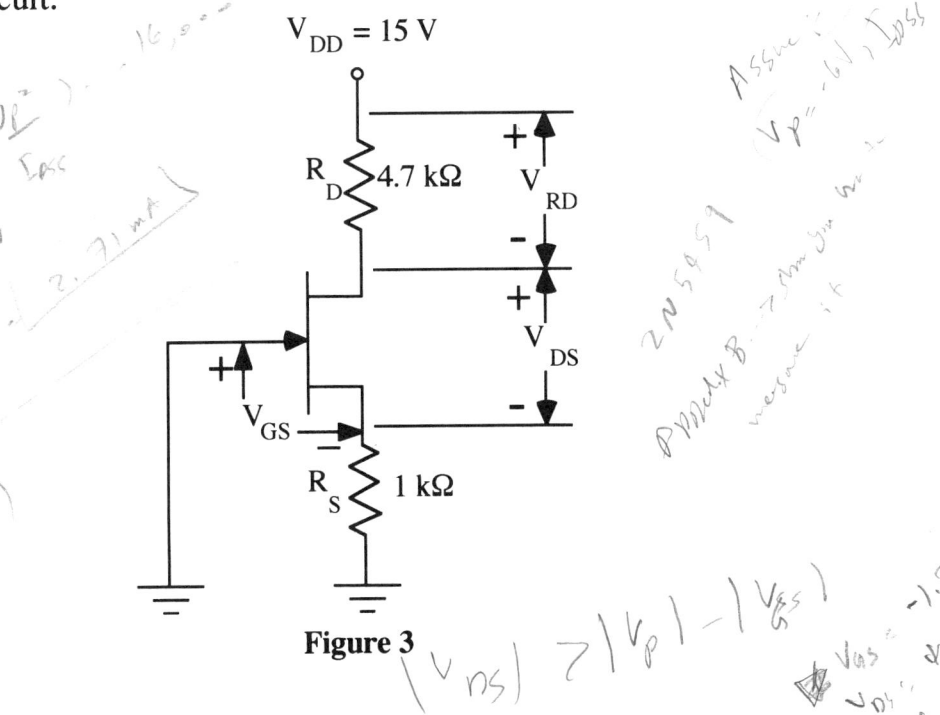

$V_{DD} = 15$ V

$R_D$ = 4.7 kΩ

$R_S$ = 1 kΩ

**Figure 3**

3. Measure and record the dc values $V_{GS}$, $V_{DS}$, and $V_{RD}$. $V_{RD}$ can be used to determine the quiescent drain current $I_D$.

51

# EXPERIMENT 7 - JFET BIASING

4. To investigate the JFET voltage-divider bias configuration, connect the following circuit:

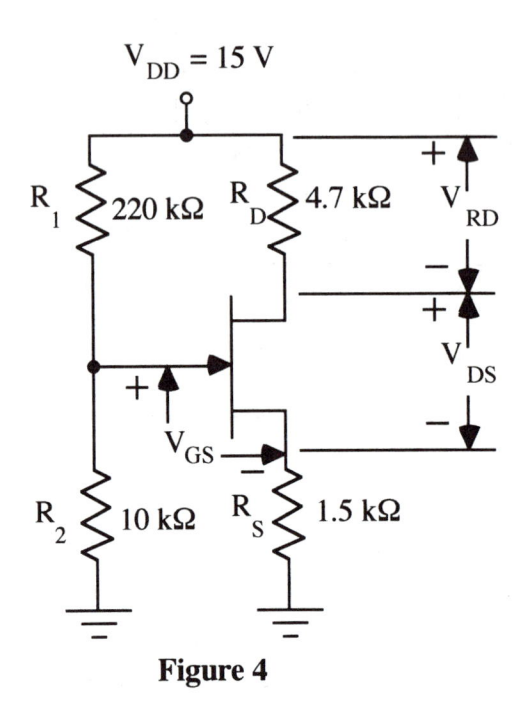

**Figure 4**

5. Measure and record the dc values $V_{GS}$, $V_{DS}$, and $V_{RD}$. $V_{RD}$ can be used to determine the quiescent drain current $I_D$.

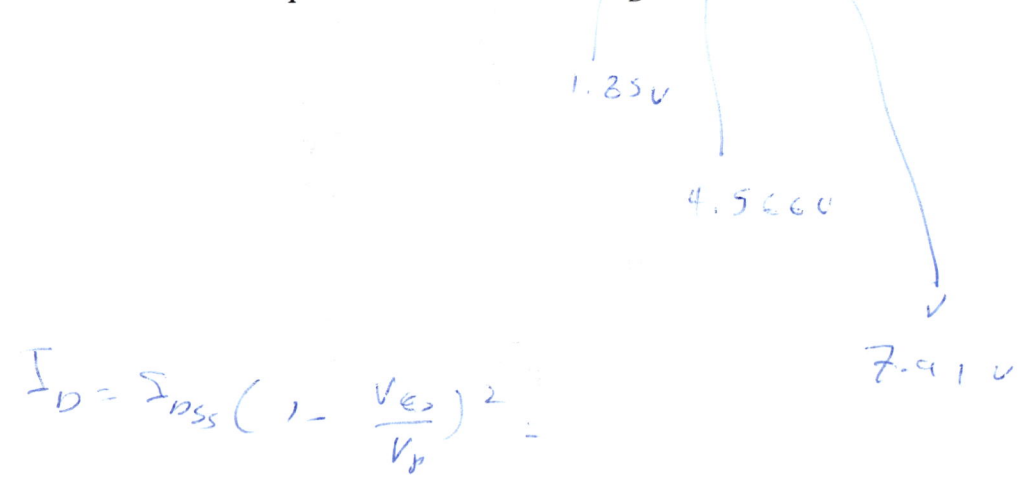

1.85 v

4.566 v

7.91 v

$$I_D = I_{DSS}\left(1 - \frac{V_{GS}}{V_p}\right)^2$$

# EXPERIMENT 7 - JFET BIASING

## *Questions*

1. Using the results obtained from Appendix B, calculate the values for $I_{DSS}$ and $V_P$.

2. For the circuit of Figure 3, calculate the dc quiescent values for $V_{GS}$, $V_{DS}$, and $I_D$. The values for $V_{GS}$ and $I_D$ are calculated by solving the simultaneous equations shown in Figure 1. The value for $V_{DS}$ can be calculated using $I_D$ and the values for $R_S$ and $R_D$. Compare the calculated values for $V_{GS}$, $V_{DS}$, and $I_D$ with the measured values obtained in procedure step 3.

3. For the circuit of Figure 4, calculate the dc quiescent values for $V_{GS}$, $V_{DS}$, and $I_D$. The values for $V_{GS}$ and $I_D$ are calculated by solving the simultaneous equations shown in Figure 2. The value for $V_{DS}$ can be calculated using $I_D$ and the values for $R_S$ and $R_D$. Compare the calculated values for $V_{GS}$, $V_{DS}$, and $I_D$ with the measured values obtained in procedure step 5.

# EXPERIMENT 7 - JFET BIASING

# JFET Current Source and Chopper

## Reference

*Electronic Devices and Circuits, Sixth Edition:* Section 5-4, The JFET Current Source; Section 5-5, The JFET as an Analog Switch

## Objectives

1. To investigate the use of a JFET as a constant current source.
2. To demonstrate the use of a JFET as an analog switch (chopper).

## Equipment List

1. 2N5459 silicon N-channel JFET or the equivalent
2. DC power supply (15 V)
3. 2-analog signal generators (200 mVp-p sine wave at 500 Hz and 6 Vp-p square wave with a −3 V dc offset at 5 kHz)
4. Resistors: 1-1.5 kΩ, 1-1 kΩ, 1-560 Ω, 1-470 Ω, 1-330 Ω, 1–220 Ω, 1-100 Ω
5. Dual-trace oscilloscope
6. VOM

## Discussion

The JFET is often used to provide constant bias current for other devices in a circuit. The most common arrangement is shown in Figure 3. Since $V_{GS} = 0$ V, the constant current that flows is equal to $I_{DSS}$. This circuit will function properly as long as the following inequality is satisfied:

$$|V_{DS}| > |V_P| - |V_{GS}|$$

# EXPERIMENT 8 - JFET CURRENT SOURCE AND CHOPPER

where:

$V_{GS} = 0$ V (in this case)

$V_P$ is the pinch-off voltage, the gate-to-source voltage when $I_D = 0$

$V_{DS}$ is the drain-to-source voltage, equal to $V_{DD} - I_{DSS}R_L$

As can be seen from the characteristic curve shown in Figure 1, this criterion places the quiescent point in the pinch-off region—the region where $I_D$ is relatively constant for all values of $V_{DS}$.

**Figure 1**

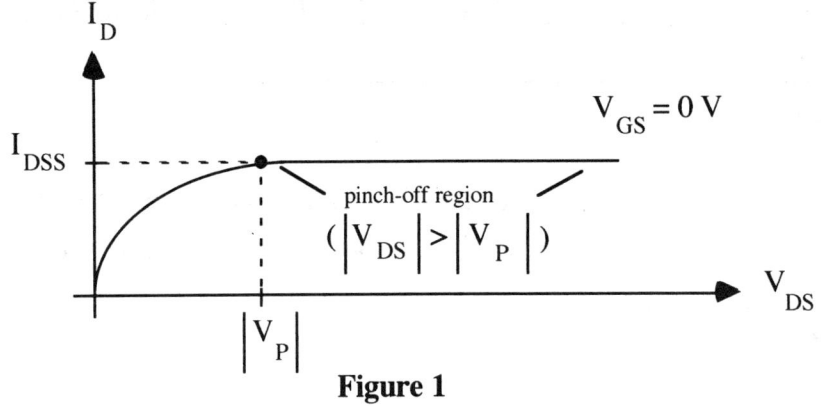

Figure 4 shows another common application for the JFET: as an analog switch in a *chopper*. This is a voltage-controlled switch that passes the input signal whenever $v_G = 0$ V and blocks the input signal whenever $v_{GS}$ is more negative than $V_P$. The output voltage obtained from a circuit of this type is commonly called a pulse-amplitude modulated signal. Figure 2 shows the JFET chopper drawn as an equivalent switch:

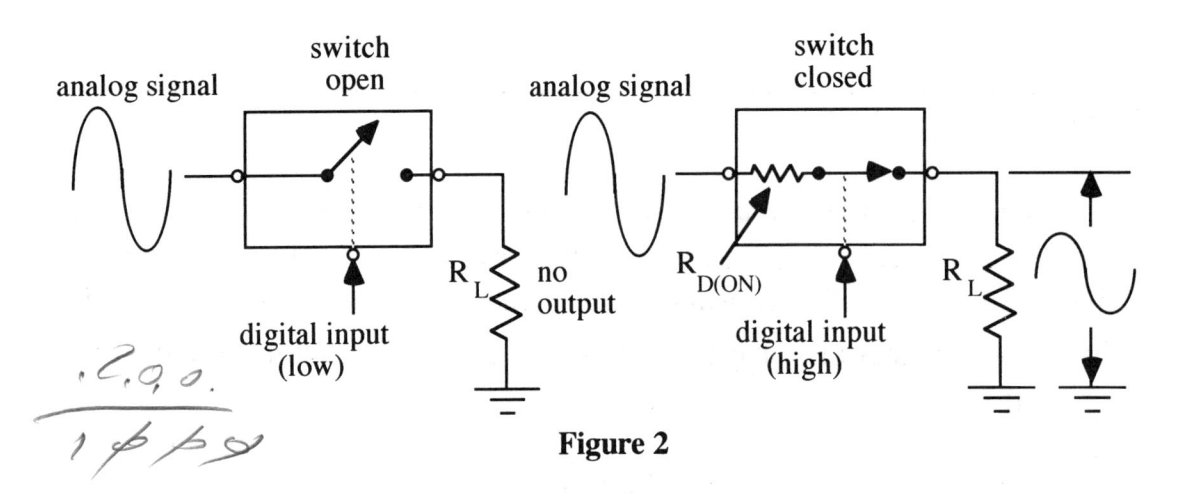

**Figure 2**

# EXPERIMENT 8 - JFET CURRENT SOURCE AND CHOPPER

## Procedure

1. To determine the values of $I_{DSS}$ and $V_P$ for the JFET to be used in this experiment, complete the procedures in Appendix B.

2. Now connect the following constant current source:

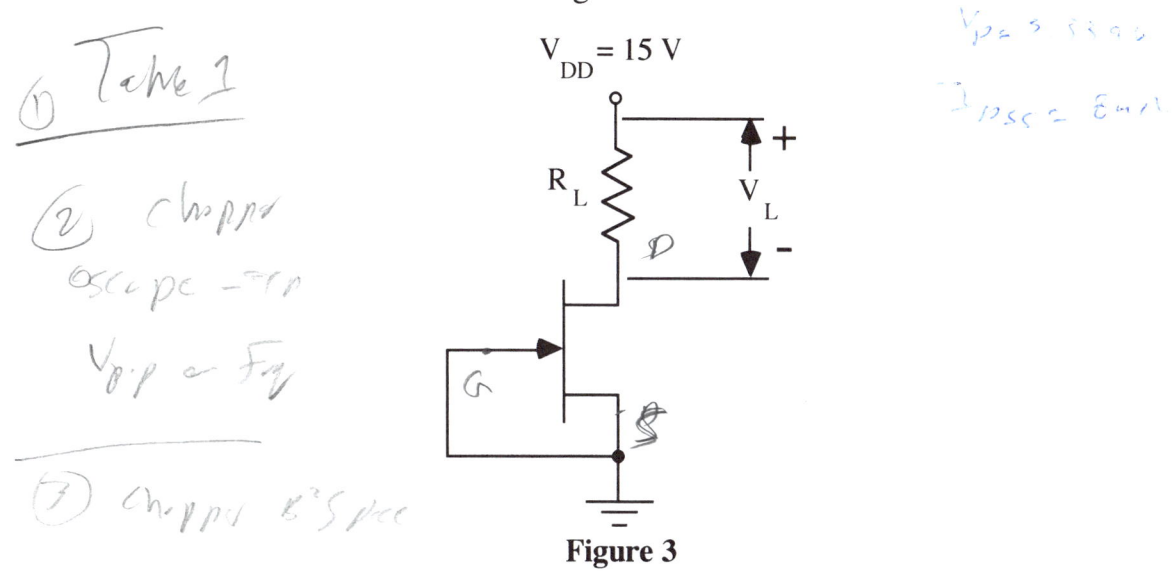

**Figure 3**

3. Measure and record $V_L$ for each value of $R_L$ shown in Table 1. The voltage and resistance values can be used to calculate $I_D$, and then determine the range of loads to which the JFET current source can supply constant current.

4. To demonstrate the use of a JFET in a chopper circuit, connect the following circuit:

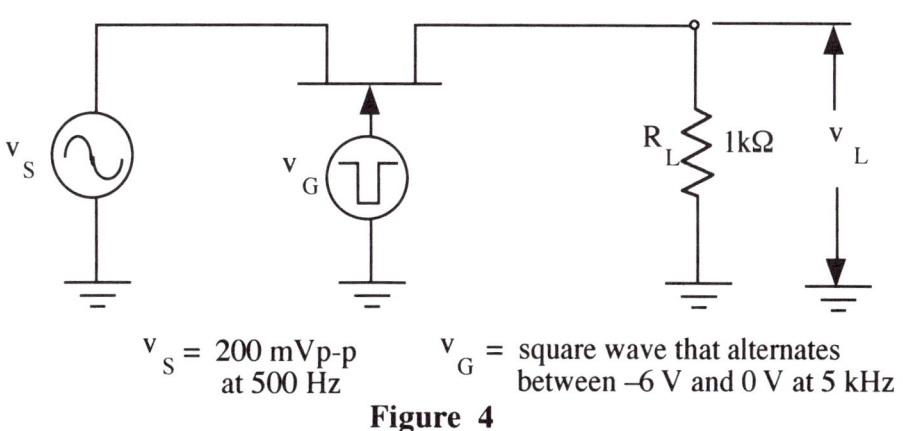

$v_S = 200$ mVp-p at 500 Hz

$v_G =$ square wave that alternates between –6 V and 0 V at 5 kHz

**Figure 4**

57

# EXPERIMENT 8 - JFET CURRENT SOURCE AND CHOPPER

5. Using a dual-trace oscilloscope, observe and sketch the waveforms $v_G$ and $v_L$. To synchronize the waveforms, it will be necessary to adjust the frequency of either $V_S$ or $V_G$ until the output waveform is stable. This will occur when the difference between $V_S$ and $V_G$ is exactly one decade.

## Questions

1. In Table 1, calculate and record the drain current $I_D$ for each value of $R_L$. Compare these values with the theoretical drain current $I_D$.

2. Using the values for $I_{DSS}$ and $V_P$ obtained in Appendix B, calculate the theoretical maximum value of load resistance for which the JFET current source can supply constant current. Comment on the measured range of load resistance in comparison to the theoretical range of load resistance.

3. Draw the equivalent circuits of the JFET chopper in Figure 4 when the chopper is on and when it is off.

4. Calculate the on resistance $R_{D(ON)}$ of the JFET chopper using the equivalent circuits from question 3.

# EXPERIMENT 8 - JFET CURRENT SOURCE AND CHOPPER

## Data

### TABLE 1

| $R_L$ (ohms) | $V_L$ (volts) | $I_D = V_L/R_L$ |
|---|---|---|
| 100 Ω | 0.84 V | 8.4 mA |
| 220 Ω | 1.75 V | 7.9 mA |
| 330 Ω | 2.65 V | 8.03 mA |
| 470 Ω | 3.76 V | 8 mA |
| 560 Ω | 4.55 V | 8.12 mA |
| 1 kΩ | 8.0 V | 8.0 mA |
| 1.5 kΩ | 11.48 V | 7.06 mA |

Sketches:

# EXPERIMENT 8 - JFET CURRENT SOURCE AND CHOPPER

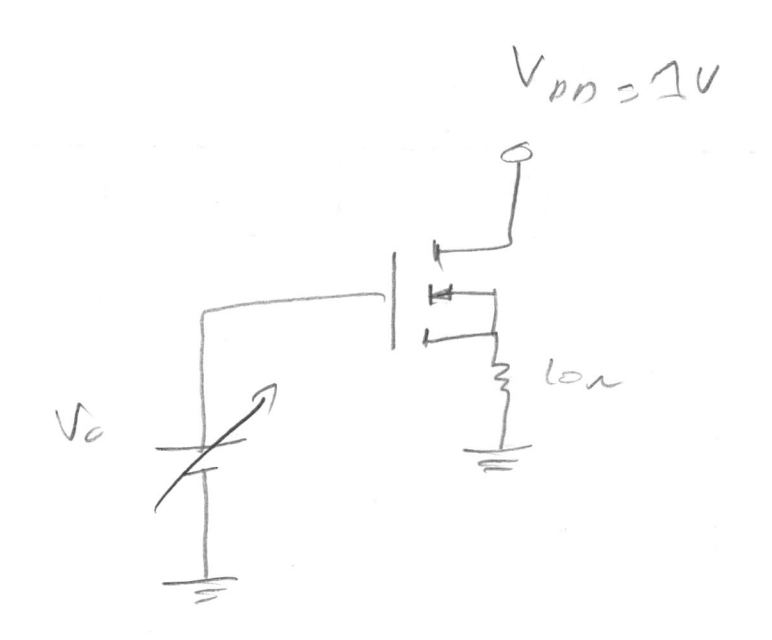

$V_{DD} = 1V$

$V_o$

10Ω

Fig 4

# MOSFET Characteristics 9

## Reference

*Electronic Devices and Circuits, Sixth Edition:* Section 5-7, Metal Oxide Semiconductor FETs

## Objectives

1. To determine the transfer characteristic of a MOSFET.
2. To investigate the MOSFET voltage-divider bias configuration.
3. To investigate the use of MOSFETs as voltage-controlled linear resistors.
4. To investigate the MOSFET biased with negative feedback.

## Equipment List

1. 2N4351 silicon N-channel MOSFET or the equivalent
2. DC power supplies (15 V and two variable supplies)
3. Resistors: 1-10 k$\Omega$, 1-8.2 k$\Omega$, 1-5.6 k$\Omega$, 2-1.5 k$\Omega$, 1-1 $\Omega$
4. VOM

## Discussion

The induced N-channel enhancement MOSFET transistor is different from the N-channel JFET because its gate-to-source voltage must be positive rather than negative to obtain conduction from drain-to-source. One of the primary uses for MOSFETs is in large-scale integration of digital circuits. The term CMOS will be familiar to engineers working with digital electronics. This technology uses complementary MOSFETs (P- and N-channel) and will be investigated in Experiment 33.

# EXPERIMENT 9 - MOSFET CHARACTERISTICS

The transfer characteristic of a typical MOSFET is shown in Figure 1. Note that the transfer characteristic of the MOSFET is similar to the characteristic of the JFET in Experiment 7, but it has been shifted to the right. This means that the voltage from gate-to-source must be greater than the *threshold* voltage $V_T$ in order for any drain current to flow. Also, the drain current is limited only by the power dissipation that the device can handle. Recall that the JFET drain current cannot exceed $I_{DSS}$.

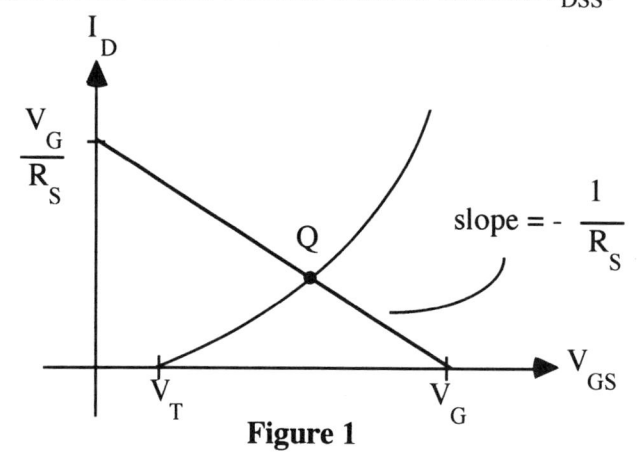

**Figure 1**

Two popular bias methods for the MOSFET are shown in Figures 3 and 5. Figure 3 shows the voltage-divider bias method. The principle behind the voltage divider bias is the same as it is with JFET transistors, except that the voltage from gate-to-source will be positive for the MOSFET instead of negative. The transfer characteristic of the MOSFET is a curve that satisfies the following equation:

$$I_D = 0.5 \beta (V_{GS} - V_T)^2$$

where:

  $\beta$ is a constant that depends on the geometry of the device

The load line in Figure 1 for the voltage-divider bias satisfies the equation $V_{GS} = V_G - I_D R_S$. The quiescent point is the point where the load line crosses the transfer characteristic curve as shown in Figure 1.

The bias method shown in Figure 5 uses the principle of negative feedback to control fluctuations in drain current. Since the gate of the MOSFET is insulated, no current will flow into the gate. Therefore, the voltage across the gate resistor is zero and $V_{DS} = V_{GS}$. Any increase in $I_D$

# EXPERIMENT 9 - MOSFET CHARACTERISTICS

will cause a decrease in $V_{DS}$, which means $V_{GS}$ will decrease. From the characteristic curve, a decrease in $V_{GS}$ will cause a decrease in $I_D$. Therefore, the original increase in $I_D$ will be corrected. The calculations for this bias method will not be discussed in this experiment.

The MOSFET can also be used as a voltage-controlled resistance. By adjusting $V_{GS}$, with $V_{DS}$ in the region where $I_D$ is not constant, the resistance from drain-to-source can be adjusted. The circuit shown in Figure 4 is an example of biasing the MOSFET in its voltage-controlled resistance region.

It is important to remember that MOSFET transistors are easily damaged by static charges. The gate insulator breaks down if excess static charges are allowed to accumulate, resulting in permanent damage. For this reason it is important to always observe certain precautions when handling MOSFETs. *Ground yourself before touching the MOSFET. Avoid handling as much as possible. Hold the device by the case, not the leads. Never insert or remove the MOSFET with the power supply on because the transient voltages can damage them as well.*

## Procedure

1. To determine the transfer characteristic of the MOSFET, connect the following circuit making sure the substrate and source are connected to the same potential (*observe handling precautions at all times*):

**Figure 2**

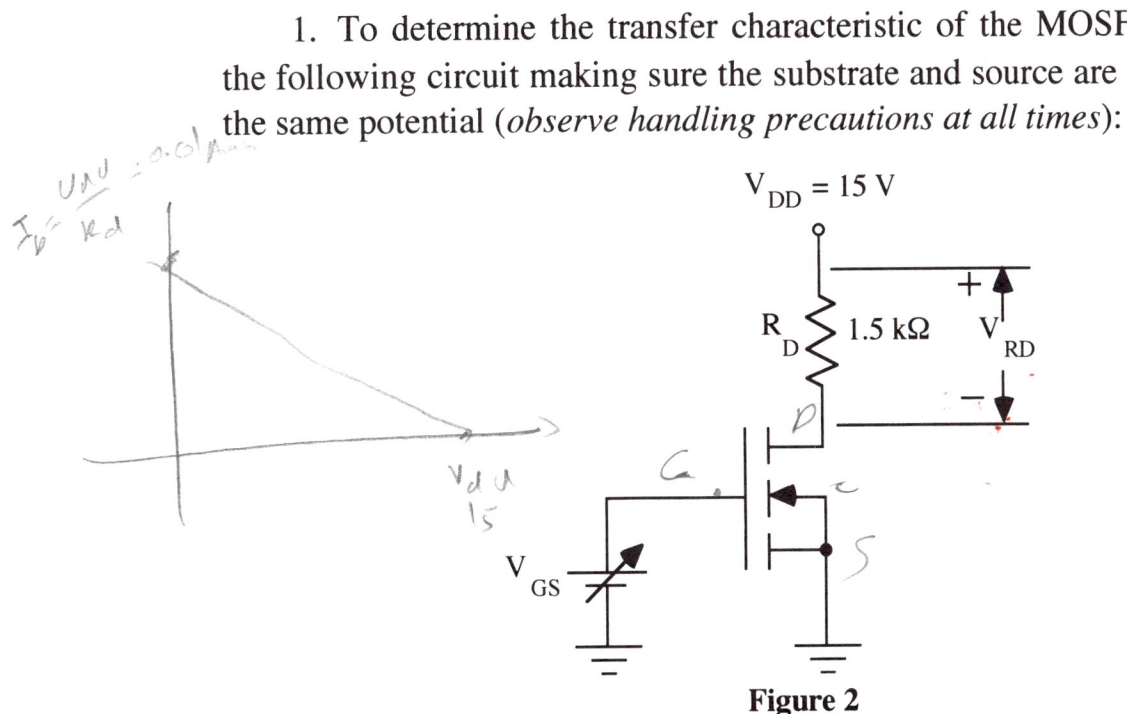

## EXPERIMENT 9 - MOSFET CHARACTERISTICS

2. Adjust $V_{GS}$ and measure and record the voltage $V_{RD}$ across the drain resistor for each value of $V_{GS}$ in Table 1. Also, measure the value of $V_{GS}$ for which drain current just starts to flow (when $V_{RD} > 0$ V). When this occurs, $V_{GS}$ is equal to the threshold voltage $V_T$. These measurements will be used to plot the transfer characteristics of the MOSFET.

3. To demonstrate the MOSFET with voltage-divider bias, connect the following circuit:

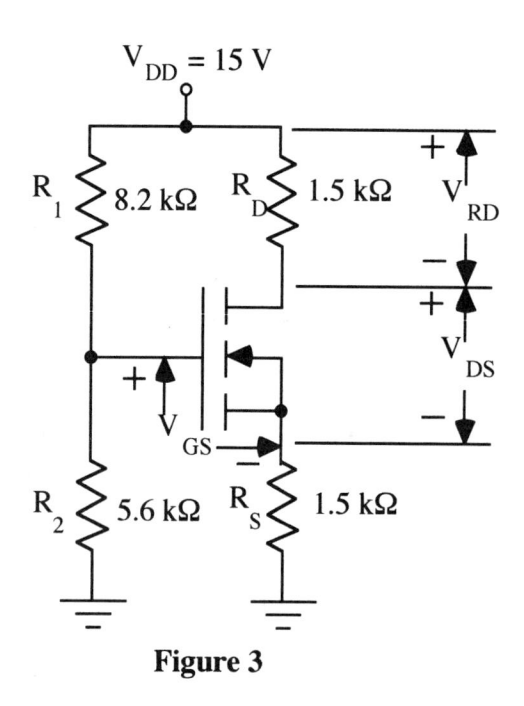

**Figure 3**

4. Measure and record $V_{DS}$, $V_{GS}$, and $V_{RD}$. These will be compared to graphically obtained values.

5. To investigate the use of the MOSFET in its voltage-controlled resistance region, connect the circuit shown in Figure 4.

# EXPERIMENT 9 - MOSFET CHARACTERISTICS

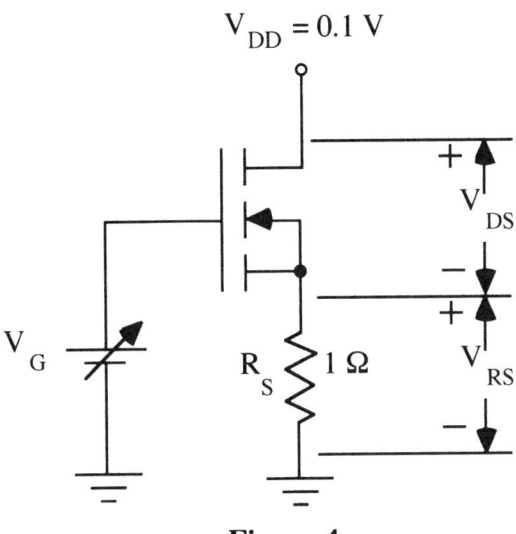

**Figure 4**

6. Adjust $V_G$ and measure and record the voltage $V_{RS}$ across the source resistor and the drain-to-source voltage $V_{DS}$ for each value of $V_G$ in Table 2. This will be used to calculate the resistance between drain and source when the MOSFET is operated in its voltage-controlled resistance region.

7. To investigate the MOSFET biased using negative feedback, connect the following circuit:

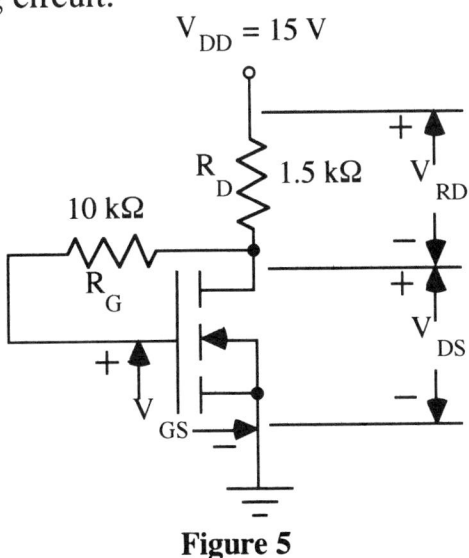

**Figure 5**

8. Measure and record the voltages $V_{GS}$, $V_{DS}$, and $V_{RD}$. Use the value of $V_{RD}$ to calculate $I_D$.

65

# EXPERIMENT 9 - MOSFET CHARACTERISTICS

## Questions

1. Calculate values for $I_D$ in Table 1. Using the results obtained from procedure step 2 and Table 1, plot the transfer characteristics of the MOSFET. Label the threshold voltage $V_T$.

2. For the circuit of Figure 3, calculate $V_G$ using the voltage-divider rule. Using this information, plot the load line on the transfer characteristic from question 1. Find the Q point graphically using this plot. Also, calculate $V_{DS}$ using the graphically obtained value for $I_D$. Compare these to the measured values of $V_{DS}$, $V_{GS}$, and $I_D$ obtained in procedure step 4.

3. Using the values recorded in Table 2, calculate $R_{DS}$ (resistance between drain and source) and record in Table 2. Construct a plot of $R_{DS}$ versus $V_{GS}$. Explain why the MOSFET in Figure 4 is said to be biased in its voltage-controlled resistance region.

4. Compare the value of $V_{GS}$ with the value of $V_{DS}$ obtained in procedure step 8. Explain why the negative feedback circuit in Figure 5 is useful. (What could cause fluctuations in drain current?)

# EXPERIMENT 9 - MOSFET CHARACTERISTICS

## *Data*

### TABLE 1

| $V_{GS}$ (volts) | $V_{RD}$ (volts) | $I_D = V_{RD}/R_D$ |
|---|---|---|
| 1 V | | |
| 2 V | | |
| 3 V | | |
| 4 V | | |
| 5 V | | |
| 6 V | | |

### TABLE 2

| $V_G$ (volts) | $V_{DS}$ (volts) | $V_{RS}$ (volts) | $I_D = V_{RS}/R_S$ | $R_{DS} = V_{DS}/I_D$ |
|---|---|---|---|---|
| 1 V | | | | |
| 2 V | | | | |
| 3 V | | | | |
| 4 V | | | | |
| 5 V | | | | |
| 6 V | | | | |

# EXPERIMENT 9 - MOSFET CHARACTERISTICS

EXPERIMENT 9 - **MOSFET CHARACTERISTICS**

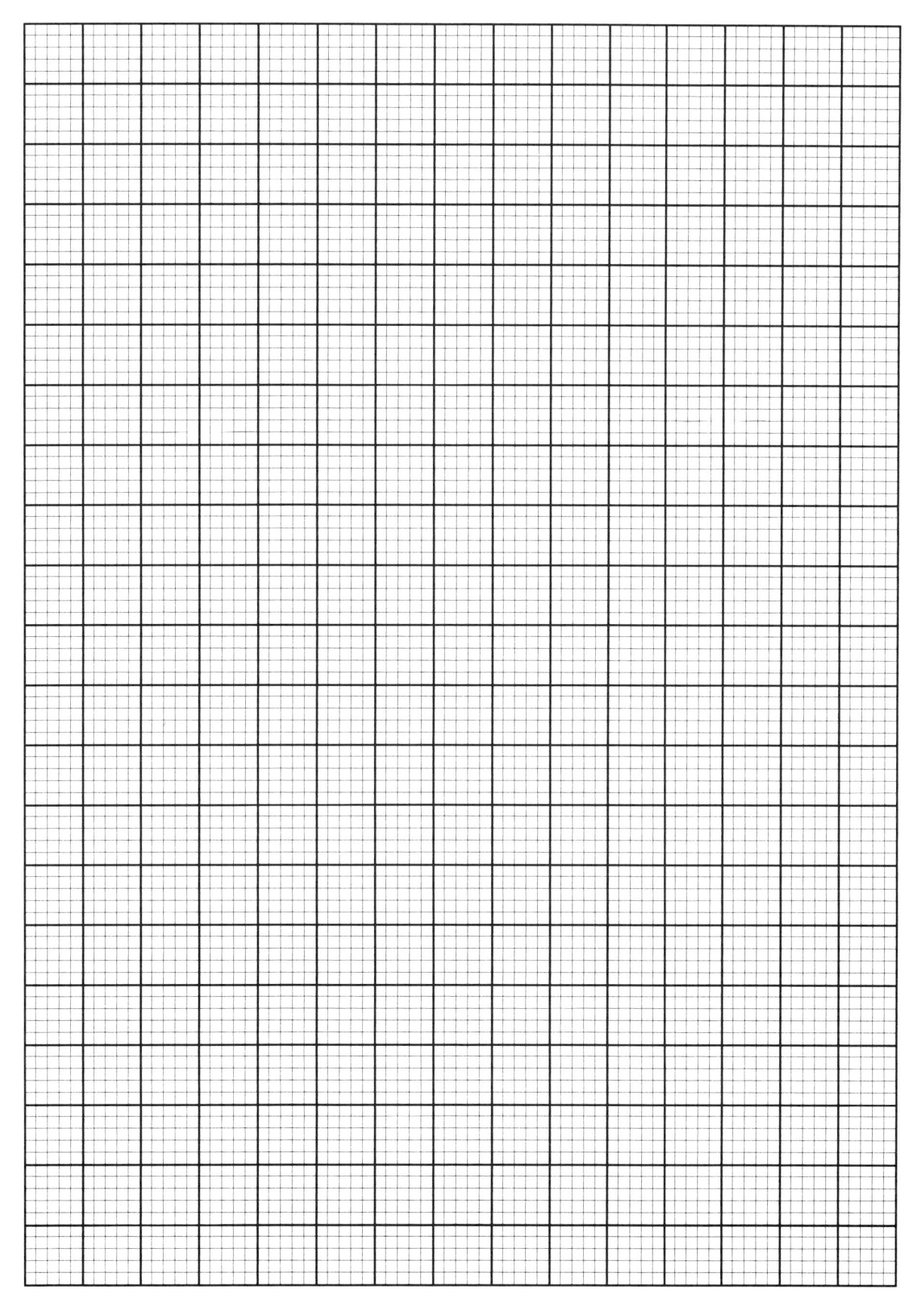

# EXPERIMENT 9 - MOSFET CHARACTERISTICS

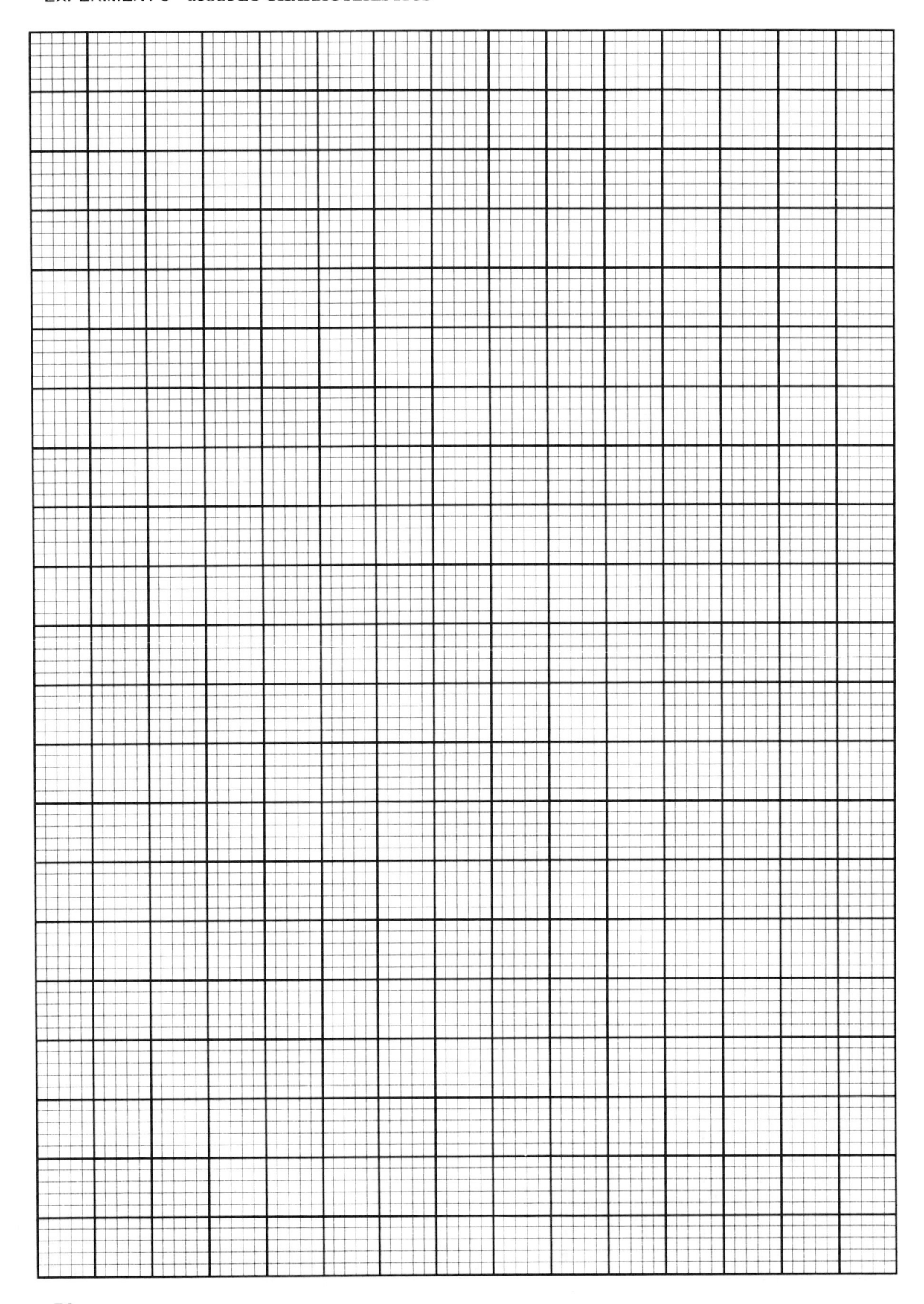

# Common-Base Amplifier 10

## Reference

*Electronic Devices and Circuits, Sixth Edition:* Chapter 6, Amplifier Fundamentals; Section 7-3, Amplifier Analysis Using Small-Signal Models

## Objectives

1. To investigate the common-base amplifier using voltage-divider bias.
2. To measure the open-circuit voltage gain, loaded voltage gain, input resistance, and output resistance of the common-base amplifier.
3. To evaluate the common-base amplifier using the small-signal equivalent model.

## Equipment List

1. 2N2222 silicon transistor or the equivalent
2. DC power supply (15 V)
3. Analog signal generator (variable sine at 10 kHz)
4. Resistors: 1-82 kΩ, 2-10 kΩ, 1-5.6 kΩ, 1-1 kΩ
5. Capacitors: 3-22 µF (25 V)
6. Potentiometers: 1-10 kΩ, 1-200 Ω
7. Dual-trace oscilloscope

## Discussion

Although it has a small input resistance, the common-base amplifier can be used in some applications requiring high voltage gain. The

## EXPERIMENT 10 - COMMON-BASE AMPLIFIER

common-base amplifier is also commonly used in conjunction with FET amplifiers, in what's called a *cascode* configuration, for high frequency amplification. When used as a small-signal amplifier, the input and output voltages and currents vary over a small range of the transistor's characteristic curves. In this situation, the amplifier is said to be operating in its *linear* region; i.e., the gain of the amplifier is the same for all amplitude variations at the input and output.

Small-signal amplifiers are often analyzed by using ac equivalent circuits. Figure 1 shows the small-signal ac equivalent circuit of the common-base amplifier in Figure 3. Notice that no capacitors or dc voltage sources appear in the equivalent circuit, because they are assumed to be short-circuits to the ac signal. $R_1$ and $R_2$ in Figure 3 are similarly shorted to ac ground.

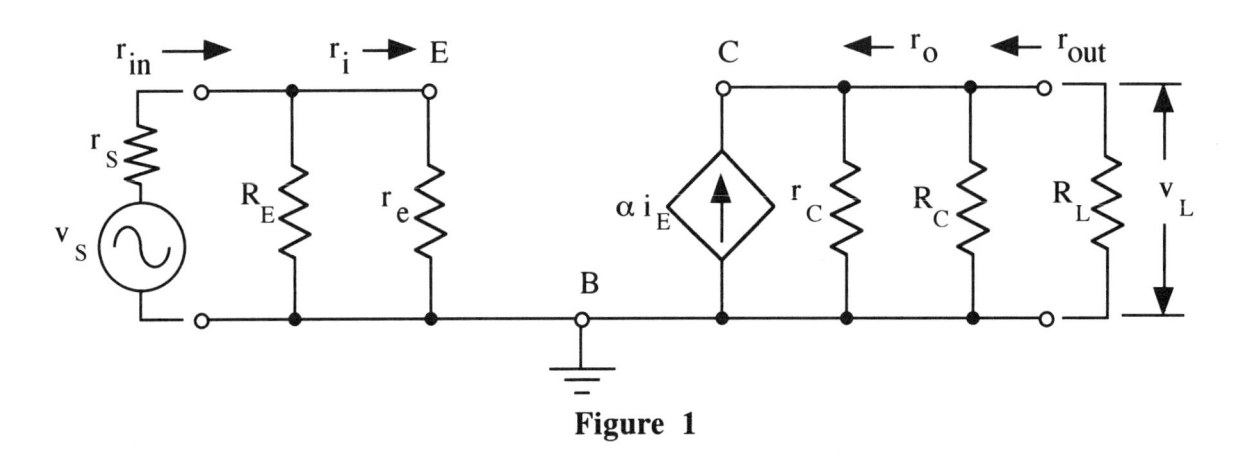

**Figure 1**

The ratio of output voltage to input voltage when the amplifier is not loaded ($R_L = \infty$, or open) is called the open-circuit voltage *gain*. The open-circuit voltage gain of the common-base amplifier can be calculated using the following equation:

$$A_V = \frac{v_O}{v_{in}} = \frac{R_C \| r_C}{R_E \| r_e} \approx \frac{R_C}{r_e}$$

where:
$R_C$ is the external collector resistor
$r_C$ is the internal collector resistance
$R_E$ is the external emitter resistor
$r_e$ is the internal emitter resistance:

$$r_i = r_e \approx \frac{0.026}{I_{EQ}}$$

where:

$I_{EQ}$ is the quiescent dc emitter current

The input resistance $r_{in}$ of the common-base amplifier is the ac resistance *looking into* the input of the amplifier stage. As can be seen in Figure 1:

$$r_{in} = R_E \parallel r_e \approx r_e$$

The output resistance $r_{out}$ of the common-base amplifier is the ac resistance looking back into the output of the amplifier stage. As can be seen in Figure 1:

$$r_{out} = R_C \parallel r_C \approx R_C$$

When a load resistor $R_L$ is connected across the output and a real signal source is connected to the input, voltage divisions take place at both the input and output. Therefore, the voltage gain from source to load is calculated as follows:

$$A_{VS} = \frac{v_L}{v_S} = \left(\frac{r_{in}}{r_s + r_{in}}\right) A_V \left(\frac{R_L}{R_L + r_{out}}\right)$$

where:

$r_S$ is the internal resistance of the signal source

# EXPERIMENT 10 - COMMON-BASE AMPLIFIER

## Procedure

1. To measure the open-circuit voltage gain, $A_V$, and the output resistance, $r_{out}$, of a common-base amplifier, connect the circuit in Figure 2. Measure the dc voltage across $R_E$. This value will be used to determine the quiescent current: $I_{EQ} = V_E/R_E$, and the internal emitter resistance: $r_e \approx 0.026/I_{EQ}$.

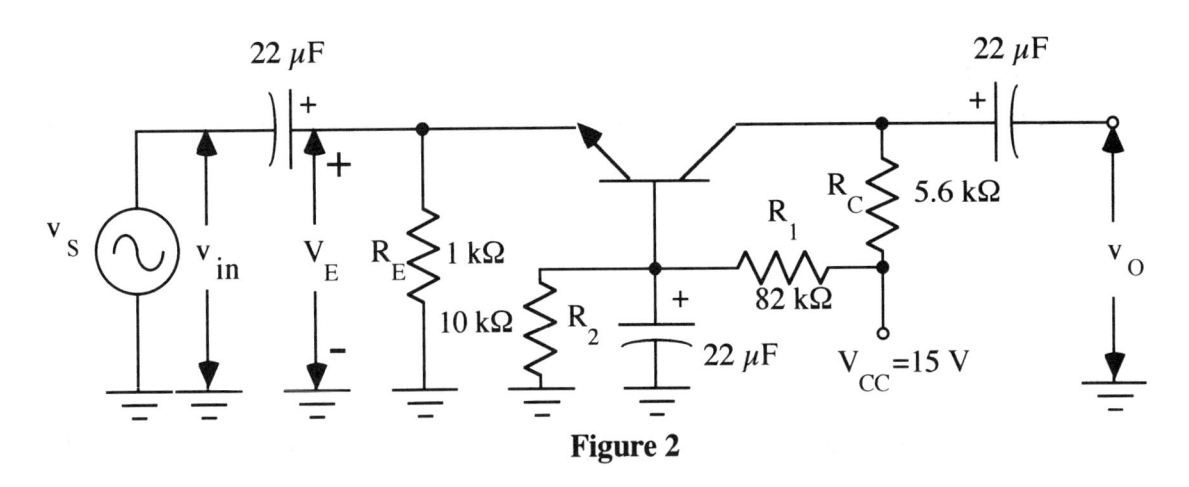

**Figure 2**

2. With the signal generator's frequency set to 10 kHz, adjust the signal generator until $v_O$ = 3 Vp-p. Measure and record the input voltage $v_{in}$ (including the phase relationship between $v_{in}$ and $v_O$). The open-circuit voltage gain $A_V$ is $v_O/v_{in}$.

3. To measure the output resistance, $r_{out}$, of the common-base amplifier, connect a 10 kΩ potentiometer connected as a rheostat between the output coupling capacitor and ground. Adjust this potentiometer until $v_O$ is 1.5 Vp-p (one-half of the previous 3 V output). Remove the potentiometer and measure its resistance. By the voltage divider rule, this resistance equals the output resistance of the common-base amplifier.

4. To measure the loaded voltage gain from source-to-load, $v_L/v_S$, and the input resistance, $r_{in}$, of the common-base amplifier, connect the circuit shown in Figure 3.

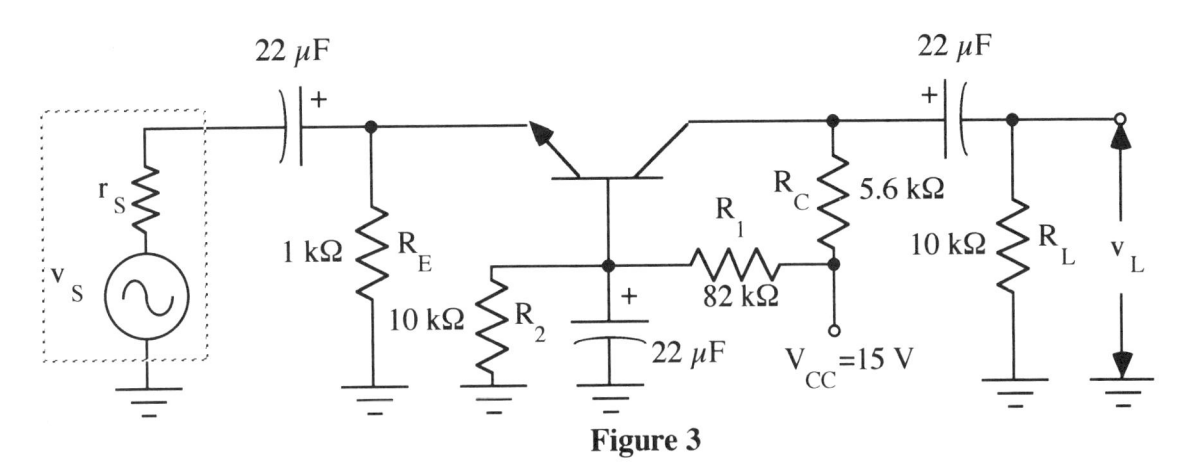

**Figure 3**

5. With the signal generator's frequency set to 10 kHz, adjust the signal generator until $v_L$ = 3 Vp-p. Remove the signal generator and measure and record the signal generator voltage $v_S$. The voltage gain from source to load is $v_L/v_S$.

6. To measure the input resistance, $r_{in}$, of the common-base amplifier, reconnect the signal generator and insert a 200 Ω potentiometer connected as a rheostat between (in series with) the input coupling capacitor and the signal generator. Adjust this potentiometer until $v_L$ = 1.5 Vp-p (one-half of the previous 3 V output). Remove the potentiometer and measure its resistance. By the voltage divider rule, this resistance, less the signal generator's internal resistance, equals the input resistance of the common-base amplifier. (Note that most signal generators used in laboratories have a 50 Ω output resistance. If the output resistance, $r_S$, of the signal generator is unknown, it can be determined as follows: With no load connected across the signal generator terminals (open-circuited output), adjust the terminal voltage to 1 Vp-p. Then connect a potentiometer (rheostat) across the terminals. Adjust the resistance until the voltage across it is 0.5 Vp-p. The resistance of the rheostat then equals $r_S$).

# EXPERIMENT 10 - COMMON-BASE AMPLIFIER

7. Reconnect the circuit of Figure 3. Now increase the amplitude of the signal source until the output voltage, $v_L$, starts to distort. Measure the peak-to-peak value of the output voltage at the point where it just starts to distort.

## Questions

1. Using the measurements made in procedure step 1, calculate the quiescent current, $I_{EQ}$, and the internal emitter resistance, $r_e$.

2. Using the values obtained in question 1, and assuming that the internal collector resistance is infinite, draw the small-signal ac equivalent circuit for the amplifier of Figure 3.

3. Using the equivalent circuit from question 2, calculate the theoretical values for $A_V$, $v_L/v_S$, $r_{in}$, and $r_{out}$. Compare these with the measured values from procedure steps 2 through 6.

4. Referring to the experimental values obtained for $A_V$ and $v_L/v_S$, do you conclude that the 10 k$\Omega$ resistor caused loading? Explain your answer. What would be the theoretical voltage gain from source-to-load, $v_L/v_S$, if the load resistor were 10 $\Omega$?

5. Explain the distortion observed in procedure step 7. Why does the output waveform distort when the amplitude of the input is increased above a certain value?

# Common-Emitter Amplifier 11

## Reference

*Electronic Devices and Circuits, Sixth Edition:* Chapter 6, Amplifier Fundamentals; Section 7-3, Amplifier Analysis Using Small-Signal Models

## Objectives

1. To measure the open-circuit voltage gain, loaded voltage gain, and input and output resistances of the common-emitter amplifier.
2. To evaluate the common-emitter amplifier using the small-signal equivalent model.
3. To demonstrate the differences in voltage gain and input resistance due to the removal of the emitter bypass capacitor.

## Equipment List

1. 2N2222 silicon transistor or the equivalent
2. DC power supply (15 V)
3. Analog signal generator (variable sine at 10 kHz)
4. Resistors: 1-56 kΩ, 1-12 kΩ, 1-3.3 kΩ, 1-2.2 kΩ, 1-1 kΩ
5. Capacitors: 1-47 µF, 2-10 µF (all 25 V)
6. Potentiometers: 1-50 kΩ, 1-10 kΩ
7. Dual-trace oscilloscope

## Discussion

The most important BJT small-signal configuration is the common-emitter amplifier. It is extremely useful because it has high voltage and

# EXPERIMENT 11 - COMMON-EMITTER AMPLIFIER

current gain, moderate input resistance, and moderate output resistance. The common-emitter amplifier will be used as the example in most general amplifier experiments in this manual.

In many common-emitter amplifiers, the emitter resistor is *bypassed* by connecting a capacitor in parallel with it. At high frequencies, the capacitor effectively shorts the emitter resistor to ground, but at dc the capacitor is a high impedance that does not affect the dc biasing of the circuit. The purpose of the emitter bypass capacitor is to increase the gain of the amplifier by eliminating *ac degeneration*, which occurs when there is a voltage present across the emitter resistor that is out of phase with the output voltage.

The small-signal ac equivalent circuit in Figure 1 can be used to calculate the gain, input resistance, and output resistance of the common-emitter amplifier of Figure 3. The equivalent circuit does not show $R_E$ because it is assumed to be completely bypassed (shorted to ground) by $C_E$ at the frequency of operation. Note that the current-controlled current source in Figure 1 is pointing down, unlike that of the common-base amplifier. This means that the output voltage is negative with respect to the input voltage, corresponding to a 180° phase shift. For this reason the common-emitter amplifier is referred to as an *inverting* amplifier.

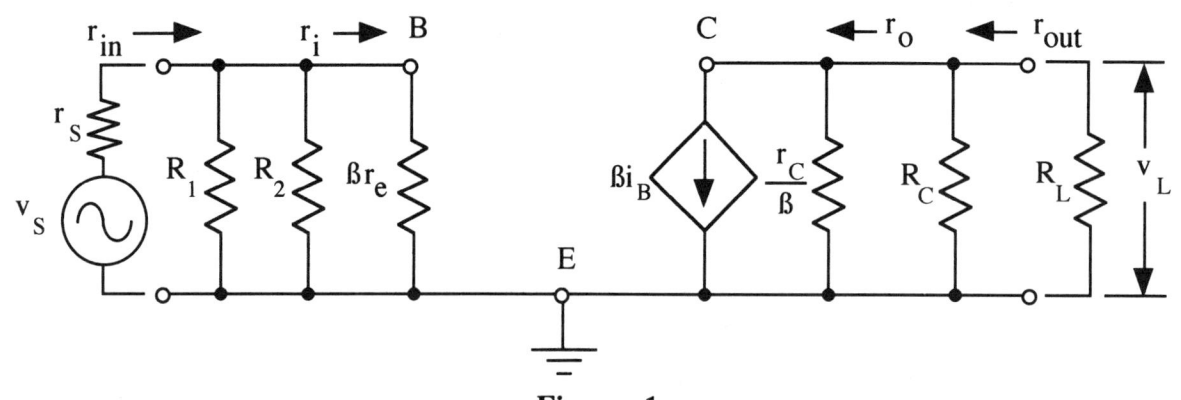

**Figure 1**

### EXPERIMENT 11 - COMMON-EMITTER AMPLIFIER

The open-circuit voltage gain $A_V$ of the common-emitter amplifier can be calculated using the appropriate one of the following equations (the minus sign means that the common-emitter amplifier is an inverting amplifier):

with $R_E$ bypassed:
$$A_v = \frac{v_o}{v_{in}} = \frac{-R_C \| \frac{r_C}{\beta}}{r_e} \approx \frac{-R_C}{r_e}$$

with $R_E$ unbypassed:
$$A_v = \frac{v_o}{v_{in}} = \frac{-R_C \| \frac{r_C}{\beta}}{r_e + R_E} \approx \frac{-R_C}{R_E}$$

The input resistance $r_{in}$ of the common-emitter amplifier can be calculated using the appropriate one of the following equations:

with $R_E$ bypassed:
$$r_{in} = \beta r_e \| R_1 \| R_2$$

with $R_E$ unbypassed:
$$r_{in} = (\beta(r_e + R_E)) \| R_1 \| R_2$$

The output resistance $r_{out}$ of the common-emitter amplifier can be calculated using the following equation:

$$r_{out} = R_C \| \frac{r_C}{\beta} \approx R_C$$

The loaded voltage gain from source-to-load $v_L/v_S$ can be calculated using the following equation:

$$\frac{v_L}{v_S} = \left(\frac{r_{in}}{r_S + r_{in}}\right) A_V \left(\frac{R_L}{R_L + r_{out}}\right)$$

# EXPERIMENT 11 - COMMON-EMITTER AMPLIFIER

## Procedure

1. Complete the procedures of Appendix A to measure the ß of the transistor.

2. To measure the open-circuit voltage gain $A_V$ and the output resistance $r_{out}$ of the common-emitter amplifier, connect the following circuit:

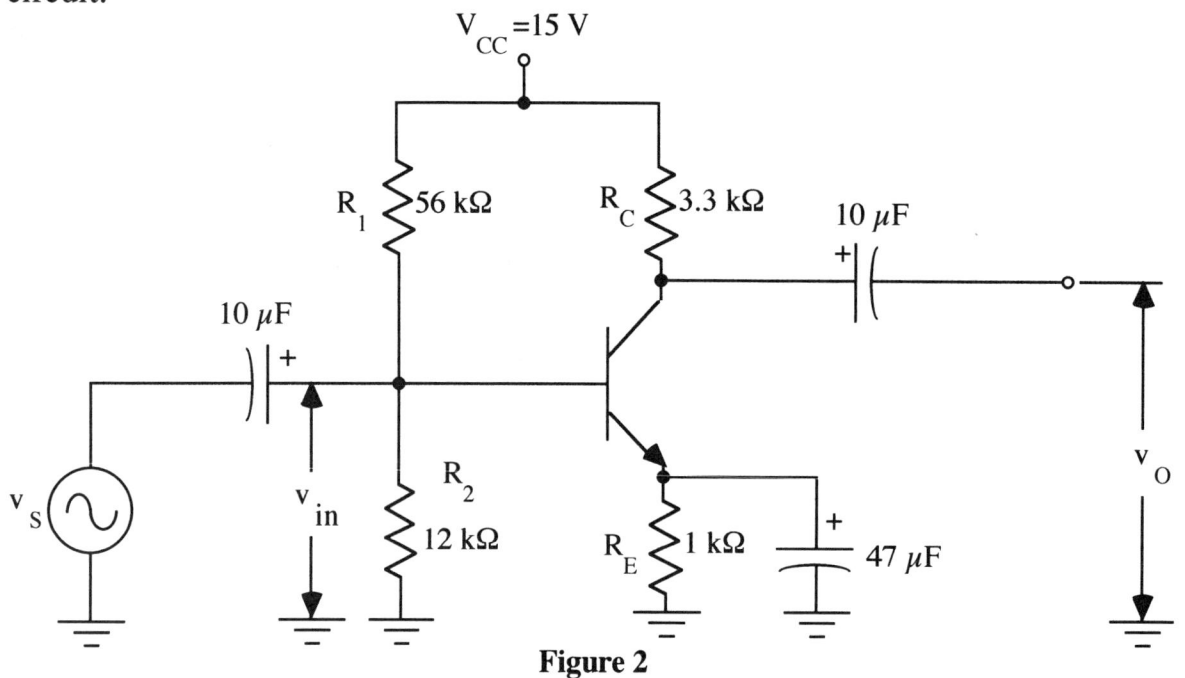

**Figure 2**

3. With the signal generator's frequency set to 10 kHz, adjust the signal generator until $v_O = 3$ Vp-p. Measure and record the peak-to-peak input voltage $v_{in}$ and the phase relationship between $v_{in}$ and $v_O$. The open-circuit voltage gain $A_V$ is $v_O/v_{in}$.

4. To measure the output resistance, $r_{out}$, of the common-emitter amplifier, connect a 10 kΩ potentiometer connected as a rheostat between the output coupling capacitor and ground. Adjust this potentiometer until $v_O$ is 1.5 Vp-p (one-half of the previous 3 Vp-p output). Remove the potentiometer and measure its resistance. By the voltage divider rule, this resistance equals the output resistance of the amplifier.

## EXPERIMENT 11 - COMMON-EMITTER AMPLIFIER

5. To measure the voltage gain from source-to-load, $v_L/v_S$, and the input resistance, $r_{in}$, of the common-emitter amplifier, connect the circuit in Figure 3.

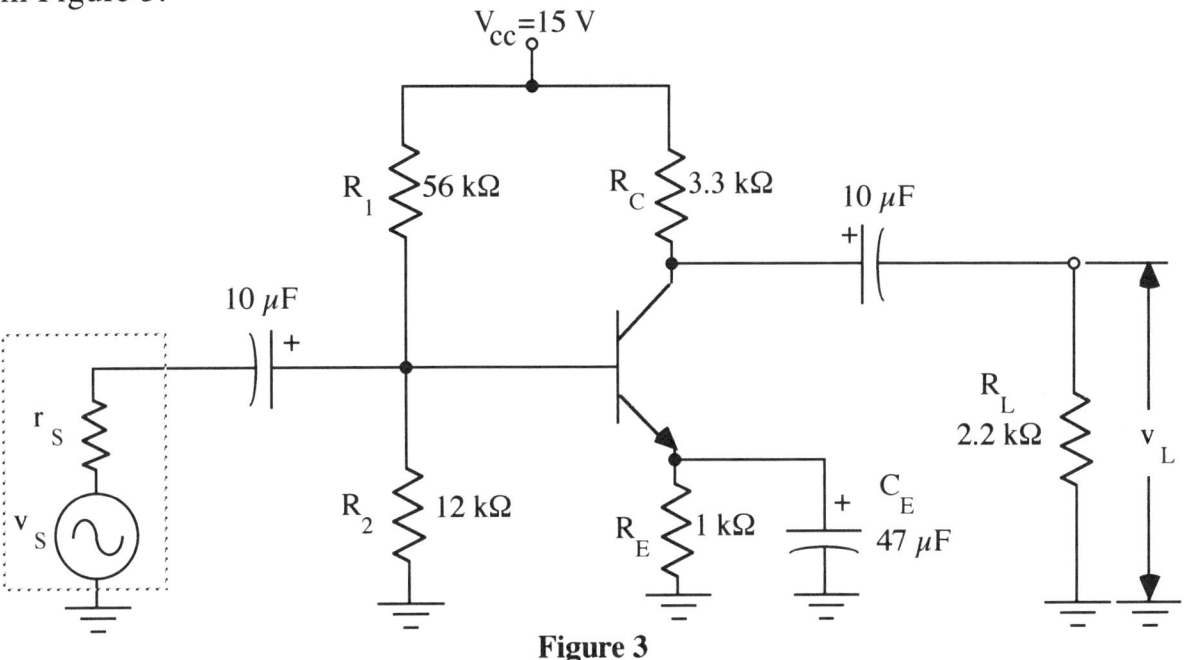

**Figure 3**

6. With the signal generator's frequency set to 10 kHz, adjust the signal generator until $v_L$ = 3 Vp-p. Remove the signal generator and measure and record the signal generator voltage, $v_S$. The voltage gain from source-to-load is $v_L/v_S$.

7. To measure the input resistance, $r_{in}$, of the common-emitter amplifier, reconnect the signal generator and insert a 50 kΩ potentiometer connected as a rheostat between (in series with) the input coupling capacitor and the signal generator. Adjust this potentiometer until $v_L$ = 1.5 Vp-p (one-half of the previous 3 V output). Remove the potentiometer and measure its resistance. By the voltage divider rule, this resistance, less the signal generator's internal resistance, $r_S$, equals the input resistance of the common-emitter amplifier. (If $r_S$ is not known, use the procedure described in step 6 of Experiment 10 to measure its value.)

8. Disconnect the emitter bypass capacitor $C_E$ and repeat procedure steps 3, 6, and 7.

# EXPERIMENT 11 - COMMON-EMITTER AMPLIFIER

## Questions

1. The theoretical dc emitter current, $I_E$, in a circuit biased like that shown in Figure 3 can be calculated as follows: First, the base-to-ground voltage $V_B$ can be determined by using the voltage divider rule: $V_B = V_{CC} R_2 / (R_1 + R_2)$. The dc emitter-to-ground voltage, $V_E$, is $V_B$ minus the drop across the base-emitter junction: $V_E = V_B - V_{BE} \approx V_B - 0.7$ V. Finally, $I_E$ is determined by: $I_E = V_E / R_E$. Calculate the theoretical values of $I_E$ and $r_e$ in Figure 3.

2. Using the values obtained in question 1 and assuming that the internal collector resistance $r_C$ is infinite, draw the small-signal ac equivalent circuit for the amplifier of Figure 3.

3. Using the equivalent circuit from question 2, calculate the theoretical values for $A_V$, $v_L/v_S$, $r_{in}$, and $r_{out}$. Compare these to the measured values from procedure steps 3 through 7.

4. Calculate the theoretical values for $A_V$, $v_L/v_S$, $r_{in}$, and $r_{out}$ for the circuit of procedure step 8, which is the same as Figure 3 with the emitter bypass capacitor removed. Compare these to the measured values from procedure step 8.

5. What are the advantages and disadvantages of an emitter bypass capacitor (in terms of gain and input impedance)?

## SPICE

To demonstrate the effect of removing the emitter bypass capacitor on the overall voltage gain, use the .AC control statement to print the output voltage in the circuit of Figure 2. With $v_S = 10$ mVp-p at 1 kHz, print the output voltage with and without the 47 $\mu$F bypass capacitor.

# Common-Collector Amplifier  12

## Reference

*Electronic Devices and Circuits, Sixth Edition:* Chapter 6, Amplifier Fundamentals; Section 7-3, Amplifier Analysis Using Small-Signal Models; Section 7-4, Direct Coupling

## Objectives

1. To measure the open-circuit voltage gain, input resistance, and output resistance of the common-collector amplifier.
2. To evaluate the common-collector amplifier using the small-signal equivalent model.
3. To demonstrate the use of the common-collector as a buffer between a high impedance source and a low impedance load.

## Equipment List

1. 2-2N2222 silicon transistors or the equivalent
2. DC power supply (15 V)
3. Analog signal generator (variable sine at 10 kHz)
4. Resistors: 1-100 kΩ, 1-47 kΩ, 1-12 kΩ, 1-10 kΩ, 1-1 kΩ, 1-470 Ω
5. Capacitors: 2-10 µF (25 V)
6. Potentiometers: 1-50 kΩ, 1-200 Ω
7. Dual-trace oscilloscope

## Discussion

Another important small-signal amplifier configuration of the BJT is the common-collector, or *emitter-follower,* amplifier. It is extremely useful because it has very high input resistance, high current gain, very

# EXPERIMENT 12 - COMMON-COLLECTOR AMPLIFIER

small output resistance, and approximately unity voltage gain. The high input resistance and low output resistance make the emitter follower an ideal *buffer* between a high impedance source and a low impedance load. A buffer is any circuit that keeps the source from being affected by a load. For example, a common-emitter amplifier with a 10 kΩ output resistance could not provide very much voltage gain to a 50 Ω load resistor.

The following small-signal ac equivalent circuit can be used to calculate the gain, input resistance, and output resistance of the common-collector amplifier of Figure 2. Note that the current-controlled current source in Figure 1 is pointing up, like that of the common-base amplifier. The load in this case is in parallel with the emitter resistor, and the output voltage is in phase with the input voltage.

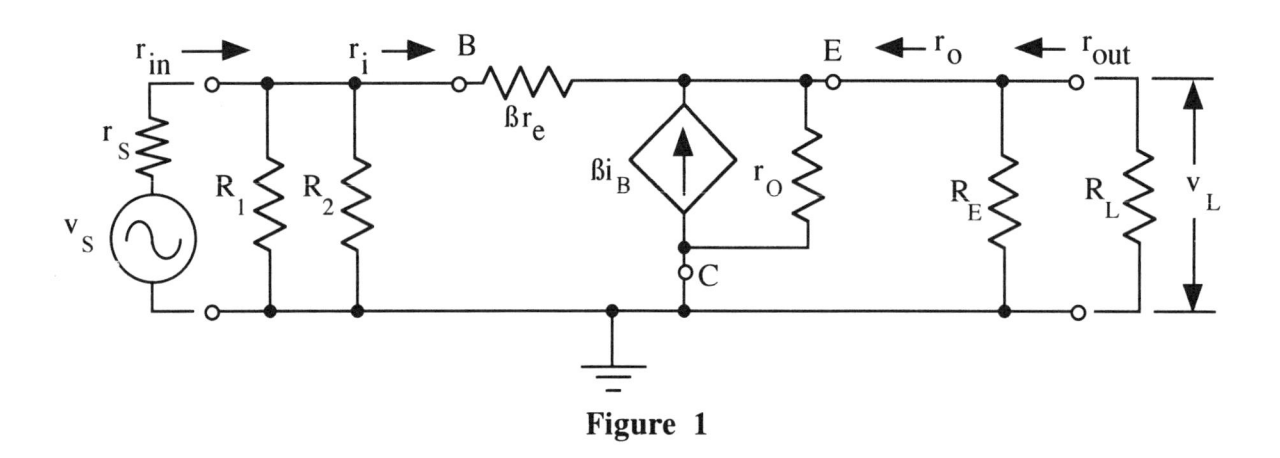

**Figure 1**

The open-circuit voltage gain $A_V$ of the emitter-follower amplifier can be calculated using the following equation (since $R_E$ is typically much larger than $r_e$, the equation can be approximated as 1):

$$A_V = \frac{R_E}{r_e + R_E} \approx 1$$

## EXPERIMENT 12 - COMMON-COLLECTOR AMPLIFIER

The input resistance, $r_{in}$, of the emitter-follower amplifier can be calculated using the following equation:

$$r_{in} = R_1 \parallel R_2 \parallel \beta(r_e + R_E \parallel R_L)$$

The output resistance, $r_{out}$, of the emitter-follower amplifier can be calculated using the following equation:

$$r_{out} = R_E \parallel \left( r_e + \frac{R_1 \parallel R_2 \parallel r_S}{\beta} \right) \approx r_e$$

## Procedure

1. Complete the procedures of Appendix A to measure the ßs of the two transistors. Keep track of which one is used for each procedure.

2. To measure the open-circuit voltage gain, $A_V$; the input resistance, $r_{in}$; and the output resistance, $r_{out}$, of the common-collector amplifier, connect the following circuit:

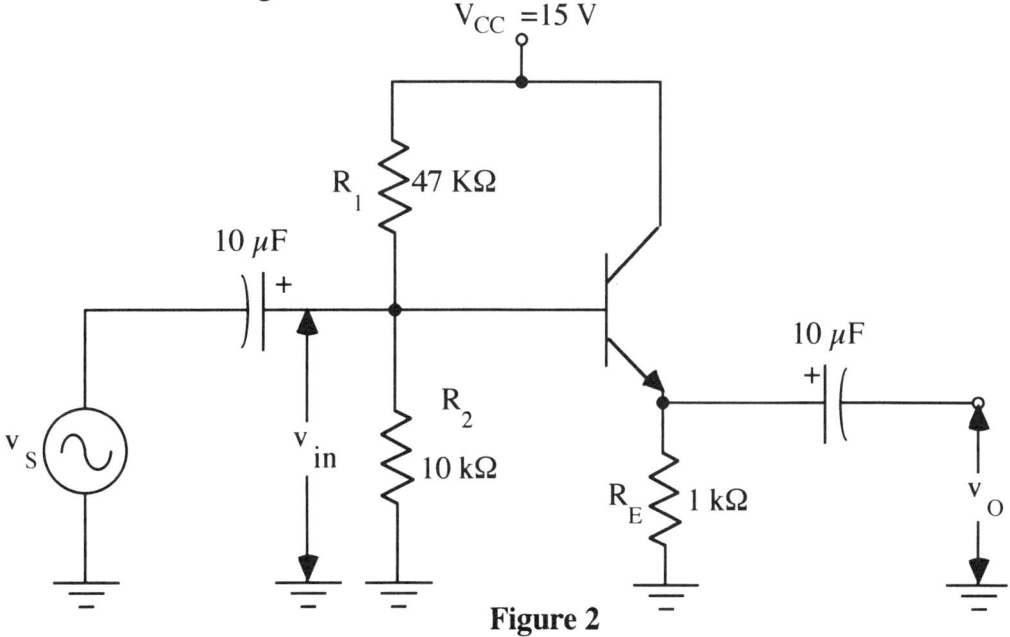

**Figure 2**

3. With the signal generator's frequency set to 10 kHz, adjust the signal generator until $v_o = 0.1$ Vp-p. Measure and record the input voltage

## EXPERIMENT 12 - COMMON-COLLECTOR AMPLIFIER

$v_{in}$ (including the phase relationship between $v_{in}$ and $v_o$). These values can be used to calculate the open-circuit voltage gain, $A_v$.

4. To measure the output resistance, $r_{out}$, of the common-collector amplifier, connect a 200 Ω potentiometer connected as a rheostat between the output coupling capacitor and ground. Adjust this potentiometer until $v_o$ is 50 mVp-p (one-half of the normal 0.1 V output). Remove the potentiometer and measure its resistance. By the voltage divider rule, this resistance equals the output resistance of the amplifier.

5. To measure the input resistance, $r_{in}$, of the common-collector amplifier, insert a 50 kΩ potentiometer connected as a rheostat between (in series with) the input coupling capacitor and the signal generator. Adjust this potentiometer until $v_o$ = 50 mVp-p (one-half of the normal 0.1 V output). Remove the potentiometer and measure its resistance. By the voltage divider rule, this resistance, less the signal generator's internal resistance, $r_s$, equals the input resistance of the common-collector amplifier (if $r_s$ is not known, use the procedure described in step 6 of Experiment 10 to measure its value).

6. To demonstrate the effects of loading on a common-emitter amplifier, connect the following circuit:

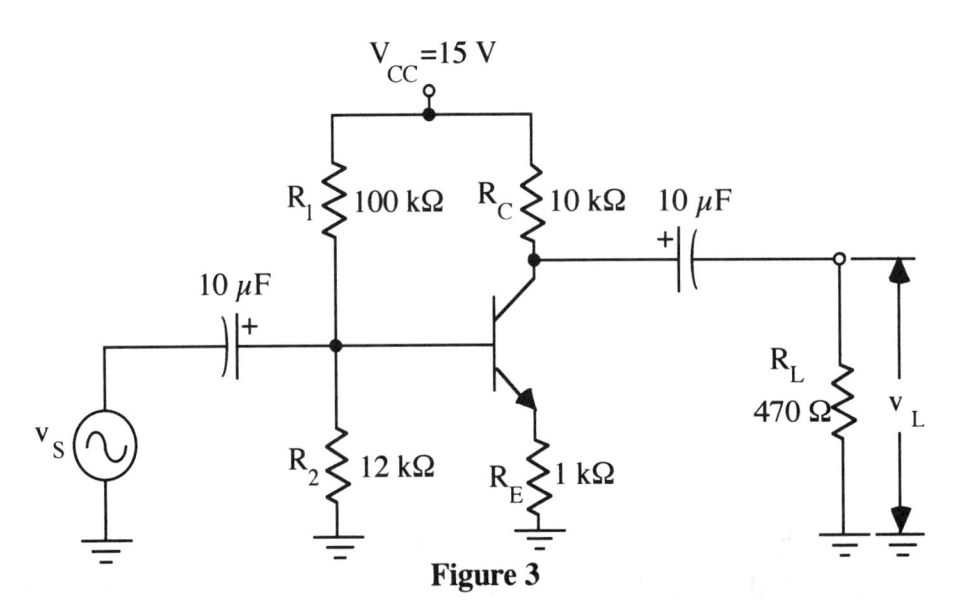

**Figure 3**

# EXPERIMENT 12 - COMMON-COLLECTOR AMPLIFIER

7. Set $v_S = 0.1$ Vp-p at 10 kHz. Measure and record $v_L$. This value can be used to calculate the voltage gain from source-to-load, $v_L/v_S$.

8. To demonstrate the use of a common-collector stage to buffer a low impedance load from the high output resistance of the common-emitter amplifier, connect the following circuit (Note that the bias of the emitter-follower stage is provided by the common-emitter amplifier's collector voltage. This eliminates the need for extra coupling capacitors or voltage divider resistors):

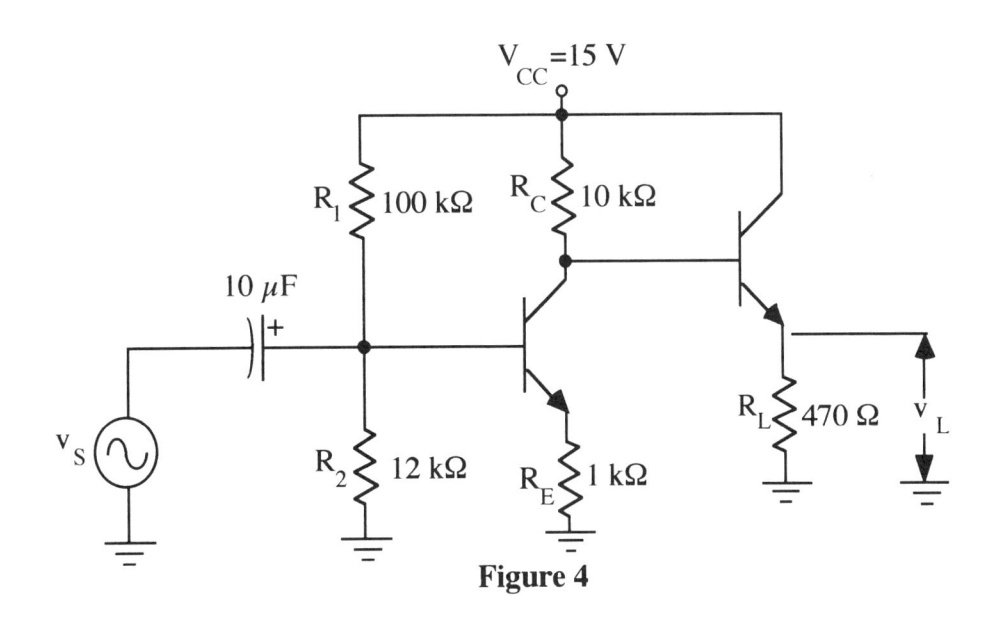

**Figure 4**

9. Repeat procedure step 7 for the circuit of Figure 4. Use ac input coupling on the oscilloscope.

# EXPERIMENT 12 - COMMON-COLLECTOR AMPLIFIER

## Questions

1. Using a technique similar to that described in question 1 of Experiment 11, calculate the dc emitter current $I_E$ and the internal emitter resistance $r_e$ for the circuit of Figure 2.

2. Using the values obtained in question 1, draw the small-signal ac equivalent circuit for the amplifier of Figure 2.

3. Using the equivalent circuit from question 2, calculate the theoretical values for $A_v$, $r_{in}$, and $r_{out}$. Compare these to the measured values from procedure steps 3 through 5.

4. Explain the results of procedure steps 7 through 9. Did the emitter-follower stage have a noticeable effect on the voltage gain from source-to-load, $v_L/v_S$?

# JFET Amplifiers   13

## Reference

*Electronic Devices and Circuits, Sixth Edition:* Section 7-6, The Common-Source JFET Amplifier; Section 7-7, The Common-Drain and Common-Gate JFET Amplifiers

## Objectives

1. To measure the voltage gain of JFET common-source and common-drain amplifiers.
2. To measure the input and output resistances of the amplifiers.
3. To investigate the effect of a source bypass capacitor.

## Equipment List

1. 2N5459 silicon N-channel JFET or the equivalent
2. DC power supply (15 V)
3. Analog signal generator (200 mVp-p sine at 1 kHz)
4. Resistors: 1-220 kΩ, 1-22 kΩ, 1-10 kΩ, 1-4.7 kΩ, 1-1.5 kΩ
5. Capacitors: 3-10 μF (25 V)
6. Potentiometers: 1-50 kΩ, 1-10 kΩ
7. Dual-trace oscilloscope
8. VOM

## Discussion

Figure 1 shows a typical JFET common-source amplifier. The JFET is biased using the combination of a voltage divider across the gate and a self-biasing resistor $R_S$ in the source circuit. This resistor is effectively short-circuited to ground, as far as ac signals are concerned, by source bypass capacitor $C_S$.

# EXPERIMENT 13 - JFET AMPLIFIERS

The transconductance $g_m$, which is the ratio of ac output current to input voltage, is given by the following equation:

$$g_m = \frac{i_d}{v_{GS}} = \frac{2I_{DSS}}{|V_P|}\left(1 - \left|\frac{V_{GS}}{V_P}\right|\right) = \frac{2I_{DSS}}{|V_P|}\sqrt{\frac{I_D}{I_{DSS}}}\text{ siemens}$$

A knowledge of the value of $g_m$ will be necessary to compute the theoretical voltage gain of both the common-source and common-drain amplifiers. It is also used to calculate the output resistance $r_{out}$ of the common-drain amplifier.

The input resistance $r_{in}$ of the common-source amplifier can be found using the following approximation:

$$r_{in} \approx R_1 \| R_2$$

where:
$R_1$ and $R_2$ form the voltage divider at the gate of the JFET

Note that the input resistance to the transistor is neglected in this approximation because it is a reverse-biased PN junction and is typically much larger than $R_1$ and $R_2$.

The voltage gain from source-to-load of the common-source amplifier is given by one of the following equations:

$$\text{bypassed}: A_{VS} = \frac{v_L}{v_S} = \left(\frac{r_{in}}{r_{in} + r_S}\right)(-g_m)(r_D \| R_D \| R_L)$$

$$\text{unbypassed}: A_{VS} = \frac{v_L}{v_S} = \left(\frac{r_{in}}{r_{in} + r_S}\right)\left(\frac{-g_m}{1 + g_m R_S}\right)(R_D \| R_L)$$

where:
$r_S$ is the internal resistance of the signal source
$r_D$ is the internal drain resistance of the JFET
$R_D$ and $R_S$ are the external drain and source resistors, respectively
$R_L$ is the load resistor

As was the case with the common-emitter BJT amplifier, the common-source JFET amplifier is an inverting amplifier.

The output resistance of the common-source amplifier can be calculated using the following equation or approximation:

$$r_{out} = r_D \parallel R_D \approx R_D$$

The approximation is valid if $r_D$ is much larger than $R_D$.

A typical JFET common-drain amplifier configuration, commonly called a *source follower,* is shown in Figure 2. The common-drain amplifier is characterized by a voltage gain of slightly less than one, a high input resistance, and a low output resistance. The input resistance is calculated by the same method used for the common-source amplifier.

By analyzing the small-signal equivalent circuit of a common-drain amplifier, it can be shown that the voltage gain from source-to-load, $v_L/v_S$, is given by:

$$\frac{v_L}{v_S} = \left(\frac{r_{in}}{r_{in} + r_S}\right)\left(\frac{(g_m)(r_D \parallel R_S \parallel R_L)}{1 + (g_m)(r_D \parallel R_S \parallel R_L)}\right)$$

The output resistance $r_{out}$ of the common-drain amplifier can be found from:

$$r_{out} = \frac{R_S}{1 + g_m R_S} \approx \frac{1}{g_m}$$

The approximation is valid when $g_m R_S \gg 1$, which is the case in most practical circuits.

# EXPERIMENT 13 - JFET AMPLIFIERS

## Procedure

1. To determine the values of $I_{DSS}$ and $V_P$ for the JFET to be used in this experiment, complete the procedures in Appendix B.

2. To investigate the common-source amplifier, connect the circuit in Figure 1. If the value of the internal resistance, $r_S$, of the signal source is not known, use the procedure described in step 6 of Experiment 10 to measure its value.

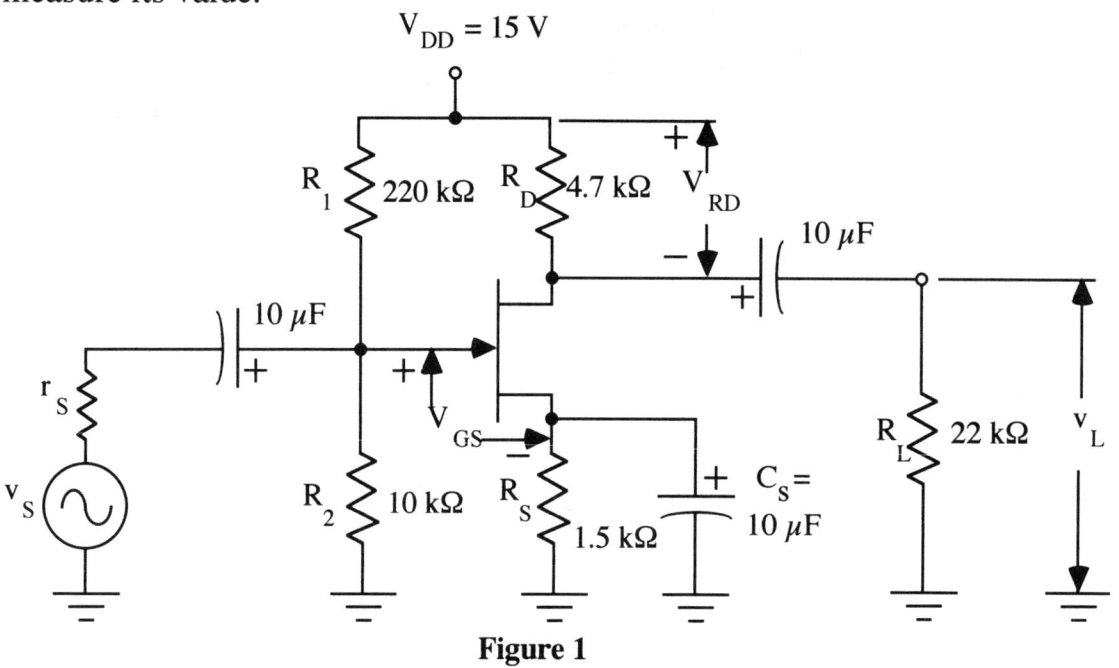

**Figure 1**

3. With $v_S = 0$ V, measure and record the dc voltages $V_{RD}$ and $V_{GS}$. These values will be used to calculate $I_D$ and $g_m$.

4. Connect a dual-trace oscilloscope so that $v_S$ and $v_L$ can be viewed simultaneously. Now adjust $v_S$ to 200 mVp-p at 1 kHz. Measure and record the peak-to-peak load voltage $v_L$ and the phase angle between $v_S$ and $v_L$.

5. Remove the source bypass capacitor $C_S$ and record the new load voltage $v_L$.

EXPERIMENT 13 - JFET AMPLIFIERS

6. Reconnect the source bypass capacitor $C_S$. To measure the input resistance of the common-source amplifier, insert a 50 kΩ potentiometer connected as a rheostat between (in series with) the input coupling capacitor and the signal source $v_S$. Adjust this potentiometer until a maximum load voltage $v_L$ occurs (when the potentiometer is set to its minimum resistance). Make a note of the amplitude of this maximum $v_L$. Then adjust the potentiometer until $v_L$ is one-half of the maximum value. Remove the potentiometer and measure its resistance. By the voltage divider rule, this resistance, less the signal generator's internal resistance, equals the input resistance of the common-source amplifier.

7. To measure the output resistance of the common-source amplifier, insert a 10 kΩ potentiometer connected as a rheostat between the output coupling capacitor and ground (after removing the 22 kΩ load resistor used previously). Measure the output resistance of the common-source amplifier using a technique similar to procedure step 4 of Experiment 11.

8. To investigate the common-drain amplifier, connect the following circuit:

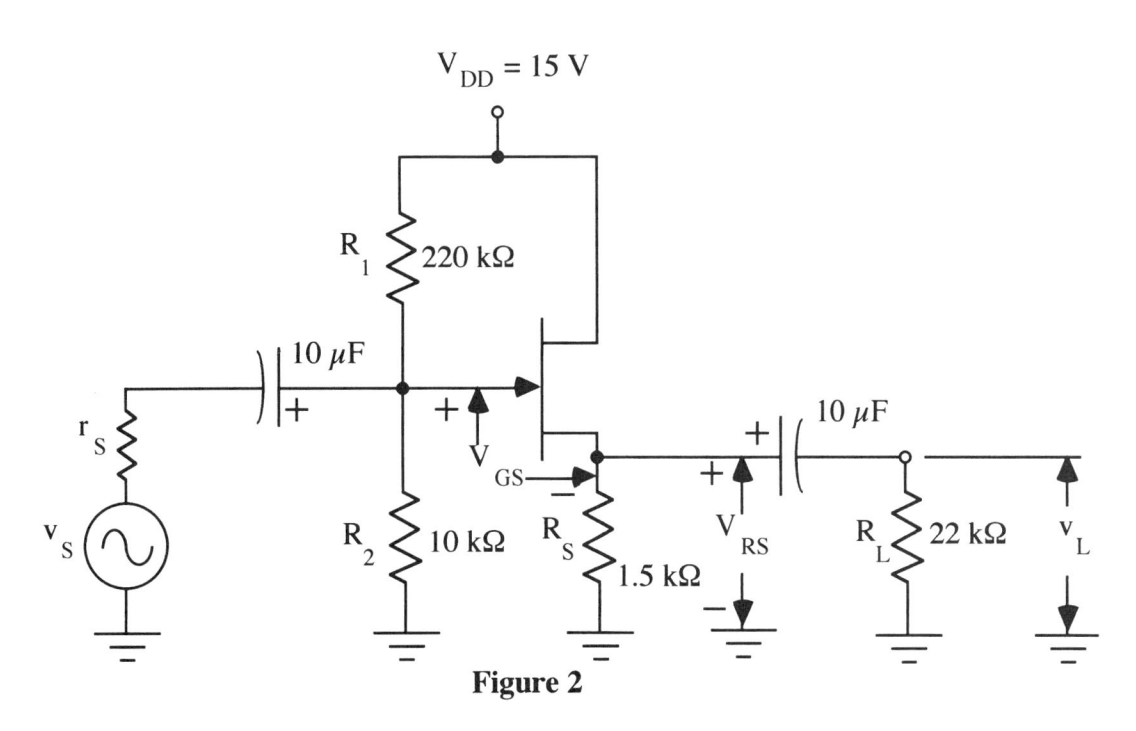

**Figure 2**

# EXPERIMENT 13 - JFET AMPLIFIERS

9. With $v_S = 0$ V, measure and record the dc voltages $V_{GS}$ and $V_{RS}$. These values will be used to calculate $I_D$ and $g_m$.

10. Repeat procedure steps 4, 6, and 7 for the common-drain amplifier.

## Questions

1. Using the results of procedure step 3 and the values for $V_P$ and $I_{DSS}$ obtained from Appendix B, calculate the drain current $I_D$ and the transconductance $g_m$.

2. Using the results of question 1, calculate the voltage gain from source-to-load and the input and output resistances for the source-bypassed circuit in Figure 1. Compare these theoretical values with the values determined experimentally.

3. Calculate the voltage gain from source-to-load for the unbypassed circuit from procedure step 5. Compare this theoretical value with the values determined experimentally.

4. Repeat questions 1 and 2 for the data obtained for the common-drain amplifier in procedure steps 9 and 10.

## SPICE

To determine the gain of the amplifier in Figure 1, use .AC to print the output voltage $v_L$ with $v_S = 200$ mVp-p at 1 kHz. Use measured values for $V_P$ and $I_{DSS}$ to determine VTO and BETA as defined in Appendix C. Then repeat the procedure with the source bypass capacitor, $C_S$, removed. Compare these results to measured results.

# Operational Amplifier 14

## Reference

*Electronic Devices and Circuits, Sixth Edition:* Section 8-1, The Ideal Operational Amplifier

## Objectives

1. To demonstrate an inverting operational amplifier circuit.
2. To demonstrate a noninverting operational amplifier circuit.
3. To investigate the operational amplifier voltage follower.

## Equipment List

1. 741 operational amplifier or the equivalent
2. 3-DC power supplies (±15 V and variable)
3. Analog signal generator (100 mVpk sine at 1 kHz, 5 Vpk sine at 1 kHz, 2 Vpk square at 500 Hz)
4. Resistors: 1-1 MΩ, 1-100 kΩ, 1-10 kΩ, 1-4.7 kΩ, 1-2.2 kΩ, 2-1kΩ, 1-470 Ω
5. Dual-trace oscilloscope

## Discussion

The operational amplifier is probably the most frequently used linear integrated circuit available. Applications for operational amplifiers range from the simple voltage amplifiers discussed in this experiment to complex circuitry that is beyond the scope of this course. The amplifier configurations investigated in this experiment are the basic building blocks of modern electronic circuits.

# EXPERIMENT 14 - OPERATIONAL AMPLIFIER

There are two basic configurations for operational amplifier circuits: the *inverting* amplifier and the *noninverting* amplifier. Operational amplifiers ideally have infinite *open-loop* gain and infinite open-loop input resistance. *Open-loop* characteristics refer to those of an amplifier having no feedback resistance between output and input. Closed-loop characteristics are those of an amplifier having an external feedback resistor. The resistor provides *negative* feedback, whereby a portion of the output voltage is subtracted from the input. Both the inverting and noninverting amplifier use the principle of negative feedback to control the overall (closed-loop) voltage gain.

Figure 1 shows a typical inverting amplifier configuration. An ideal inverting amplifier's voltage gain is determined by:

$$A_V = -\frac{R_F}{R_1}$$

where:
   $R_1$ is the input resistor
   $R_F$ is the feedback resistor
   As usual, the minus sign signifies phase inversion.

Figure 2 shows a typical noninverting amplifier configuration. The voltage gain of an ideal noninverting amplifier is determined by:

$$A_V = 1 + \frac{R_F}{R_1}$$

Like the emitter follower and source follower, the output of an operational amplifier voltage follower is the same as its input (voltage gain = +1). However, the operational amplifier version is superior to its discrete counterparts because it has a much larger input resistance and a much smaller output resistance.

The voltage follower shown in Figure 3 is actually a special case of a noninverting amplifier. Note from the above equation that as $R_F$ approaches 0 (short) and as $R_1$ approaches ∞ (open), the voltage gain of the noninverting amplifier approaches 1.

# EXPERIMENT 14 - OPERATIONAL AMPLIFIER

## Procedure

1. To investigate an operational amplifier used as an inverting amplifier, connect the circuit in Figure 1. The small numbers in the diagram correspond to the integrated circuit's (chip's) pin numbers, as shown in specification sheets. (NOTE: If oscillation occurs it may be necessary to add 0.1 $\mu$F capacitors from each supply pin to ground. Also keep this in mind when performing all future op-amp experiments.)

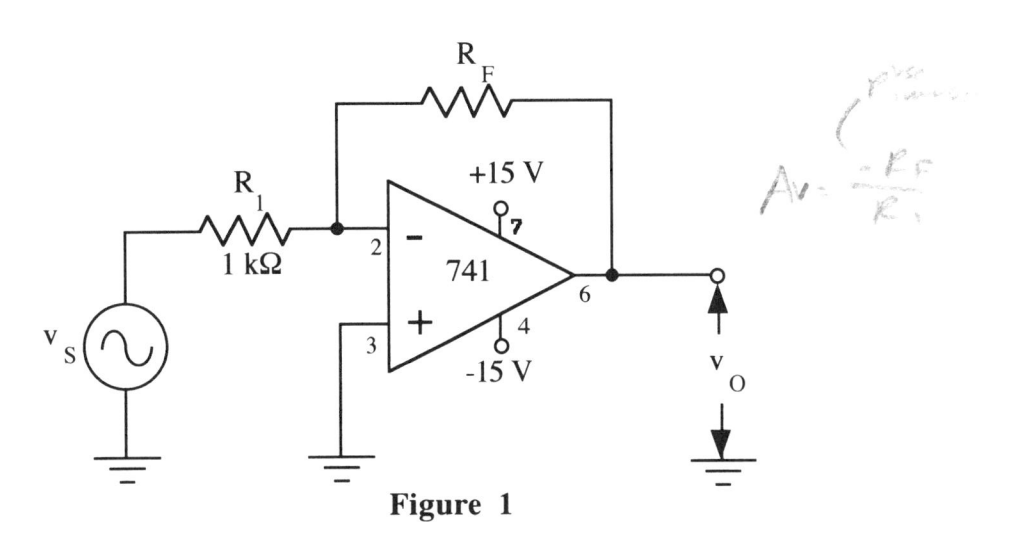

**Figure 1**

2. Connect a dual-trace oscilloscope to observe both the input $v_S$ and the output $v_O$. With $v_S$ = 100 mVpk at 1 kHz, measure and record in Table 1 the output voltage $v_O$ for each value of $R_F$ listed in Table 1. Also note the phase angle of the output $v_O$ with respect to the input $v_S$.

3. To verify that the inverting amplifier is a dc amplifier, replace the signal generator with a dc power supply. With $R_F$ = 10 k$\Omega$, and $v_S$ = 1 Vdc measure the output voltage $v_O$ and note its polarity with respect to $v_S$.

4. Now replace $R_F$ with a 1 M$\Omega$ resistor and sketch the resulting output waveform $v_O$ as well as the input waveform $v_S$.

## EXPERIMENT 14 - OPERATIONAL AMPLIFIER

5. To investigate an operational amplifier used as a noninverting amplifier, connect the following circuit:

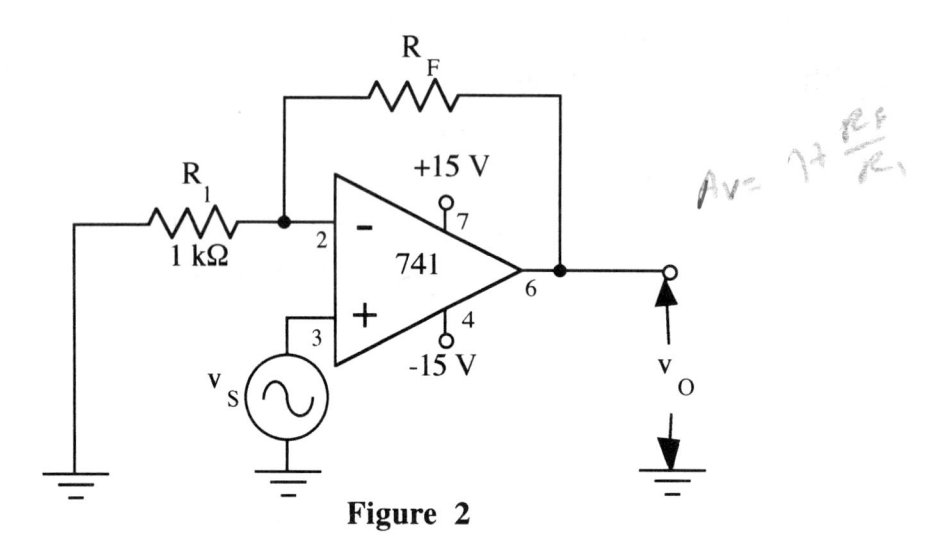

**Figure 2**

6. Connect a dual-trace oscilloscope to observe both the input $v_S$ and the output $v_O$. Repeat procedure step 2 for the noninverting amplifier using the values of $R_F$ in Table 2.

7. To verify that the noninverting amplifier is a dc amplifier, replace the signal generator with a dc power supply. With $R_F = 10$ k$\Omega$ and $v_S = 1$ Vdc, measure the output voltage $v_O$ and note its polarity with respect to $v_S$.

8. To investigate the operational amplifier voltage follower, connect the following circuit:

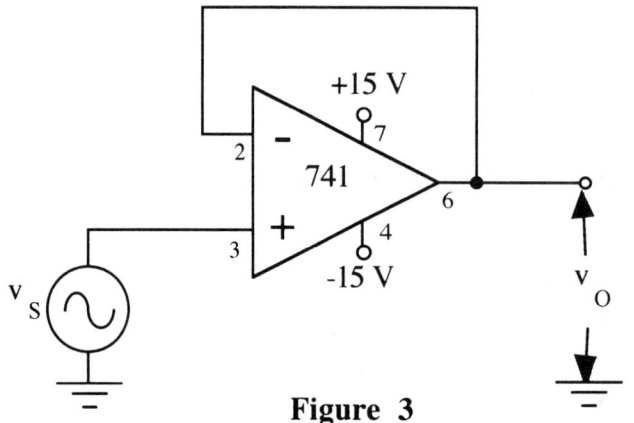

**Figure 3**

# EXPERIMENT 14 - OPERATIONAL AMPLIFIER

9. With $v_S = 5$ Vpk at 1 kHz, measure the output voltage $v_O$. Note the phase angle of the output $v_O$ with respect to the input $v_S$. Repeat this procedure with $v_S = 10$ Vdc and again with $v_S = 2$ Vpk square wave.

## Questions

1. Calculate the voltage gain for each value of $R_F$ in Table 1 using the voltage values obtained in procedure step 2. Also calculate the voltage gain for the inverting amplifier using the results of procedure step 3. Compare these values with the theoretical voltage gain for each value of $R_F$. Do the phase and polarity relationships hold true to theory?

2. Explain the results of procedure step 4. What would the output voltage $v_O$ have looked like if the input voltage $v_S$ had been only 50 mVpk?

3. Repeat question 1 for the values of $R_F$ in Table 2 using the voltage values obtained in procedure steps 6 and 7.

4. Calculate the voltage gain of the voltage follower using the voltage values obtained in procedure step 9. Given this information, why would a voltage follower ever be useful?

# EXPERIMENT 14 - OPERATIONAL AMPLIFIER

## Data

### TABLE 1

mV

| $R_F$ (ohms) | $v_O$ (volts) | $A_V = v_O/v_S$ |
|---|---|---|
| 470 Ω | −104.7 | 0.49 |
| 1 kΩ | −203.1 | 0.92 |
| 2.2 kΩ | −481.2 | 1.97 |
| 4.7 kΩ | −921.9 | 4.4 |
| 10 kΩ | −1.938 V | 8.5 |
| 100 kΩ | −19.38 | 86.1 |

### TABLE 2

| $R_F$ (ohms) | $v_O$ (volts) | $A_V = v_O/v_S$ |
|---|---|---|
| 470 Ω | 543.7 | 1.4 |
| 1 kΩ | 872.5 | 2.07 |
| 2.2 kΩ | 1.281 | 3.2 |
| 4.7 kΩ | 2.312 | 5.178 |
| 10 kΩ | 4.5 | 11.25 |
| 100 kΩ | 20 | 106 |

# EXPERIMENT 14 - OPERATIONAL AMPLIFIER

# *Summing and Difference Amplifier* 15

## Reference

*Electronic Devices and Circuits, Sixth Edition:* Section 8-2, Voltage Summation, Subtraction, and Scaling

## Objective

To demonstrate the use of operational amplifiers for performing mathematical operations—summation and difference.

## Equipment List

1. 741 operational amplifier or the equivalent
2. DC power supplies (±15 V, 5 V)
3. Analog signal generator (1 Vpk sine at 1 kHz)
4. Resistors: 2-100 kΩ, 2-47 kΩ
5. Dual-trace oscilloscope

## Discussion

When the first operational amplifiers were constructed, their primary function was to perform mathematical *operations* in analog computers. These included summation, subtraction, multiplication, division, integration, and differentiation. The summation circuit is also used to mix or combine analog signals together, for example, at a rock concert. The huge mixing board in the center of the coliseum contains many operational amplifiers connected as summation amplifiers that combine the guitar, vocals, and other instrument signals into a single signal to send to the power amplifiers and speakers.

Figure 1 shows an example of how an operational amplifier is connected to perform voltage summation. (In this figure, an ac and a dc voltage are summed.) In general,

# EXPERIMENT 15 - SUMMING AND DIFFERENCE AMPLIFIER

$$v_O = -\left(v_{in1}\frac{R_F}{R_{in1}} + v_{in2}\frac{R_F}{R_{in2}} + ....etc.\right)$$

The circuit in Figure 2 is a difference amplifier. This design is useful for performing mathematical subtraction, or to connect two parts of an electrical system that need ground isolation. The differential amplifier provides excellent common mode rejection, and this fact makes it useful for canceling out unwanted signals that get onto both the signal and ground, for example.

It can be shown that the gain of the difference amplifier can be calculated using the following:

$$v_O = \left(v_{in2}\left(1 + \frac{R_F}{R_{in1}}\right)\left(\frac{R_G}{R_{in2} + R_G}\right)\right) - \left(v_{in1}\frac{R_F}{R_{in1}}\right)$$

This circuit can be simplified by making $R_G = R_F = R_{in1} = R_{in2}$, yielding a simple differential amplifier with unity gain:

$$v_O = v_{in2} - v_{in1}$$

## Procedure

1. To demonstrate the use of an operational amplifier as a summing amplifier, connect the following circuit:

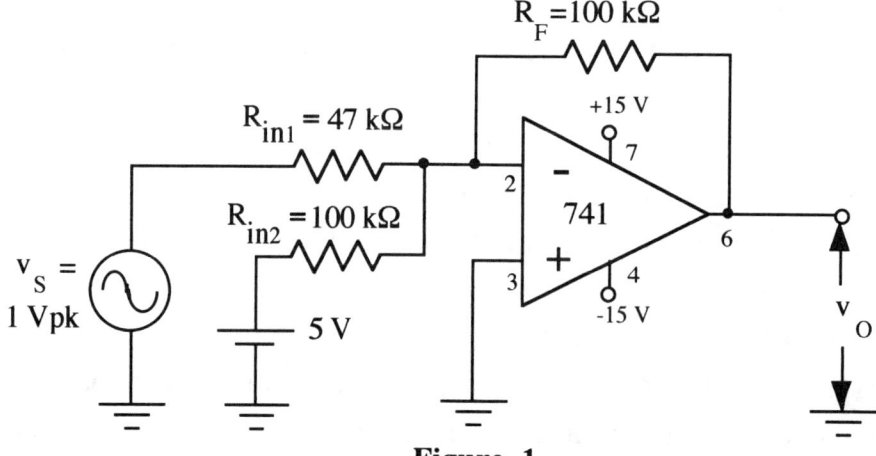

**Figure 1**

# EXPERIMENT 15 - SUMMING AND DIFFERENCE AMPLIFIER

2. With $v_S$ adjusted to produce a 1 Vpk sine wave at 1 kHz, observe the output voltage $v_O$ (and $v_S$ to note the phase relationship) on an oscilloscope set to dc input coupling. Sketch the output waveform. Be sure to note the dc level in the output.

3. Interchange the 5 V dc power supply and the 1 Vpk signal generator. Repeat procedure step 2.

4. To investigate the use of an operational amplifier in a difference amplifier configuration, connect the following circuit:

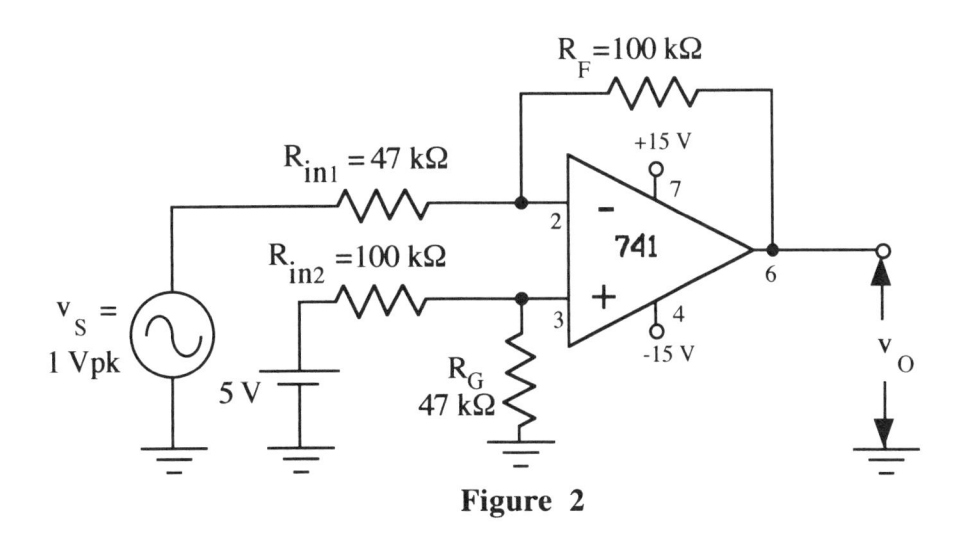

**Figure 2**

5. With $v_S$ adjusted to produce a 1 Vpk sine wave at 1 kHz, observe the output voltage $v_O$ (and $v_S$ to note the phase relationship) on an oscilloscope set to dc input coupling. Sketch the output waveform. Be sure to note the dc level in the output.

6. Interchange the 5 V dc power supply and the 1 Vpk signal generator. Repeat procedure step 5.

# EXPERIMENT 15 - SUMMING AND DIFFERENCE AMPLIFIER

## Questions

1. Write the theoretical equation for the output voltage in the circuit of Figure 1 with the input voltages prescribed by procedure step 2. Compare this equation with the equation based on the measurements obtained in procedure step 2.

2. Repeat question 1 for procedure step 3.

3. Write the theoretical equation for the output voltage in the circuit of Figure 2 with the input voltages prescribed by procedure step 2. Compare this equation with the equation based on the measurements obtained in procedure step 5.

4. Repeat question 3 for procedure step 6.

5. Design a summing amp with three inputs having gains $A_v = 2$, 3, and 4 respectively.

# Lower Cutoff Frequency 16

## Reference

*Electronic Devices and Circuits, Sixth Edition:* Section 9-1, Definitions and Basic Concepts; Section 9-2, Decibels and Logarithmic Plots; Section 9-3, Series Capacitance and Low Frequency Response; Section 9-6, Frequency Response of BJT Amplifiers

## Objectives

1. To measure the lower cutoff frequency of a common-emitter amplifier.
2. To measure the lower cutoff frequencies due to each coupling and bypass capacitor.

## Equipment List

1. 2N2222 silicon transistor or the equivalent
2. DC power supply (15 V)
3. Analog signal generator (50 mVp-p at 50 Hz to 10 kHz)
4. Resistors: 1-82 k$\Omega$, 1-15 k$\Omega$, 1-6.8 k$\Omega$, 1-2.2 k$\Omega$, 1-1.5 k$\Omega$
5. Capacitors: 2-100 $\mu$F, 1-4.7 $\mu$F, 1-0.22 $\mu$F, 1-0.1 $\mu$F (all 25 V)
6. Dual-trace oscilloscope

## Discussion

Since the impedance of coupling capacitors increases as frequency decreases, the voltage gain of a BJT amplifier decreases as frequency decreases. At very low frequencies, the capacitive reactance of the coupling capacitors may become large enough to drop some of the input voltage or output voltage. Also, the emitter-bypass capacitor may become large enough so that it no longer *shorts* the emitter resistor to ground.

## EXPERIMENT 16 - LOWER CUTOFF FREQUENCY

The following equations can be used to determine the lower cutoff frequency, where the voltage gain drops 3 dB from its midband value ($\approx 0.707$ times the midband $A_V$):

$$f_1 = \frac{1}{2\pi(r_{in} + r_S)C_1}$$

where:
- $f_1$ = lower cutoff frequency due to $C_1$
- $C_1$ = input coupling capacitance
- $r_{in}$ = input resistance of the amplifier
- $r_S$ = source resistance

$$f_2 = \frac{1}{2\pi(r_{out} + R_L)C_2}$$

where:
- $f_2$ = lower cutoff frequency due to $C_2$
- $C_2$ = output coupling capacitance
- $r_{out}$ = output resistance of the amplifier
- $R_L$ = load resistance

$$f_L = \frac{1}{2\pi R_e C_E}$$

where:
- $f_L$ = lower cutoff frequency due to $C_E$
- $C_E$ = emitter-bypass capacitance
- $R_e$ = Thévenin resistance parallel to the capacitor:

$$R_e = R_E \parallel \left( r_e + \frac{R_B \parallel r_S}{\beta} \right)$$

where:
- $R_B$ = parallel combination of all the input bias resistors

Provided that $f_1$, $f_2$, and $f_L$ are not close in value, the actual lower cutoff frequency is approximately equal to the largest of the three.

## EXPERIMENT 16 - LOWER CUTOFF FREQUENCY

## Procedure

1. Complete the procedures of Appendix A to measure the ß of the transistor.

2. To measure the low frequency response of the common-emitter amplifier, connect the following circuit. (The plus (+) signs show the polarities of the electrolytic capacitors used in procedure steps 5 through 8)

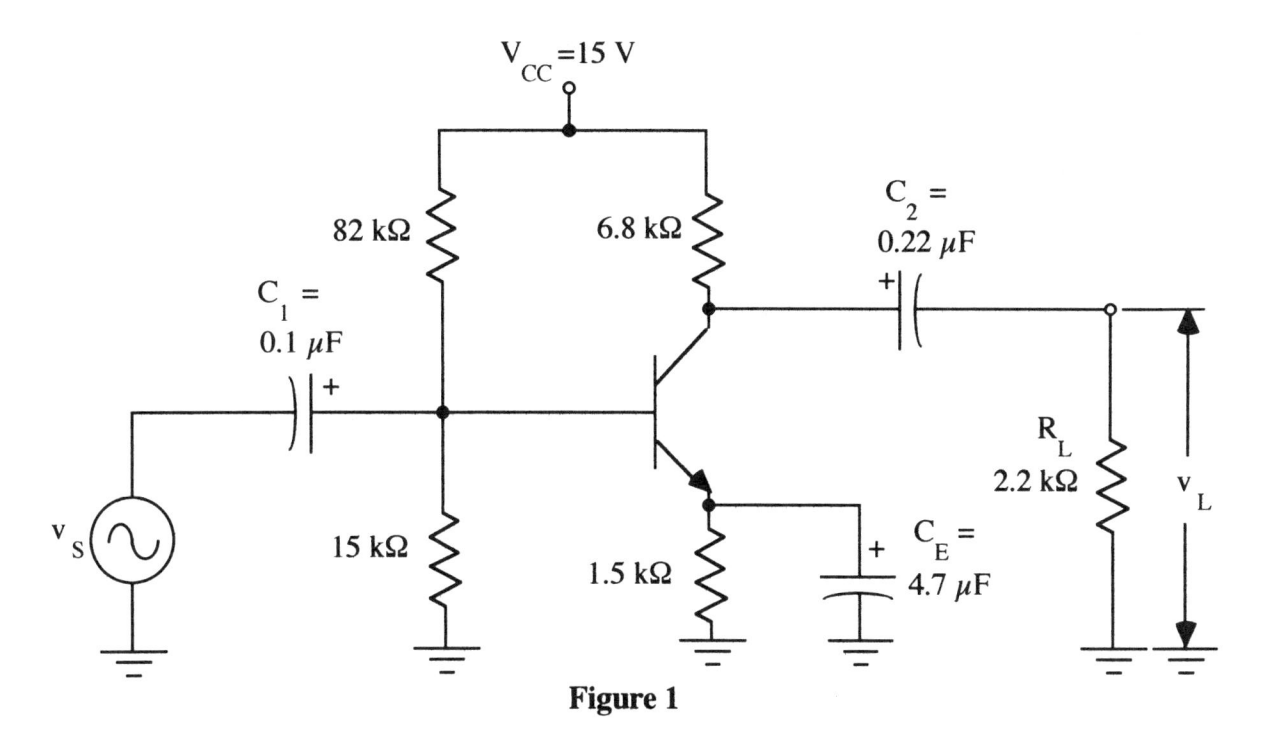

**Figure 1**

3. With $v_S$ = 50 mVp-p at 10 kHz, measure and record $v_L$. This value can be used to determine the midband voltage gain, $v_L/v_S$.

4. Now decrease the frequency of the signal generator to each frequency in Table 1 and measure the value of $v_L$ at each frequency. Make sure the output voltage from the signal generator is constant. These values will be used to plot the low-frequency response of the amplifier.

# EXPERIMENT 16 - LOWER CUTOFF FREQUENCY

5. By making two capacitors very large, the effects of those capacitors on the lower cutoff frequency can be made negligible. The cutoff frequency due to the third capacitor can then be measured. With this in mind, reconnect the circuit of Figure 1 with the following capacitor values (observe the polarities as shown in Figure 1):

$$C_1 = 0.1 \; \mu F, \; C_2 = 100 \; \mu F, \; C_E = 100 \; \mu F$$

6. Making certain that $v_S$ remains at 50 mVp-p, adjust the frequency of the signal generator until the output voltage (and therefore the voltage gain) equals 0.707 times that measured in procedure step 3. The frequency where this occurs is $f_1$.

7. Repeat procedure steps 5 and 6 to determine $f_2$ using the following capacitor values:

$$C_1 = 100 \; \mu F, \; C_2 = 0.22 \; \mu F, \; C_E = 100 \; \mu F$$

8. Repeat procedure steps 5 and 6 to determine $f_L$ using the following capacitor values:

$$C_1 = 100 \; \mu F, \; C_2 = 100 \; \mu F, \; C_E = 4.7 \; \mu F$$

# EXPERIMENT 16 - LOWER CUTOFF FREQUENCY

## Questions

1. Using the results obtained in Appendix A, calculate the ß of the transistor. Use the method described in question 1 of Experiment 11 to determine $I_E$ and the resulting value of $r_e$. Then use these values to calculate the midband ac parameters ($r_{in}$, $r_{out}$, $v_L/v_S$) of the circuit in Figure 1.

2. Calculate the values for $v_L/v_S$ at each frequency in Table 1. Then plot these values on log-log graph paper. Include asymptotic lines that show the break frequency due to each capacitor. From this graph of frequency response, obtain the lower cutoff frequency (−3 dB point) and label the graph accordingly.

3. Calculate $f_1$, $f_2$, and $f_L$ for the common-emitter amplifier. Compare these with the lower cutoff frequencies measured in procedure steps 5 through 8.

4. Which capacitor had the most effect on the lower cutoff frequency? Compare the lower cutoff frequency due to this capacitor with the overall cutoff frequency determined in question 2. Comment and explain.

## SPICE

Use the .AC command to plot the frequency response of the circuit in Figure 1. Plot from 50 Hz to 10 kHz, with adequate steps to compare to data measured in lab.

# EXPERIMENT 16 - LOWER CUTOFF FREQUENCY

# EXPERIMENT 16 - LOWER CUTOFF FREQUENCY

## Data

### TABLE 1

| Frequency | $v_L$ (volts) | $A_{VS} = v_L/v_S$ |
|---|---|---|
| 10 kHz | | |
| 7.5 kHz | | |
| 5 kHz | | |
| 2 kHz | | |
| 1.5 kHz | | |
| 1 kHz | | |
| 900 Hz | | |
| 750 Hz | | |
| 500 Hz | | |
| 250 Hz | | |
| 200 Hz | | |
| 100 Hz | | |
| 50 Hz | | |

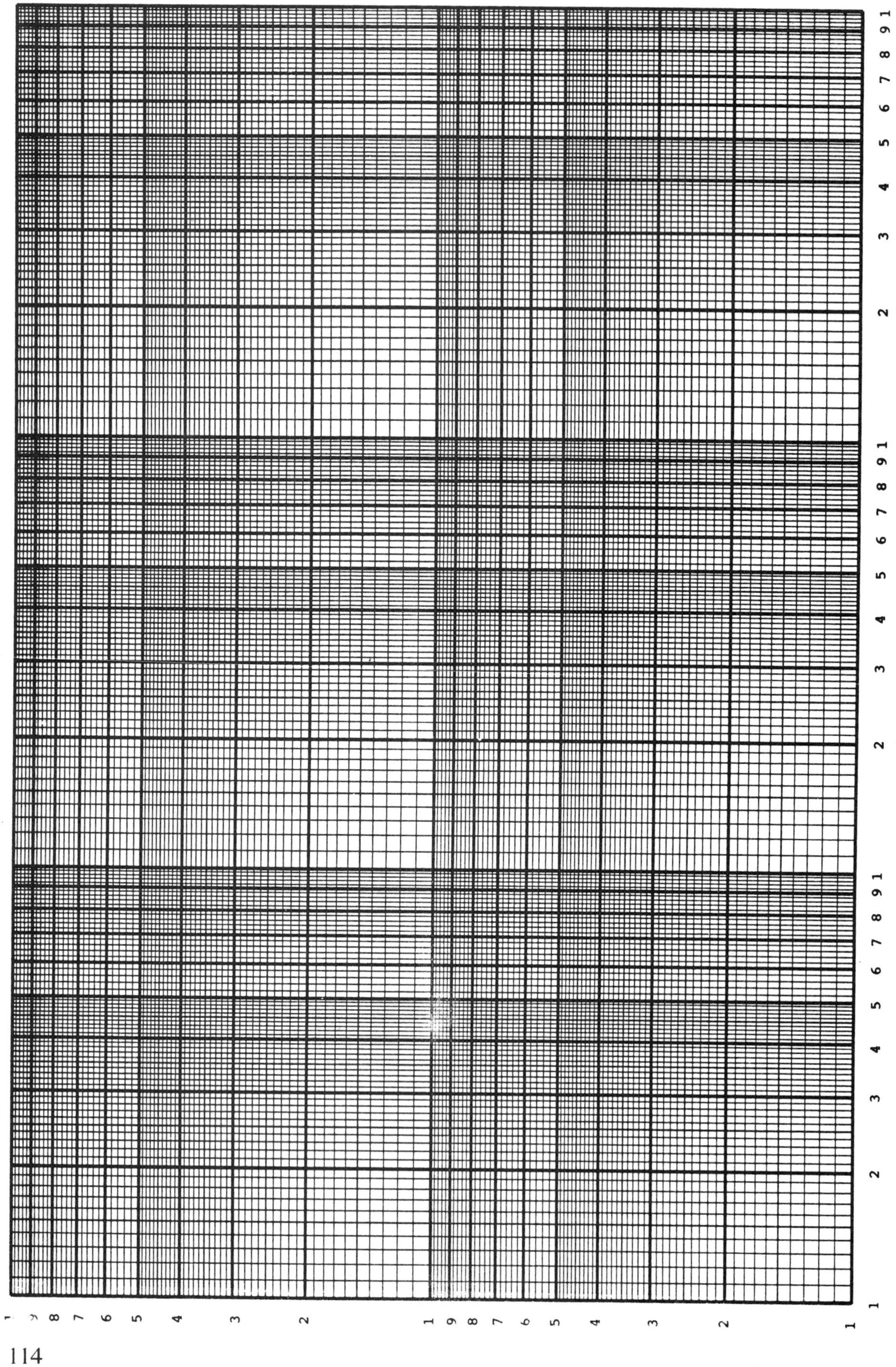

# Upper Cutoff Frequency 17

## Reference

*Electronic Devices and Circuits, Sixth Edition:* Section 9-1, Definitions and Basic Concepts; Section 9-2, Decibels and Logarithmic Plots; Section 9-4, Shunt Capacitance and High-Frequency Response; Section 9-6, Frequency Response of BJT Amplifiers

## Objectives

1. To measure the upper cutoff frequency of a common-emitter amplifier.
2. To measure the upper cutoff frequencies due to shunt capacitances.
3. To demonstrate the effect of Miller capacitance on upper cutoff frequency.

## Equipment List

1. 2N2222 silicon transistor or the equivalent
2. DC power supply (15 V)
3. Analog signal generator (25 mVp-p at 400 Hz to 50 kHz)
4. Resistors: 1-100 kΩ, 1-15 kΩ, 1-10 kΩ, 1-5.6 kΩ, 2-1 kΩ
5. Capacitors: 1-100 µF, 2-22 µF, 1-0.0022 µF, 1-0.068 µF, 1-100 pF (all 25 V)
6. Dual-trace oscilloscope

## Discussion

As was discussed in Experiment 16, the capacitive reactance of a capacitor decreases as frequency increases. This can lead to problems for amplifiers used for high-frequency amplification. Transistors have

# EXPERIMENT 17 - UPPER CUTOFF FREQUENCY

inherent *shunt* capacitances between each pair of terminals. At high frequencies, these capacitances effectively short (shunt) the ac signal voltage. Therefore, for high frequency amplifiers, transistors with low shunt capacitance are preferred.

In this experiment, artificial shunt capacitors will be installed in the amplifier circuit because it is extremely difficult to measure the actual interelectrode capacitances of the transistor. It is equally difficult to measure *stray* shunt capacitance due to the wiring of the circuit. Since the artificial capacitors are much larger than the real capacitance already present, the parallel combination of real capacitance and artificial capacitors is approximately equal to the value of the artificial capacitors. The objective is to investigate the high-frequency response of the amplifier to gain insight into the problems associated with shunt capacitance, and to obtain practice measuring the upper cutoff frequency of an amplifier.

The upper cutoff frequency is the larger of the two frequencies where the voltage gain of the amplifier is –3 dB or 0.707 times the midband value (the lower cutoff frequency is the other frequency where this occurs). For the circuit in Figure 1, the upper cutoff frequency $f_H$ due to input shunt capacitance $C_A$ ($C_{BE}$), output shunt capacitance $C_B$ ($C_{CE}$), and feedback capacitance $C_C$ ($C_{CB}$), can be closely approximated using the following general equations:

$$f_H = \frac{1}{\frac{1}{f'_A} + \frac{1}{f'_B}}$$

where:

$$f'_A = \frac{1}{2\pi(r_S \| r_i)C'_A} \qquad f'_B = \frac{1}{2\pi(r_O \| r_L)C'_B}$$

where $C_A$ and $C_B$ are modified by adding the *Miller-effect* capacitance, which is the interelectrode feedback capacitance $C_{CB}$ modified by the gain $A_V$ as follows:

$$C'_A = C_A + (1 - A_V)C_C \qquad C'_B = C_B + (1 - 1/A_V)C_C$$

where:

$A_V$ = the voltage gain from input-to-load in the midband

Miller capacitance only occurs in inverting amplifiers, so noninverting amplifiers are most often used in very high-frequency amplification. It is important to notice that $A_v$ does not take into account the voltage divider between the internal signal-source resistance and the input resistance of the amplifier. Therefore, the value of $A_v$ is not equal to the overall gain from source-to-load, $v_L/v_S$.

It is common practice to represent frequency response data in terms of decibels (dB). The voltage gain $v_L/v_S$ can be converted to gain in dB using the following equation:

$$A_{vs}(dB) = 20 \log(A_{vs})$$

where:

$A_{vs}$ is the voltage gain, $v_L/v_S$

The resulting gain values are plotted on semi-log graph paper, which has a linear scale for gain and a logarithmic scale for frequency.

# EXPERIMENT 17 - UPPER CUTOFF FREQUENCY

## Procedure

1. Complete the procedures of Appendix A to measure the ß of the transistor.

2. To measure the high-frequency response of the common-emitter amplifier, connect the following circuit. The capacitors $C_{BC}$, $C_{BE}$, and $C_{CE}$ shown in the circuit represent interelectrode capacitances. They, along with $R_S$, are intentionally made much larger than the normal device capacitances and source resistances for reasons outlined in the discussion section.

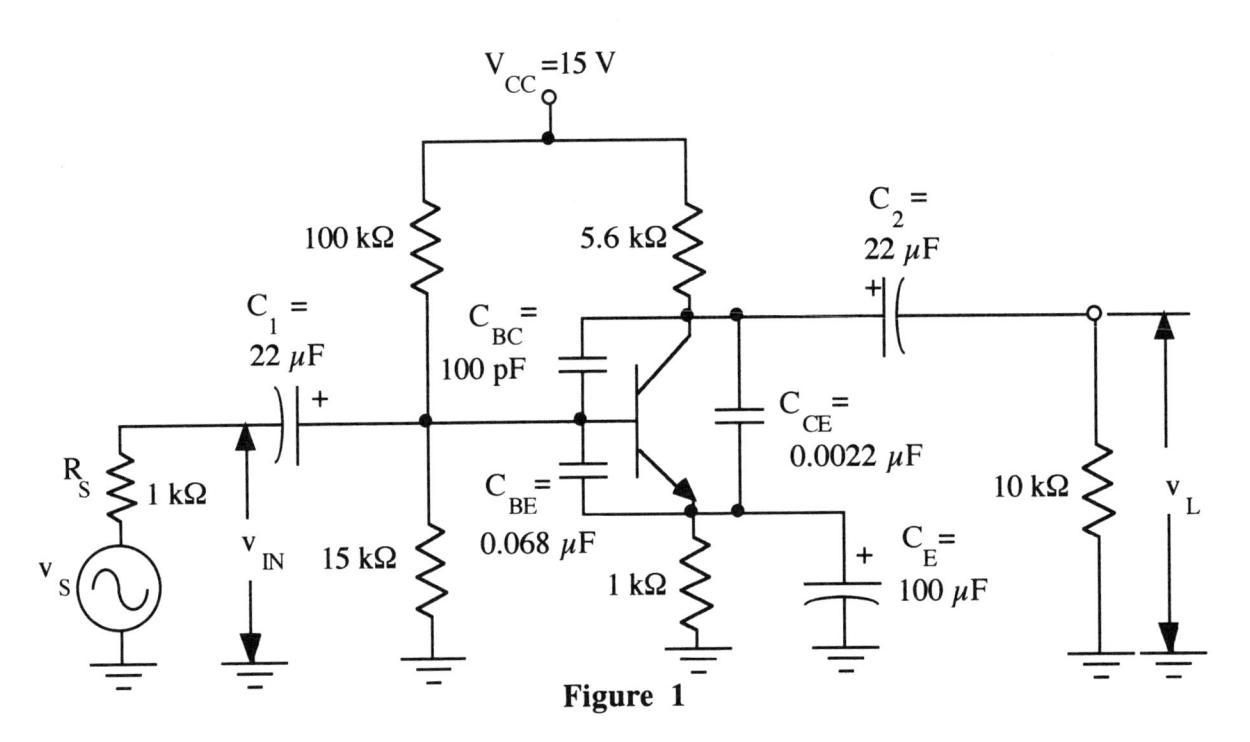

**Figure 1**

3. With $v_S$ = 25 mVp-p at 400 Hz, measure and record $v_{IN}$ and $v_L$. These values can be used to determine the midband voltage gain $A_V$ and the voltage gain from load-to-source, $v_L/v_S$.

4. Now increase the frequency of the signal generator to each frequency in Table 1 measuring values of $v_L$ at each frequency.

EXPERIMENT 17 - **UPPER CUTOFF FREQUENCY**

Periodically remove the signal generator and measure its output voltage to ensure that it remains at 25 mVp-p as frequency is changed. The values of $v_L$ will be used to plot the high-frequency response of the amplifier.

## Questions

1. Using the results obtained in Appendix A, calculate the ß of the transistor. Then use this value of ß to calculate the midband ac parameters ($r_e$, $r_{in}$, $r_{out}$, $A_v$, $v_L/v_S$) for the circuit of Figure 1. Use these values to calculate the Miller capacitance.

2. Calculate the values for $A_v$ at each frequency in Table 1 derived from procedure steps 3 and 4. Then convert these values to decibels (dB). Plot the decibel equivalents on semi-log graph paper. From this graph of frequency response, obtain the upper cutoff frequency (–3 dB point) and label the graph accordingly.

3. Compare the theoretical and measured results for upper cutoff frequency $f_H$ for the example in the experiment. Would this circuit be used in a high fidelity audio amplifier? Explain.

# EXPERIMENT 17 - UPPER CUTOFF FREQUENCY

# EXPERIMENT 17 - UPPER CUTOFF FREQUENCY

## Data

### TABLE 1

| Frequency | $v_L$ (volts) | $A_{VS} = v_L/v_S$ |
|---|---|---|
| 400 Hz | | |
| 600 Hz | | |
| 1 kHz | | |
| 2 kHz | | |
| 4 kHz | | |
| 8 kHz | | |
| 16 kHz | | |
| 20 kHz | | |
| 40 kHz | | |

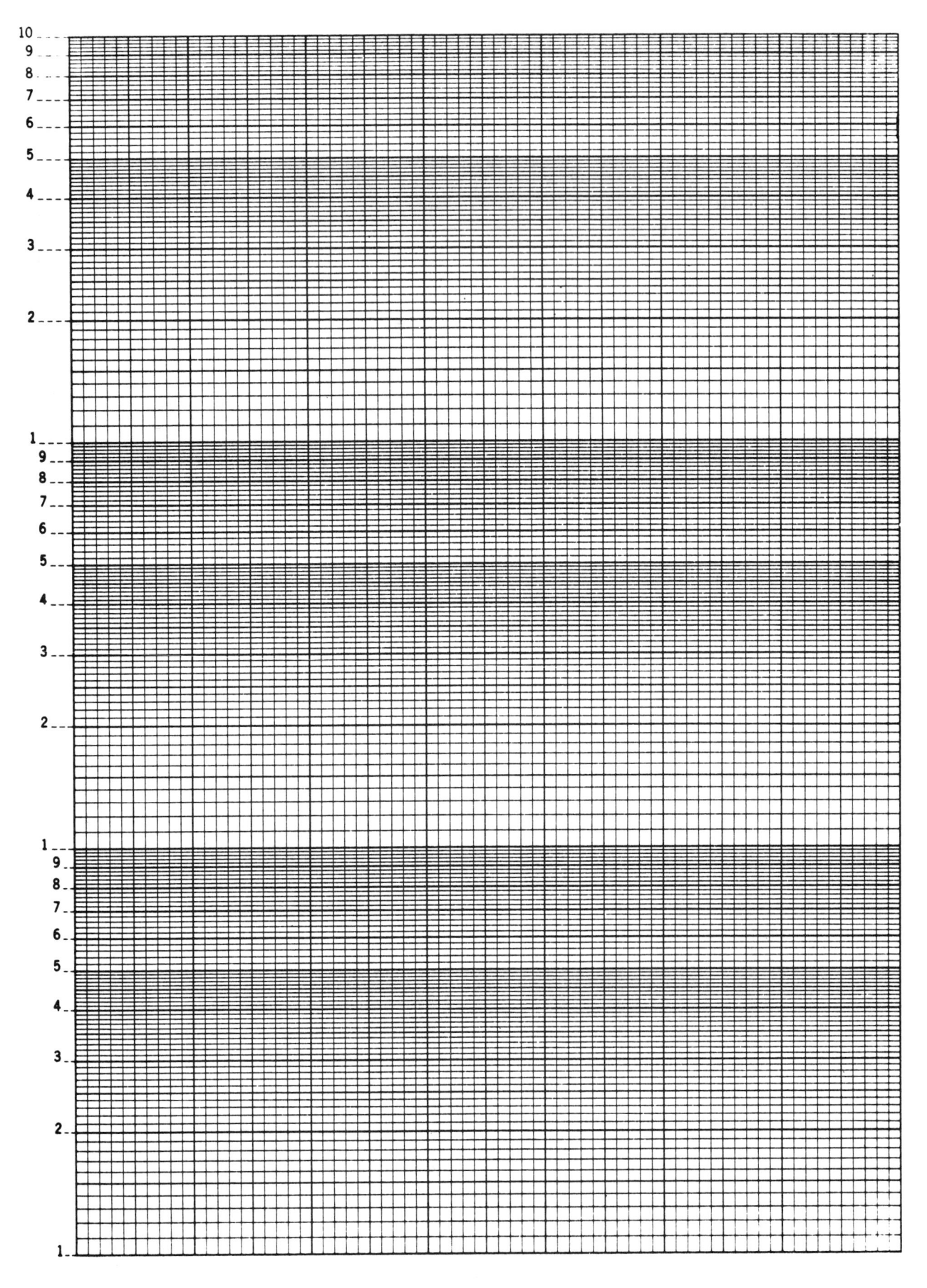

# Bandwidth, Slew Rate, and Offsets  18

## Reference

*Electronic Devices and Circuits, Sixth Edition:* Section 10-3, Frequency Response; Section 10-4, Slew Rate and Rise Time; Section 10-5, Offset Currents and Voltages

## Objectives

1. To investigate the bandwidth of an operational amplifier as a function of gain.
2. To determine the slew rate of an operational amplifier.
3. To investigate the output offset voltage at the output of an operational amplifier.

## Equipment List

1. 741 operational amplifier or the equivalent
2. DC power supplies (±15 V)
3. Analog signal generator (50 mVpk sine, 10 Vpk sine, 1 Vpk square—all with variable frequency)
4. Resistors: 2-1 MΩ, 1-470 kΩ, 1-100 kΩ, 1-47 kΩ, 2-10 kΩ
5. Potentiometer: 1-10 kΩ
6. Dual-trace oscilloscope
7. DVM

## Discussion

The operational amplifier has a few limitations. This experiment will investigate the operational amplifier's bandwidth as a function of gain, the slew rate of the operational amplifier, and output offset voltages. Unlike a

# EXPERIMENT 18 - BANDWIDTH, SLEW RATE, AND OFFSETS

real operational amplifier, the ideal operational amplifier has an infinite voltage gain, perfectly matched internal transistors, and no output offset voltage.

The bandwidth of an operational amplifier is inversely proportional to the closed-loop gain of the amplifier. The following equation shows the relationship between bandwidth and the feedback ratio, ß:

$$f_T = \frac{BW_{CL}}{\beta}$$

where:

$f_T$ is the *gain-bandwidth product* or *unity-gain frequency*
$BW_{CL}$ is the closed-loop bandwidth of the amplifier
ß is the feedback ratio:

$$\beta = \frac{R_1}{R_1 + R_F}$$

Another factor that limits the high-frequency response of an operational amplifier is its maximum permissible *slew rate*. The maximum slew rate is the maximum value of:

$$S = \frac{\Delta V}{\Delta t}$$

where:

$\Delta V$ is a change in output voltage
$\Delta t$ is the time interval over which the output voltage changes

The slew rate limits the high frequency response because at high frequencies, there is a large rate-of-change of voltage. The maximum sinusoidal frequency at which an operational amplifier having slew rate S can be operated without producing distortion is:

$$f_S(max) = \frac{S}{2\pi K}$$

where:

$f_S(max)$ is the maximum frequency imposed by the slew rate limitation
K is the peak value of the *output* waveform

Output offset voltage is the dc voltage that appears at the output when both inputs are zero volts. The output offset voltage of an operational amplifier is caused by input offset voltage, due to slightly mismatched transistors in the differential amplifier input stage, and differences in input bias currents, I⁻ and I⁺. The output offset voltage due to mismatched bias currents I⁺ and I⁻ can be reduced by connecting a *compensating* resistor, $R_C$, in series with the noninverting input. This resistor does not affect the closed-loop gain of the amplifier. The optimum value of $R_C$ is:

$$R_C = R_1 \| R_F$$

When this compensating resistor is used, the magnitude of the output offset voltage due to input offset current is:

$$|V_{os}| = (I^+ + I^-) R_F = I_{io} R_F$$

where:
  $|V_{os}|$ is the magnitude of the output offset voltage
  I⁻ is the input bias current at the inverting terminal
  I⁺ is the input bias current at the noninverting terminal
  $I_{io}$ is the input offset current (I⁺ − I⁻)

Note that $V_{os}$ may be either positive or negative, depending on which of I⁺ and I⁻ is larger.

The 741 operational amplifier has externally accessible terminals that can be used to *null*, or *balance*, the amplifier, i.e., to adjust the output offset to zero when the inputs are zero. A potentiometer is connected across pins 1 and 5 for this purpose, as shown in Figure 5.

# EXPERIMENT 18 - BANDWIDTH, SLEW RATE, AND OFFSETS

## Procedure

1. To measure the unity-gain frequency of the operational amplifier, connect the following circuit:

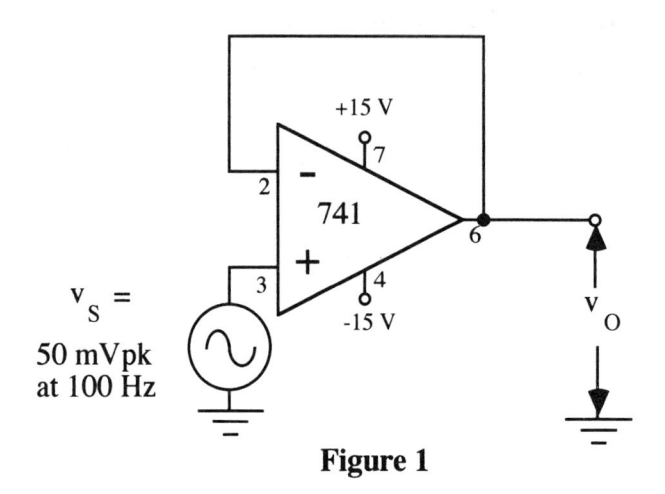

**Figure 1**

2. Using a dual-trace oscilloscope, observe $v_S$ and $v_O$. Increase the frequency of the signal generator, and record the frequency where $v_O$ decreases to 0.707 times its value at 100 Hz. This frequency is the unity-gain frequency of the amplifier, or its gain-bandwidth product.

3. To demonstrate that the gain-bandwidth product is constant, connect the following circuit:

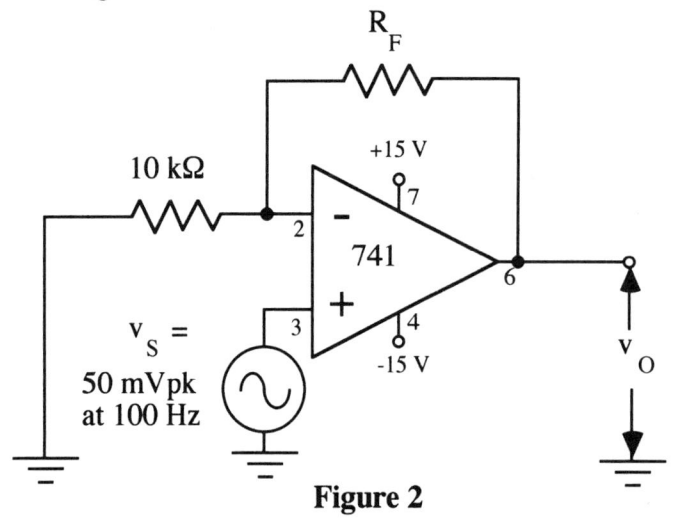

**Figure 2**

# EXPERIMENT 18 - BANDWIDTH, SLEW RATE, AND OFFSETS

4. With $R_F = 47$ k$\Omega$, measure the output voltage, $v_O$. Increase the frequency of the signal generator until the output voltage decreases to 0.707 times its value at 100 Hz. Remove the signal generator and make sure its output voltage has not changed. Record this frequency. Repeat this procedure with $R_F = 100$ k$\Omega$.

5. To measure the slew rate of the operational amplifier, connect the circuit in Figure 3. $V_S$ is a square-wave having very small rise and fall times.

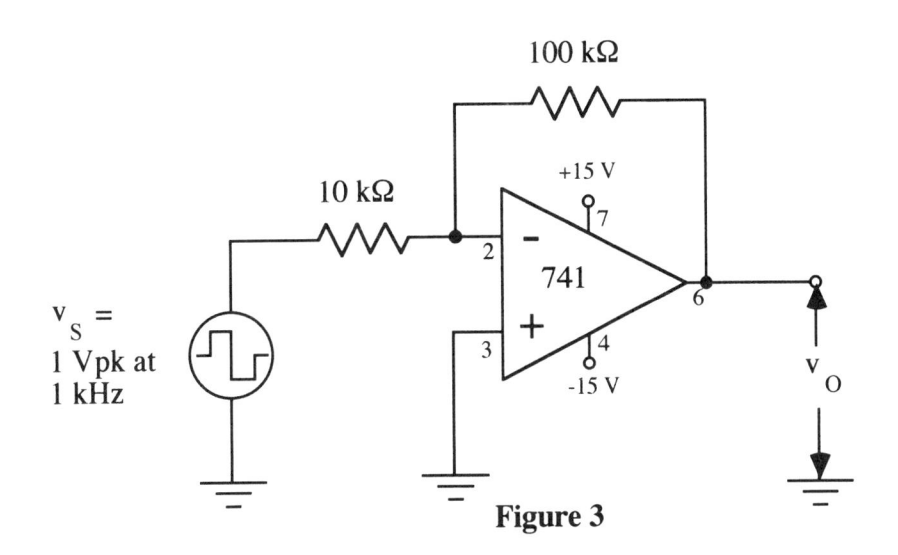

**Figure 3**

6. With a dual-trace oscilloscope, measure the slew rate in the following manner: Adjust the time-base of the oscilloscope so that only one changing edge of the output waveform $v_O$ can be viewed (either a low-to-high voltage change or a high-to-low change). Expand the time base on the oscilloscope so that the change in time $\Delta t$ can be observed. Then measure both the change in voltage $\Delta V$ and the change in time $\Delta t$. Use these values to calculate the slew rate $S = \Delta V/\Delta t$.

7. Calculate the maximum frequency imposed by the slew rate using the equation given in the discussion. With $v_S$ changed to a 10 Vpk sine wave at 1 kHz and $R_F$ changed to 10 k$\Omega$, increase the signal generator frequency beyond this calculated maximum frequency and note the changes in the waveform of $v_O$.

127

# EXPERIMENT 18 - BANDWIDTH, SLEW RATE, AND OFFSETS

8. To measure the total output offset voltage of the operational amplifier, connect the following circuit:

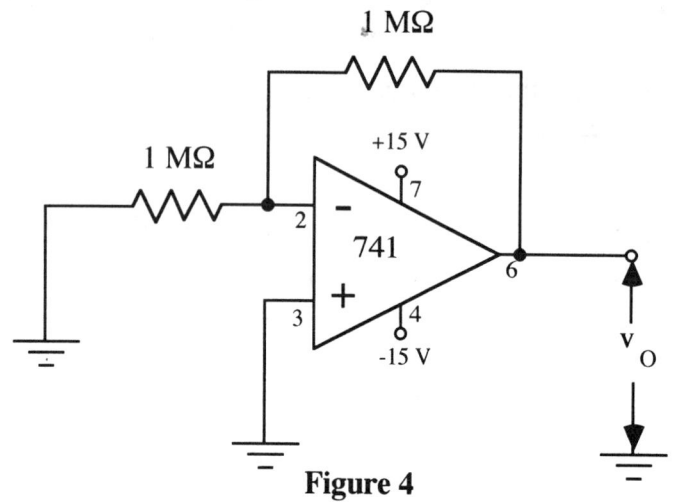

**Figure 4**

9. Using a digital voltmeter (or any active voltmeter), measure the dc output voltage, $v_O$.

10. Now replace the short-circuit to ground on the noninverting terminal with a 470 kΩ resistor to ground. Repeat procedure step 9.

11. To demonstrate how a 741 amplifier can be balanced, connect a potentiometer as shown in Figure 5:

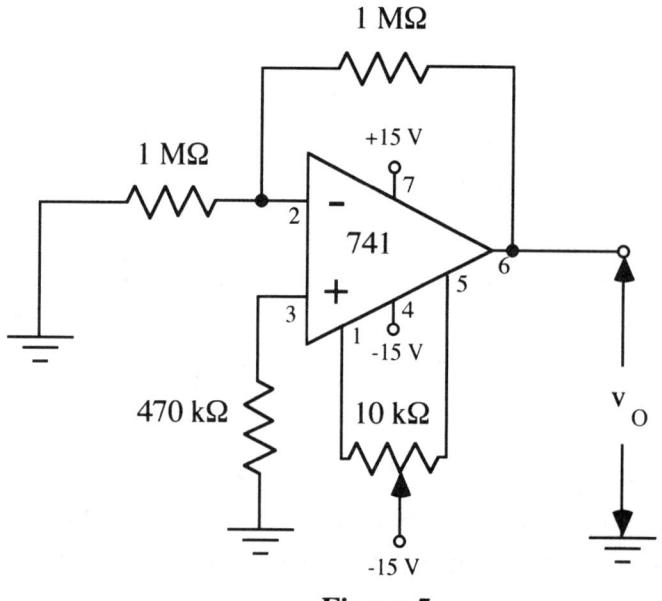

**Figure 5**

EXPERIMENT 18 - BANDWIDTH, SLEW RATE, AND OFFSETS

12. While measuring $v_O$ with a DVM, adjust the 10 kΩ potentiometer until the output offset voltage is as close to 0 V as possible. Measure and record this total output offset voltage.

## Questions

1. Using the results of procedure steps 2 through 4, verify that the gain-bandwidth product is constant. Compare this constant to the manufacturer's specifications.

2. Compare the slew rate calculated in procedure step 6 with the manufacturer's specifications. Using the results of procedure step 7, describe the effects that exceeding the maximum frequency imposed by the slew rate, $f_S$, had on the output waveform $v_O$.

3. Compare the total output offset voltage measured in procedure step 9 with the manufacturer's specifications. How well did the modification of procedure step 10 decrease the total output offset voltage? Explain why.

4. How does the modification of procedure step 12 *null* the input bias currents? Study the internal schematic diagram from the manufacturer's specification sheet.

## SPICE

To demonstrate high-frequency compensation of operational amplifiers, use the EOP as a model for the op-amp in Figure 3. Plot the .AC response as high as necessary to show the upper cutoff frequency. Then add 100 pF in parallel with the 100 kΩ feedback resistor. What happens to the upper cutoff frequency?

# EXPERIMENT 18 - BANDWIDTH, SLEW RATE, AND OFFSETS

# Integration and Differentiation    19

## Reference

*Electronic Devices and Circuits, Sixth Edition:* Section 11-1, Electronic Integration; Section 11-2, Electronic Differentiation

## Objective

To demonstrate the use of operational amplifiers for performing mathematical operations—integration and differentiation.

## Equipment List

1. 741 operational amplifier or the equivalent
2. DC power supplies (±15 V, 5 V)
3. Analog signal generator ( 1 Vpk to 5 Vpk sine, 1 Vpk to 5 Vpk square—all with variable frequency)
4. Resistors: 1-470 k$\Omega$, 1-47 k$\Omega$, 1-10 k$\Omega$, 1-470 $\Omega$
5. Capacitors: 1-0.22 $\mu$F, 1-0.001 $\mu$F (25 V)
6. Dual-trace oscilloscope

## Discussion

As discussed in earlier experiments, the first operational amplifiers were constructed to perform mathematical *operations* in analog computers. This experiment investigates the use of operational amplifiers to perform integration and differentiation.

As shown in Figure 1, the output of an electronic *integrator* is proportional to the total *area under the input waveform* up to that point in time. To perform integration, a capacitor is connected in the feedback path of the amplifier. However, any dc voltage appearing at the input of an integrator will cause the output voltage to rise (or fall) until it reaches its maximum (or minimum) possible value. To prevent this undesirable

## EXPERIMENT 19 - INTEGRATION AND DIFFERENTIATION

occurrence, a resistor, $R_F$, is connected in parallel with the feedback capacitor. Any dc input voltage, such as the input offset voltage of the amplifier, is then simply amplified by the dc gain, $R_F/R_1$.

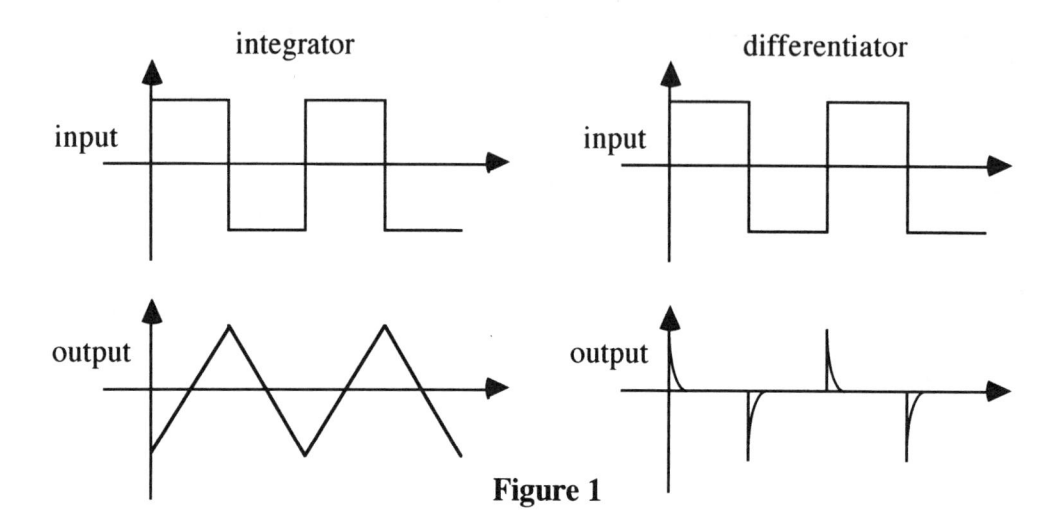

**Figure 1**

The following equation can be used to determine the output voltage of the operational amplifier integrator with a sine wave input:

$$v_O = \frac{-1}{R_{in}C_F}\int v_{in} dt = \frac{-1}{R_{in}C_F}\int A\sin(\omega t)dt = \frac{-1}{(\omega R_{in}C_F)}A\cos\omega t$$

Integration will be performed only at frequencies well above the *break frequency* caused by the feedback resistor:

$$f_B = \frac{1}{2\pi R_F C_F}$$

As shown in Figure 1, the output of an electronic *differentiator* is proportional to the *rate-of-change* of the input waveform at any point in time. To perform differentiation, a capacitor is connected in series with the input. The following equation can be used to determine the output voltage of the operational amplifier differentiator with a sine wave input:

$$v_O = -R_F C_{in}\frac{dv_{in}}{dt} = -R_F C_{in}\frac{dA\sin(\omega t)}{dt} = -(\omega R_F C_{in})A\cos\omega t$$

## EXPERIMENT 19 - INTEGRATION AND DIFFERENTIATION

Since the output voltage of a differentiator is proportional to the input frequency, high-frequency signals (such as electrical noise) may saturate or cutoff the amplifier. For this reason, a resistor is placed in series with the capacitor in the input. This establishes a high-frequency limit beyond which differentiation no longer occurs:

$$f_B = \frac{1}{2\pi R_{in} C_{in}}$$

To achieve greater attenuation at higher frequencies (to prevent oscillation), a feedback capacitor is added in parallel with the feedback resistor. This establishes another break frequency that can be calculated like the one in the integrator.

## Procedure

1. To investigate the use of an operational amplifier to perform mathematical integration, connect the following circuit:

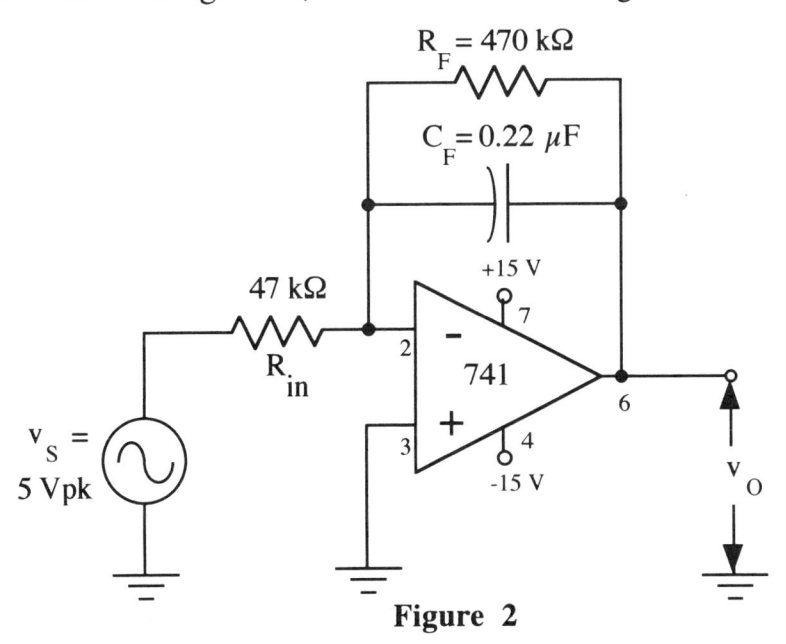

**Figure 2**

2. With $v_S$ adjusted to produce a 5 Vpk sine wave at 20 Hz and using a dual-trace oscilloscope set to ac input coupling, measure and record the

## EXPERIMENT 19 - INTEGRATION AND DIFFERENTIATION

peak value of the output voltage $v_O$ in Table 1. Note any phase shift of the output voltage $v_O$ with respect to the input voltage $v_S$. Repeat this procedure for the remaining frequencies in Table 1.

3. Set $v_S$ to a ±5 Vpk square wave at 100 Hz. Using a dual-trace oscilloscope, sketch the output voltage $v_O$ with respect to the input voltage $v_S$.

4. To demonstrate the use of an operational amplifier as a differentiator, connect the following circuit:

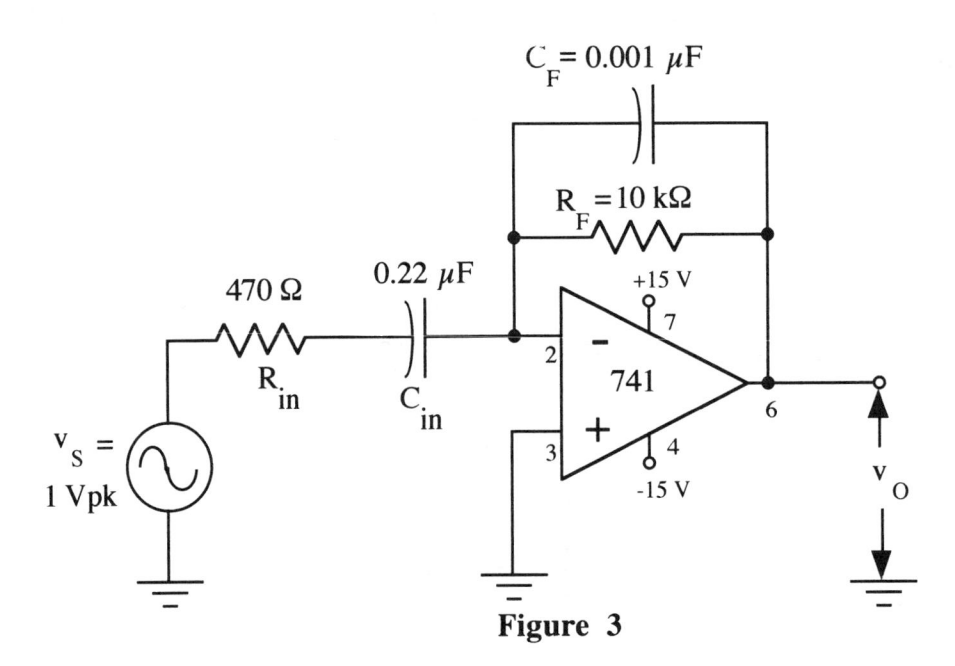

**Figure 3**

5. With $v_S$ adjusted to produce a 1 Vpk sine wave at 500 Hz and using a dual-trace oscilloscope set to ac input coupling, measure and record the peak value of the output voltage $v_O$ in Table 2. Note any phase shift of the output voltage $v_O$ with respect to the input voltage $v_S$. Repeat this procedure for the remaining frequencies in Table 2.

6. Set $v_S$ to a ±1 Vpk square wave at 200 Hz. Using a dual-trace oscilloscope, sketch the output voltage $v_O$ with respect to the input voltage $v_S$.

134

# EXPERIMENT 19 - INTEGRATION AND DIFFERENTIATION

## Questions

1. Write the theoretical equation for the output of the integrator circuit of Figure 2 for each of the input frequencies in Table 1. Compare these with the equations based on experimental voltage measurements obtained in procedure step 2. Explain any phase shift of the output voltage with respect to the input voltage.

2. Did the results of procedure step 3 verify an integrator's response to a square wave input? What differences, if any, were there between the sketches obtained in procedure step 3 and Figure 1?

3. Repeat question 2 for Table 2 and the measurements obtained in procedure step 5.

4. Did the results of procedure step 6 verify a differentiator's response to a square wave input? What differences, if any, were there between the sketches obtained in procedure step 6 and Figure 1?

5. Calculate the theoretical break frequencies for both the integrator of Figure 2 and the differentiator of Figure 3.

# EXPERIMENT 19 - INTEGRATION AND DIFFERENTIATION

# EXPERIMENT 19 - INTEGRATION AND DIFFERENTIATION

## Data

### TABLE 1

| Frequency | $v_O$ (volts) | Phase shift |
|---|---|---|
| 20 Hz | | |
| 50 Hz | | |
| 100 Hz | | |
| 500 Hz | | |
| 1 kHz | | |

### TABLE 2

| Frequency | $v_O$ (volts) | Phase shift |
|---|---|---|
| 500 Hz | | |
| 200 Hz | | |
| 100 Hz | | |

Sketches:

# EXPERIMENT 19 - INTEGRATION AND DIFFERENTIATION

# Active Filters 20

## Reference

*Electronic Devices and Circuits, Sixth Edition:* Section 11-5, Active Filters

## Objectives

1. To demonstrate the use of operational amplifiers in active filters.
2. To design active low- and high-pass filters using coefficient tables.

## Equipment List

1. 741 operational amplifier or the equivalent
2. DC power supplies (±15 V)
3. Analog signal generator (1 Vpk sine at variable frequencies)
4. Resistors: 2-4.7 kΩ, 1-3.3 kΩ, 2-2.2 kΩ, 1-1.5 kΩ, 1-680 Ω, 1-330 Ω
5. Capacitors: 2-0.1 μF, 1-0.033 μF (all 25 V)
6. Dual-trace oscilloscope

## Discussion

Another important application for operational amplifiers is in the construction of active filters. Low-pass filters are circuits that allow low-frequency voltages to pass through them while blocking high frequencies. High-pass filters, as one might expect, perform exactly the opposite role; they pass high frequencies and block low frequencies.

The frequency response of a filter is often classified as either a *Butterworth* or a *Chebyshev* design. As shown in Figure 1, all voltages whose frequencies are within the passband of a Butterworth filter have

# EXPERIMENT 20 - ACTIVE FILTERS

approximately the same gain. The cutoff frequency is the frequency at which the voltage gain drops by 3 dB from the passband amount of gain.

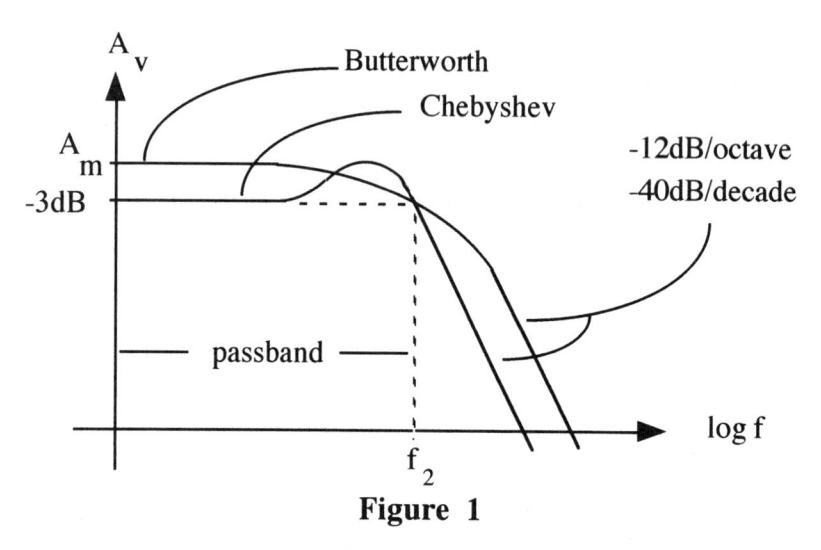

**Figure 1**

As shown in Figure 1, the attenuation produced by a Chebyshev filter at any frequency outside the passband is greater than the attenuation produced by a Butterworth filter at the same frequency, assuming both filters have the same order and the same cutoff frequency. However, the voltage gain of the Chebyshev filter in its passband is not constant. The total variation of the gain in the passband is called the *ripple width* (RW) of the filter. The cutoff frequency of the Chebyshev filter is the frequency at which the gain is equal to the lowest value of passband gain and is changing at a slope of –12 dB/octave for a 2-pole filter, as shown in Figure 1. Note that both second-order Chebyshev and Butterworth filters attenuate signals outside the passband at a rate of 12 dB/octave.

One of the most commonly used filters is the VCVS (voltage-controlled voltage source) filter or *Sallen-Key* circuit. These filters can be simplified greatly by designing for unity gain in the passband, whereby the op-amp is simply a follower and basically buffers the filters from loading each other. These are cascaded for even-order filters, and for odd-order filters an additional first-order stage is added. Figure 2 shows the general configuration for the low-pass filter using a single resistor value R and capacitor values calculated using the coefficient tables in Figure 3.

# EXPERIMENT 20 - ACTIVE FILTERS

**Figure 2**

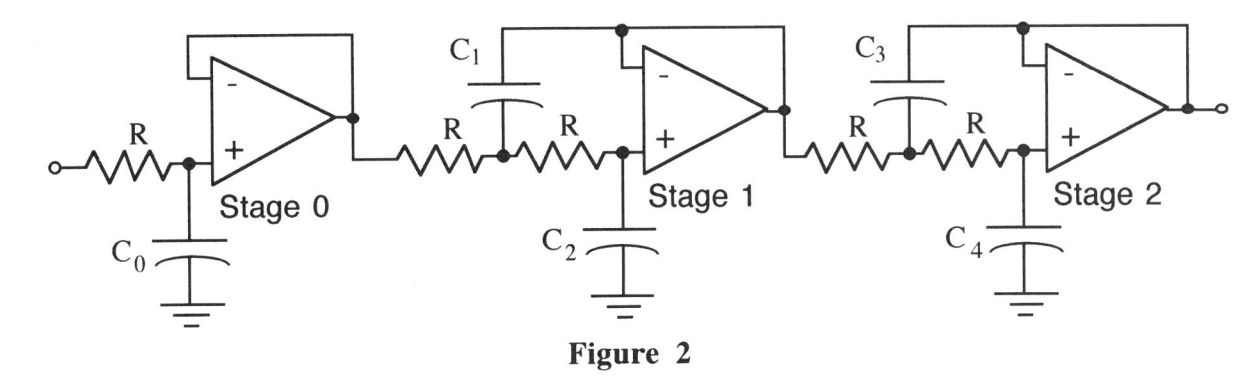

When designing filters using this technique, the designer uses one stage per even-order filter (Stage 0 is added for odd-ordered filters). These stages can be cascaded for more than 5-pole filters but have been limited for the purposes of simplicity. (For a more detailed look at these filters and for higher-ordered filters refer to Section 11-5 of *Electronic Devices and Circuits, Sixth Edition*.) The designer decides which filter characteristics are appropriate; picks a nominal value for R in the design; and calculates the values for $C_1$, $C_2$, and so on, for whatever order filter is desired. Sometimes, an iterative process, where new resistors are chosen, is necessary if the calculated capacitor values are impractical.

For Low-Pass Filters:

(Stage 0)　　　　　　(Stage 1)　　　　　　(Stage 2) . . .

$$C_0 = \frac{1}{2\pi a_0 f_C R}　　　C_1 = \frac{1}{\pi a_1 f_C R}　　　C_3 = \frac{1}{\pi a_3 f_C R}$$

$$C_2 = \frac{a_1}{4\pi a_2 f_C R}　　　C_4 = \frac{a_3}{4\pi a_4 f_C R}$$

where:
　　$C_0$, $C_1$, $C_2$, $C_3$ and $C_4$ are the capacitors in Figure 2
　　$f_C$ is the filter's desired cutoff frequency
　　$a_0$, $a_1$, $a_2$, $a_3$ and $a_4$ are coefficients from the table in Figure 3

Figure 3 shows the table of coefficients for Butterworth and Chebyshev low-pass and high-pass filters.

# EXPERIMENT 20 - ACTIVE FILTERS

## Coefficients for Butterworth and Chebyshev Filter Designs

| Butterworth | Stage 0 | Stage 1 | | Stage 2 | |
|---|---|---|---|---|---|
| | $a_0$ | $a_1$ | $a_2$ | $a_3$ | $a_4$ |
| 2-pole | | 1.4142 | 1.0000 | | |
| 3-pole | 1.0000 | 1.0000 | 1.0000 | | |
| 4-pole | | 0.76537 | 1.0000 | 1.8478 | 1.0000 |
| 5-pole | 1.0000 | 0.61803 | 1.0000 | 1.6180 | 1.0000 |

| Chebyshev (2 dB RW) | Stage 0 | Stage 1 | | Stage 2 | |
|---|---|---|---|---|---|
| | $a_0$ | $a_1$ | $a_2$ | $a_3$ | $a_4$ |
| 2-pole | | 0.80382 | 0.82306 | | |
| 3-pole | 0.36891 | 0.36891 | 0.8861 | | |
| 4-pole | | 0.20977 | 0.92868 | 0.50644 | 0.22157 |
| 5-pole | 0.21831 | 0.13492 | 0.95217 | 0.35323 | 0.39315 |

**Figure 3**

Figure 4 shows the VCVS filter design for a high-pass filter (even-ordered filters don't use Stage 0):

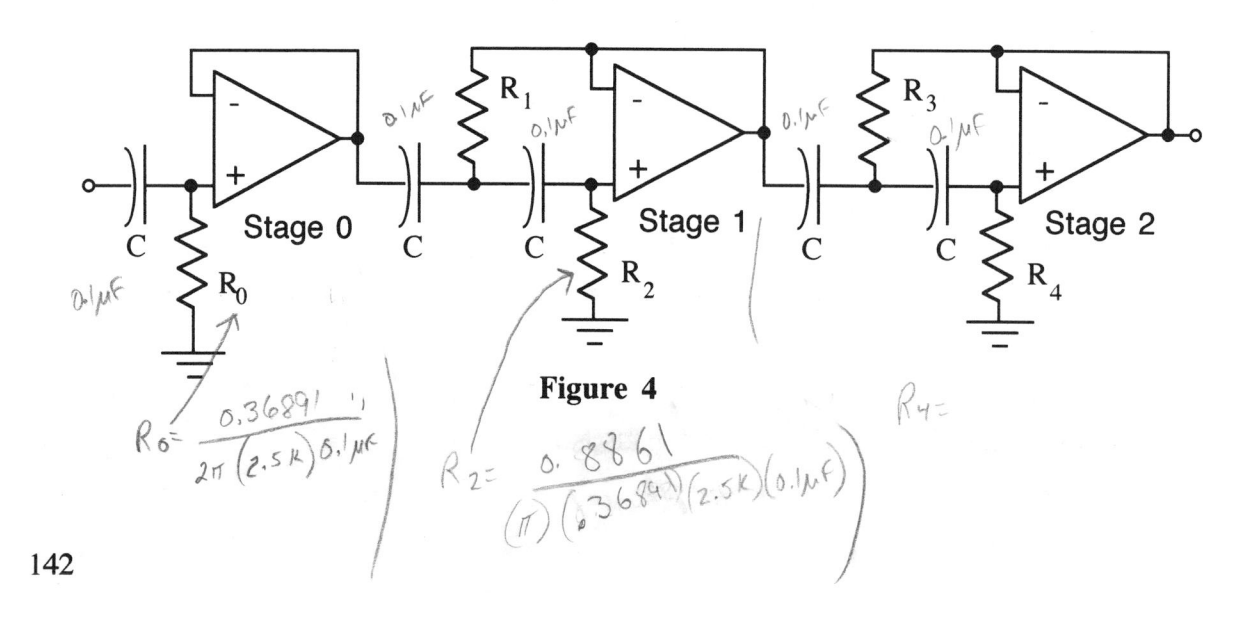

**Figure 4**

$$R_0 = \frac{0.36891}{2\pi (2.5k)(0.1\mu F)}$$

$$R_2 = \frac{0.8861}{(\pi)(.36891)(2.5k)(0.1\mu F)}$$

$R_4 =$

# EXPERIMENT 20 - ACTIVE FILTERS

The design of a high-pass filter is done in much the same way as the low-pass filter—except in this case the capacitor value is chosen, usually around 0.1 µF or so. Then the characteristic Butterworth or Chebyshev filter approach is chosen, along with the number of poles or order of the filter. After selecting the appropriate coefficients from the table in Figure 3, the following equations are used to determine the resistor values to be used:

For High-Pass Filters:

(Stage 0)        (Stage 1)           (Stage 2) . . .

$$R_0 = \frac{a_0}{2\pi f_C C} \qquad R_1 = \frac{a_1}{4\pi f_C C} \qquad R_3 = \frac{a_3}{4\pi f_C C}$$

$$R_2 = \frac{a_2}{\pi a_1 f_C C} \qquad R_4 = \frac{a_4}{\pi a_3 f_C C}$$

where:
$R_0$, $R_1$, $R_2$, $R_3$ and $R_4$ are the resistors in Figure 2
$f_C$ is the filter's desired cutoff frequency
$a_0$, $a_1$, $a_2$, $a_3$ and $a_4$ are coefficients from the table in Figure 3

There are many other approaches to filter design, including IGMF (infinite-gain multiple feedback) filters, state-variable, and biquad. Each one has its advantages, but the VCVS is the most commonly used and uses the fewest components.

Note that all of these filters rely on the same basic RC time constant, and once a filter is designed, its cutoff frequency can be changed simply by multiplying by constants. In other words, doubling all the resistor values in the design will yield half the cutoff frequency. This speeds up the design process because resistors are available in many different standard values, and the designer can simply double, triple, etc., the resistor values to get alternate filters.

# EXPERIMENT 20 - ACTIVE FILTERS

## Procedure

1. To demonstrate the operational amplifier used in a VCVS, second-order, low-pass filter with Butterworth characteristics, connect the circuit in Figure 5:

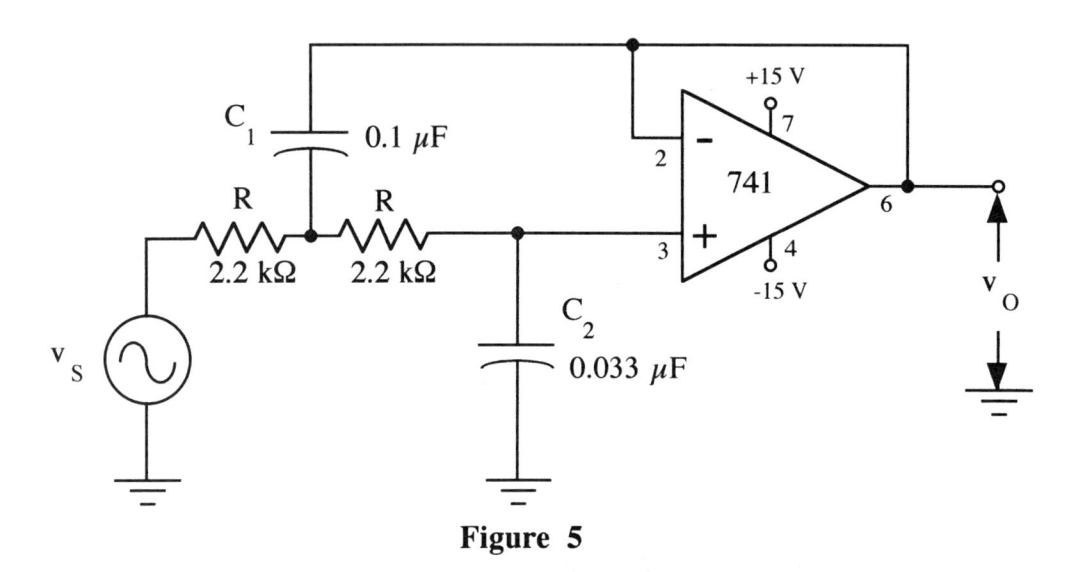

**Figure 5**

2. With $v_S$ adjusted to produce a 1 Vpk sine-wave at 500 Hz, measure and record the peak value of $v_O$. Since 500 Hz is within the passband of this filter, these values can be used to determine the passband voltage gain $A_m$.

3. Now increase the frequency of the signal generator until the output voltage $v_O$ (and therefore the voltage gain) equals 0.707 times that measured in procedure step 2. The frequency where this occurs is the cutoff frequency $f_2$ of the filter.

4. Replace each resistor R in Figure 5 with a 4.7 k$\Omega$ resistor. With $v_S$ adjusted to produce a 1 Vpk sine-wave at 100 Hz, measure and record the peak value of $v_O$. Measure the cutoff frequency $f_2$ of the filter as described in procedure step 3.

EXPERIMENT 20 - ACTIVE FILTERS

5. Using the tables in Figure 3 and the design procedure in the discussion, design a VCVS low-pass filter having Butterworth characteristics and a cutoff frequency of 2.5 kHz (a typical value for passing only low-frequency signals to a low-frequency *woofer* speaker in a 2-speaker high-fidelity enclosure). Use standard capacitor and resistor values. Connect the designed circuit and test for cutoff frequency by using the previous procedure steps as guidelines.

6. To demonstrate the operational amplifier used in a VCVS, second-order, high-pass filter with Chebyshev characteristics and 2 dB ripple width, connect the following circuit:

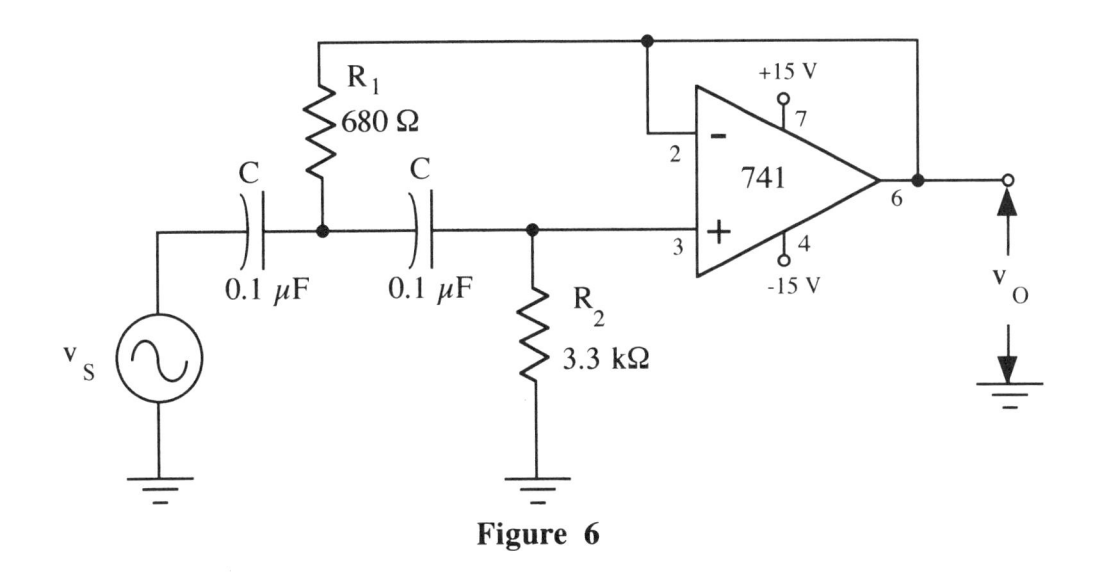

**Figure 6**

7. Note that the technique for determining the cutoff frequency for a Chebyshev filter is different than that for a Butterworth filter. With $v_S$ = 1 Vpk at 5 kHz, measure the peak value of $v_O$. Then decrease the frequency of the signal generator until $v_O$ reaches a maximum value. Record the peak value of $v_O$ when it is a maximum. The ratio of these two peak values of $v_O$ can be used to calculate the ripple width in dB. Continue to decrease the frequency of the signal generator until the output voltage $v_O$

# EXPERIMENT 20 - ACTIVE FILTERS

equals that measured at 5 kHz. Measure the frequency where this occurs, which is the cutoff frequency $f_1$ of the Chebyshev filter.

8. Replace $R_1$ and $R_2$ in Figure 4 with 330 Ω and 1.5 kΩ, respectively. With $v_S = 1$ Vpk at 10 kHz, repeat procedure step 7.

9. Using the tables in Figure 3 and the design procedure in the discussion, design a high-pass filter with Chebyshev characteristics, a gain of unity, a ripple width of 2 dB, and a cutoff frequency of 2.5 kHz (a typical value for passing only high-frequency signals and blocking potentially harmful low-frequency signals to a high-frequency *tweeter* speaker in a 2-speaker high-fidelity enclosure). Use standard capacitor and resistor values. Connect the designed circuit and test for cutoff frequency using the previous procedure steps as guidelines.

HIGH PASS - CHEBYSHEV
$F_c = 2.5k$

## Questions

1. The four filters demonstrated in the procedure were designed using the following criteria:

| Filter | Procedure Step(s) | Cutoff Frequency | Resistor(R) |
|---|---|---|---|
| Low-pass | 2–3 | 1 kHz | 2.2 kΩ |
| Low-pass | 4 | 500 Hz | 4.7 kΩ |

| Filter | Procedure Step(s) | Cutoff Frequency | Capacitor(C) |
|---|---|---|---|
| High-pass | 7 | 1 kHz | 0.1 $\mu$F |
| High-pass | 8 | 2 kHz | 0.1 $\mu$F |

Using the guidelines in the discussion, show the procedure for designing each of these filters. Compare the measured cutoff frequencies with the designed cutoff frequencies. Explain any discrepancies and comment on ways to reduce the discrepancy between the theoretical and experimentally observed cutoff frequencies.

2. Show the design work done for procedure step 5. Include a schematic diagram for the filter. How well did the filter function? Redesign the low-pass filter from procedure step 5 as a 4-pole filter.

3. Repeat question 2 for the filter of procedure step 9.

# EXPERIMENT 20 - ACTIVE FILTERS

# Comparators  21

## Reference

*Electronic Devices and Circuits, Sixth Edition:* Section 12-1, Voltage Comparators

## Objectives

1. To demonstrate the voltage comparator and to investigate the effects of adding hysteresis.
2. To demonstrate the use of voltage comparators in astable multivibrators.

## Equipment List

1. 741 operational amplifier or the equivalent
2. DC power supplies (±15 V, 5 V)
3. Analog signal generator (10 Vpk sine at 1 kHz)
4. Resistors: 1-470 kΩ, 1-100 kΩ, 1-4.7 kΩ, 2-1 kΩ
5. Capacitor: 1-0.1 µF (25 V)
6. Potentiometer: 1 kΩ
7. Dual-trace oscilloscope

## Discussion

Another important application of operational amplifiers is that of voltage comparison. This function is as simple as it sounds—the operational amplifier can *compare* the amplitudes of two voltage inputs. To compare voltage levels, the amplifier is operated open-loop so that the voltage gain is extremely large. When the voltage connected to the

# EXPERIMENT 21 - COMPARATORS

noninverting terminal is slightly greater than the voltage connected to the inverting terminal (v+ > v−), the large open-loop gain causes the output of the amplifier to be driven to its maximum positive value. Similarly, when the voltage connected to the inverting terminal is slightly greater than the voltage connected to the noninverting terminal (v− > v+), the output of the amplifier is driven to its maximum negative value. A zero detector can be constructed by simply connecting one of the input terminals to ground. This makes the comparator ideal for shaping sinusoidal waveforms for digital purposes, since the output will be a square wave.

A useful modification to the basic comparator circuit is the addition of circuitry that introduces *hysteresis*. Hysteresis means that the high-to-low transition of the output occurs at one input voltage level and the low-to-high transition occurs at a different input voltage level. The relationship between the input levels and resulting output transitions can be seen in Figure 1:

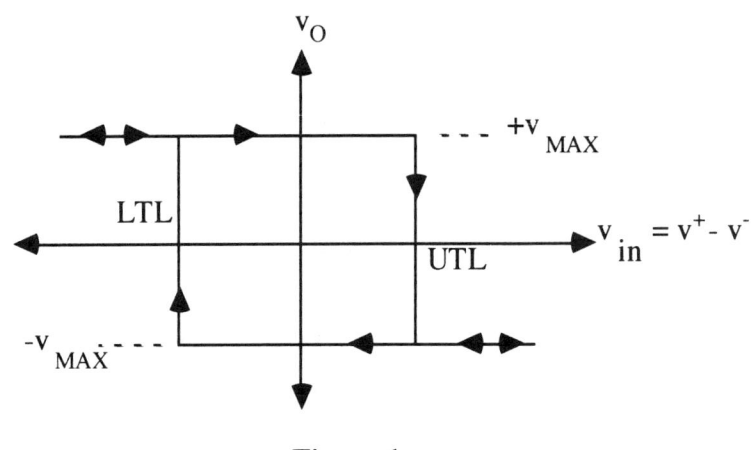

**Figure 1**

The lower and upper trigger levels (LTL and UTL) in Figure 1 can be calculated using the following equations (based on the Schmitt trigger in Figure 3):

$$LTL = \frac{R_2}{R_1 + R_2} V_{REF} + \frac{R_1}{R_1 + R_2}(-V_{MAX})$$

$$UTL = \frac{R_2}{R_1 + R_2} V_{REF} + \frac{R_1}{R_1 + R_2}(+V_{MAX})$$

where:
- $R_1$ and $R_2$ form the feedback voltage divider to the noninverting terminal of the operational amplifier circuit
- $V_{REF}$ is the reference voltage connected to $R_1$
- $+V_{MAX}$ is the maximum positive output voltage of the amplifier (usually the same as the positive supply voltage)
- $-V_{MAX}$ is the maximum negative output voltage of the amplifier (usually the same as the negative supply voltage)

When substituting values into these equations, note that $-V_{MAX}$ is a negative number.

Another useful application of the voltage comparator is in an *astable multivibrator*, as shown in Figure 4. The astable multivibrator is a free-running oscillator whose output waveform is a square wave. The period of the oscillation can be calculated using the following formula:

$$T = 2RC \ln\left(\frac{1+\beta}{1-\beta}\right)$$

where:
- R is the feedback resistor
- C is the capacitor connected to the inverting terminal
- ß is the feedback ratio:

$$\beta = \frac{R_1}{R_1 + R_2}$$

## EXPERIMENT 21 - COMPARATORS

### Procedure

1. To investigate the use of an operational amplifier as a voltage comparator, connect the circuit in Figure 2. Connect a dual-trace oscilloscope so $v_S$ and $v_O$ can be observed simultaneously.

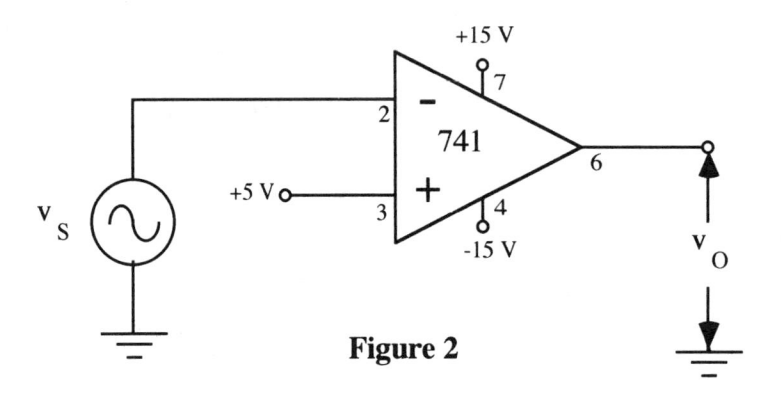

**Figure 2**

2. With $v_S$ set to produce a 10 Vpk sine wave at 1 kHz, sketch the output voltage $v_O$ and the input voltage $v_S$. Be sure to note the levels of $v_S$ at which the output voltage $v_O$ changes levels.

3. Connect the Schmitt trigger shown in Figure 3:

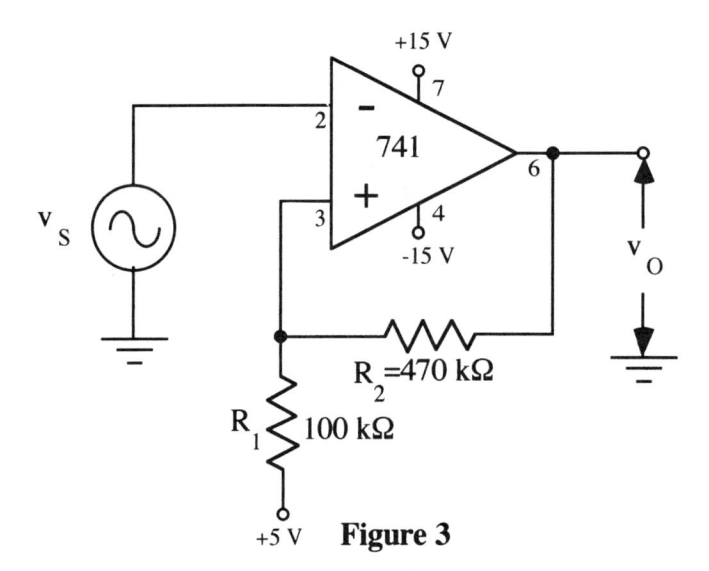

**Figure 3**

4. Repeat procedure step 2 for the circuit of Figure 3.

EXPERIMENT 21 - **COMPARATORS**

5. To demonstrate the use of the comparator in an astable multivibrator, connect the circuit in Figure 4:

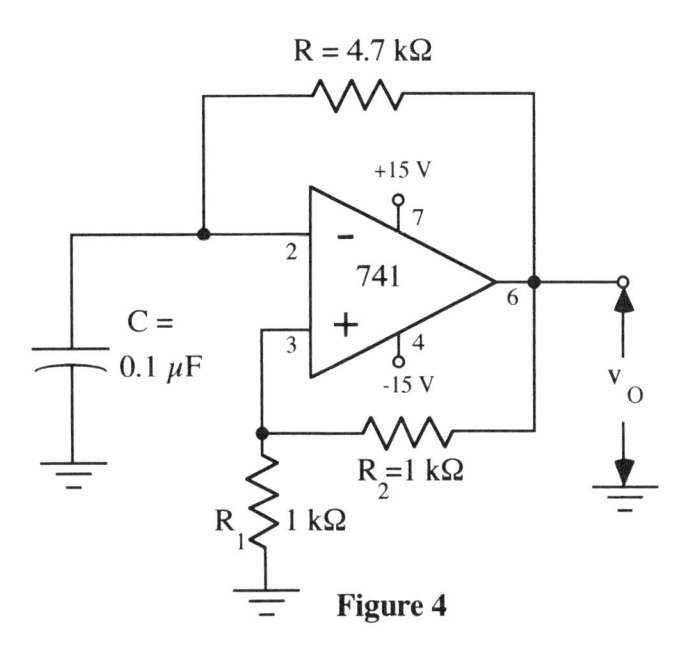

**Figure 4**

6. Measure and record the frequency of the output waveform $v_O$. Sketch the output waveform $v_O$.

153

# EXPERIMENT 21 - COMPARATORS

## Questions

1. Explain the results of procedure step 2. Sketch the output waveform that would result if the reference voltage were changed to 2 V. What difference would be observed in the output waveform if the input voltages at the terminals of the operational amplifier in Figure 2 were reversed?

2. Calculate the theoretical lower and upper trigger levels for the circuit of Figure 3. Compare the calculated values with the values obtained from the sketch drawn in procedure step 4.

3. Calculate the theoretical oscillation frequency of the multivibrator of Figure 4. Compare the calculated value with the measured frequency obtained in procedure step 6. Suggest a simple change in the circuit of Figure 4 that would enable the oscillation frequency to be adjusted.

# Oscillators 22

## Reference

*Electronic Devices and Circuits, Sixth Edition:* Section 12-3, Oscillators

## Objectives

1. To demonstrate the Wien bridge oscillator.
2. To demonstrate the RC phase-shift oscillator.

## Equipment List

1. 741 operational amplifier or the equivalent
2. DC power supplies (±15 V)
3. Resistors: 2-10 kΩ, 3-1 kΩ, 3-560 Ω
4. Capacitors: 3-0.47 μF, 3-0.22 μF, 2-0.1 μF (25 V)
5. Potentiometers: 1-500 kΩ, 1-1 kΩ
6. Dual-trace oscilloscope

## Discussion

Oscillators are circuits that spontaneously generate a periodic output voltage due to *positive feedback*. Two important types of sinusoidal oscillators are the Wien bridge and the RC phase-shift oscillator. An operational amplifier is ideal for use in oscillator circuits because of its large input impedance, large gain, and the ease with which positive feedback can be introduced around it. The positive feedback required for oscillation is specified by the *Barkhausen* criterion: the total gain from input to output and back through the feedback circuitry must equal at least one, and the total phase shift from input to output and back through the feedback circuitry must equal 0°, or a multiple of 360°.

# EXPERIMENT 22 - OSCILLATORS

A Wien bridge oscillator is shown in Figure 1. It may be regarded as a bridge whose two branches are the resistive voltage divider across the inverting terminal and the reactive voltage divider across the noninverting terminals of the operational amplifier. The circuit oscillates at the frequency at which the ac voltages at the two input terminals are equal. If $R_1$ and $R_2$ (see Figure 1) are resistors of equal value and $C_1$ and $C_2$ are capacitors of equal value, then the ratio of $R_f$ to $R_{in}$ must be 2:1 to satisfy the Barkhausen criterion. The oscillation frequency for the Wien bridge oscillator, given these stipulations, can be calculated from:

$$f = \frac{1}{2\pi RC}$$

where:
$$R = R_1 = R_2 \quad \text{and} \quad C = C_1 = C_2$$

An example of an RC phase-shift oscillator is shown in Figure 2. The RC phase-shift oscillator uses three cascaded stages of RC high-pass filters, with the output of the last stage fed back to the inverting input of the operational amplifier. The purpose of the RC filters is to provide a phase shift of 180°. Since the output of these filters is fed back to the inverting terminal, the amplifier itself provides another phase shift of 180°. The total phase shift of the circuit is therefore 360° or 0°. Given the stipulations that $R_1$, $R_2$, and $R_3$ are all equal-valued resistors and that $C_1$, $C_2$, and $C_3$ are all equal-valued capacitors, the oscillation frequency of the RC phase-shift oscillator can be calculated using the following equation:

$$f = \frac{1}{2\pi RC\sqrt{6}}$$

where:
$$R = R_1 = R_2 = R_3$$
$$C = C_1 = C_2 = C_3$$

This equation is exact only if the input resistor on the inverting terminal (10 k$\Omega$ in Figure 2) is large enough to prevent any loading of the cascaded RC stages.

# EXPERIMENT 22 - OSCILLATORS

## Procedure

1. To demonstrate the Wien bridge oscillator, connect the following:

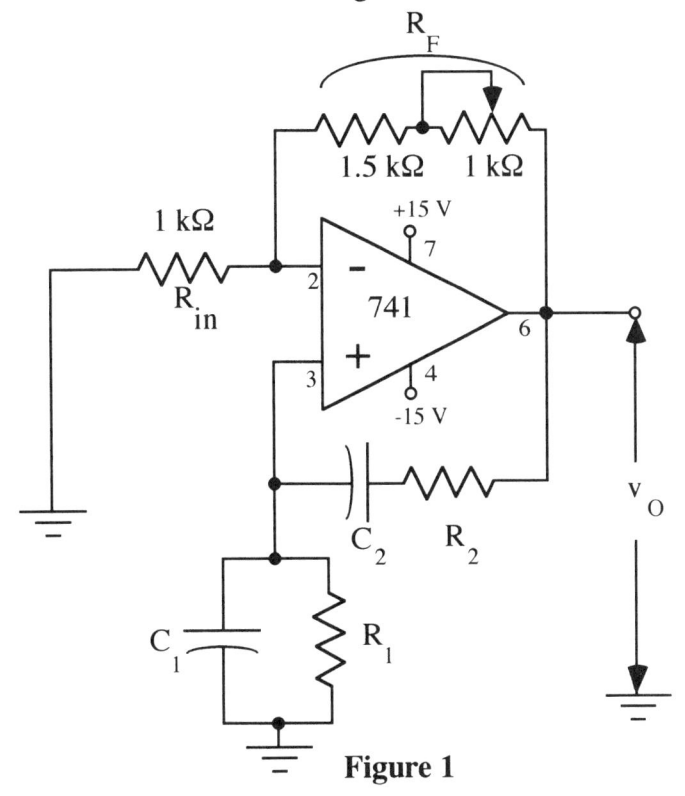

**Figure 1**

2. Connect an oscilloscope set to ac input coupling so that $v_O$ can be viewed. With $R_1 = R_2 = 10$ kΩ and $C_1 = C_2 = 0.1$ μF, carefully adjust the 1 kΩ potentiometer until the output waveform has the least amount of distortion. Measure and record the frequency of this waveform.

3. Replace $C_1$ and $C_2$ with 0.22 μF capacitors and repeat procedure step 2.

4. Replace $C_1$ and $C_2$ with 0.47 μF capacitors and repeat procedure step 2.

5. Replace $R_1$ and $R_2$ with 1 kΩ resistors and repeat procedure steps 2 through 4 using the capacitors specified.

# EXPERIMENT 22 - OSCILLATORS

6. To demonstrate the RC phase-shift oscillator, connect the following circuit:

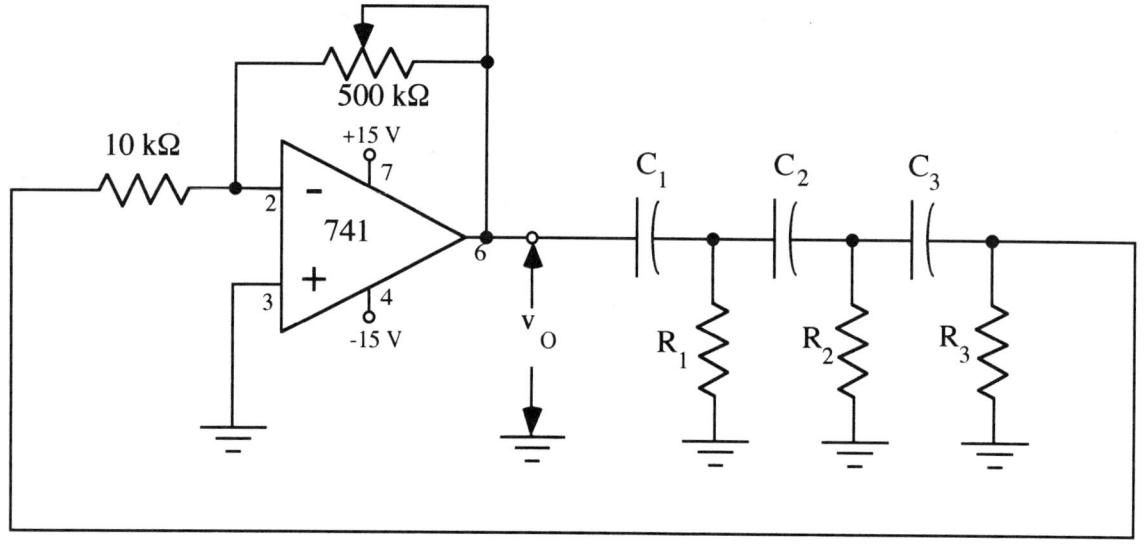

**Figure 2**

7. Connect an oscilloscope set to ac input coupling so that $v_O$ can be viewed. With $R_1 = R_2 = R_3 = 1$ k$\Omega$ and $C_1 = C_2 = C_3 = 0.22$ $\mu$F, carefully adjust the 500 k$\Omega$ potentiometer until the output waveform has the least amount of distortion. Measure and record the frequency of this waveform.

8. Replace $C_1$, $C_2$, and $C_3$ with 0.47 $\mu$F capacitors and repeat procedure step 7.

9. Replace $R_1$, $R_2$, and $R_3$ with 560 $\Omega$ resistors and repeat procedure steps 7 and 8 using the capacitors specified.

## Questions

1. For each of the capacitor values in procedure steps 2 through 4, calculate the theoretical oscillation frequency for the Wien bridge oscillator of Figure 1. Compare these calculated values to the measured results obtained in procedure steps 2 through 4.

2. Repeat question 1 for procedure step 5.

3. For each of the capacitor values in procedure steps 7 and 8, calculate the theoretical oscillation frequency for the RC phase-shift oscillator of Figure 2. Compare these calculated values to the measured results obtained in procedure steps 7 and 8.

4. Repeat question 3 for procedure step 9.

5. Using Figures 1 and 2 as examples, design a Wien bridge and an RC phase-shift oscillator each of which will oscillate at a frequency of 1 kHz. Use standard values for capacitors and inductors, and use potentiometers connected as rheostats, if necessary, for resistors.

# EXPERIMENT 22 - OSCILLATORS

# Clipping and Clamping Circuits 23

## Reference

*Electronic Devices and Circuits, Sixth Edition:* Section 12-5, Clipping and Rectifying Circuits; Section 12-6, Clamping Circuits

## Objectives

1. To demonstrate passive and active clipping circuits.
2. To demonstrate passive and active clamping circuits.

## Equipment List

1. 741 operational amplifier or the equivalent
2. 1N4004 (NTE116) silicon diode or the equivalent
3. 1N4736 (NTE6410) silicon 6.8 V zener diode or the equivalent
4. DC power supplies (±15 V and 6.8 V with isolated ground and current sinking capability)
5. Analog signal generator (5–10 Vp-p sine wave at 1 kHz)
6. Resistors: 1-100 kΩ, 2-10 kΩ, 1-1 kΩ
7. Capacitor: 1-1 $\mu$F (25 V)
8. Dual-trace oscilloscope

## Discussion

The two types of circuits described in this experiment are the clipping circuit and the clamping circuit. Figure 1 shows an example of the input and output waveforms of a clipping circuit. The circuits in Figures 3 and 4 are examples of *passive* clipping circuits. The output voltage will not change when the input voltage is such that the diode remains forward-biased. As a consequence, the output voltage is *limited* to a fixed positive

## EXPERIMENT 23 - CLIPPING AND CLAMPING CIRCUITS

or negative value. The half-wave rectifier of Experiment 2 is an example of a passive clipping circuit.

An active clipping circuit is one that incorporates an active device, such as an operational amplifier, to produce a clipped output. Figures 5 and 6 show examples. Here, a zener diode is used to establish a clipping level. The advantage of an active clipper is that it has a low output impedance and can drive heavier loads than a passive clipper can. The diode in series with each zener diode prevents current flow when the zener diode is forward-biased.

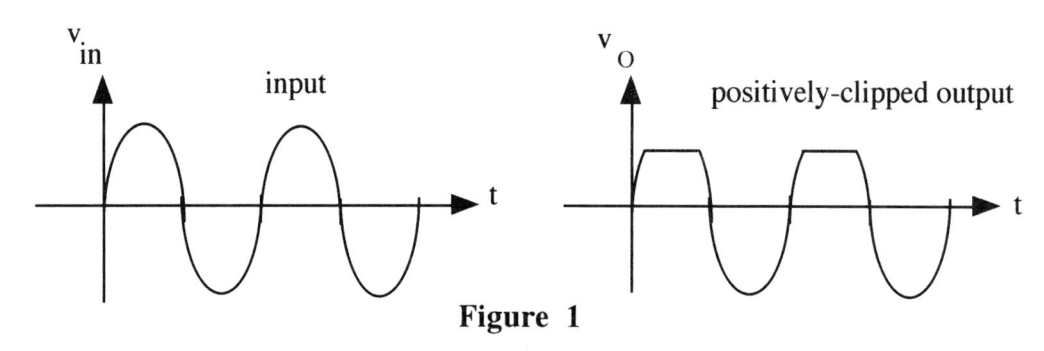

**Figure 1**

A clamping circuit is a circuit that *shifts* a waveform to remove negative variations. It is sometimes called a *level restorer* because it effectively adds a dc level (previously removed by capacitor-coupling) to a waveform. Figure 2 shows typical input and output waveforms of a clamping circuit.

**Figure 2**

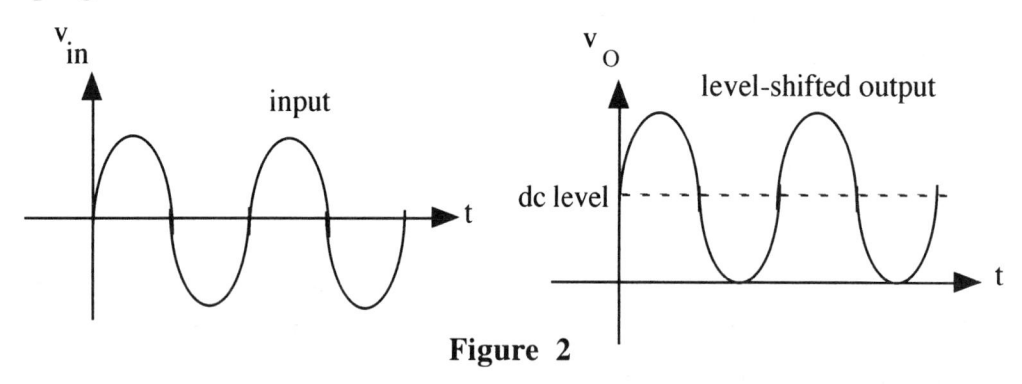

Figure 7 is an example of a passive clamping circuit. The capacitor charges through the diode when the input voltage is negative. The capacitor charges to the peak value of the input voltage. When the input voltage is positive, the load voltage equals the dc voltage across the capacitor plus the input voltage. If the RC time constant of the capacitor and the load is much

### EXPERIMENT 23 - CLIPPING AND CLAMPING CIRCUITS

greater than the period of the input voltage, the capacitor will not have enough time to discharge through the load resistor. Therefore, the load voltage is the input voltage shifted by enough dc to keep the entire waveform positive.

Figure 8 shows an example of an active clamping circuit. The important advantage of the active clamping circuit is that the 0.7 V drop across the forward-biased diode does not affect the output voltage. This means that voltages smaller than 0.7 V can be clamped using the active clamping circuit.

## Procedure

1. To demonstrate a passive clipping circuit, connect the circuit in Figure 3:

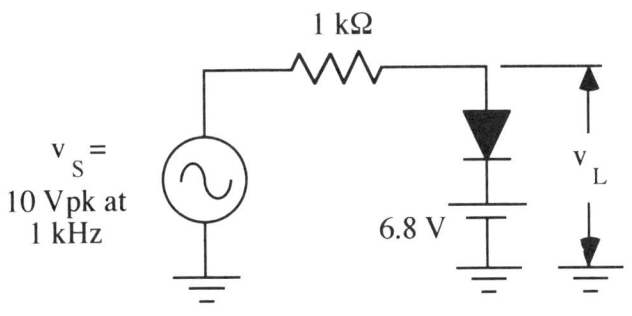

**Figure 3**

2. With a dual-trace oscilloscope set to dc input coupling, sketch the input voltage $v_S$ and the output voltage $v_L$. Record the voltage level at which clipping occurs.

3. Connect the following circuit:

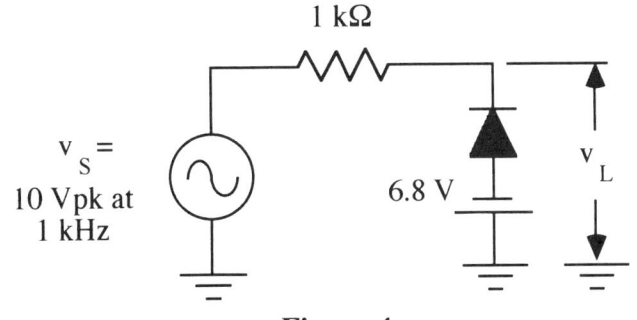

**Figure 4**

4. Repeat procedure step 2 for the circuit of Figure 4.

EXPERIMENT 23 - CLIPPING AND CLAMPING CIRCUITS

5. To demonstrate the operational amplifier used in an active clipping circuit, connect the following circuit using a 6.8 V zener diode:

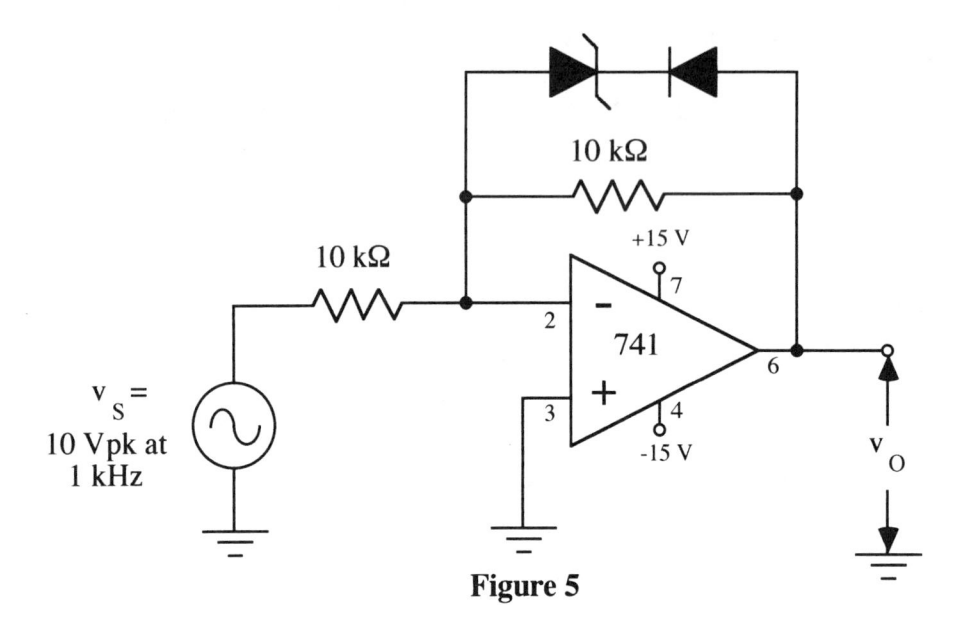

**Figure 5**

6. Repeat procedure step 2 for the circuit of Figure 5.

7. Reverse the diode connections so the circuit appears as shown in Figure 6:

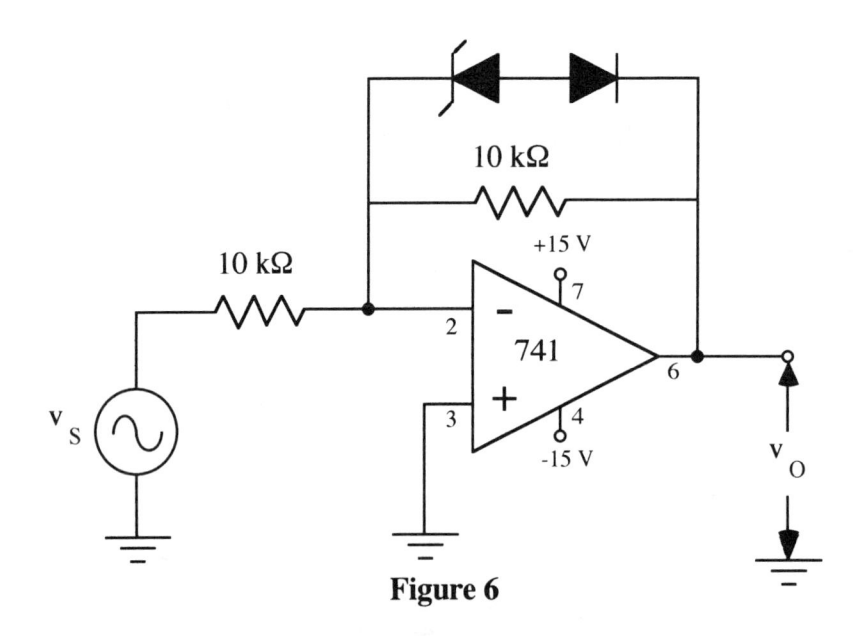

**Figure 6**

8. Repeat procedure step 2 for the circuit of Figure 6.

EXPERIMENT 23 - **CLIPPING AND CLAMPING CIRCUITS**

9. To demonstrate a passive clamping circuit, connect the following circuit:

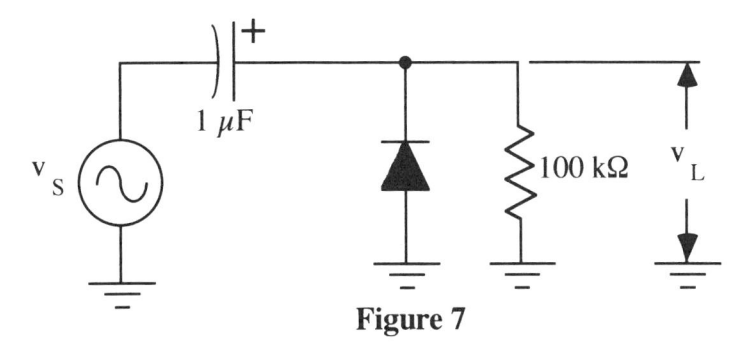

**Figure 7**

10. Set $v_S$ to 5 Vp-p at 1 kHz. With a dual-trace oscilloscope set to dc coupling, sketch the input and output voltages $v_S$ and $v_L$. Be sure to note the dc level of the output voltage $v_L$. Change $v_S$ to 1 Vp-p at 1 kHz and repeat the measurements. Repeat the measurements again with $v_S = 0.1$ Vp–p at 1 kHz.

11. To demonstrate an operational amplifier in an active clamping circuit, connect the following circuit:

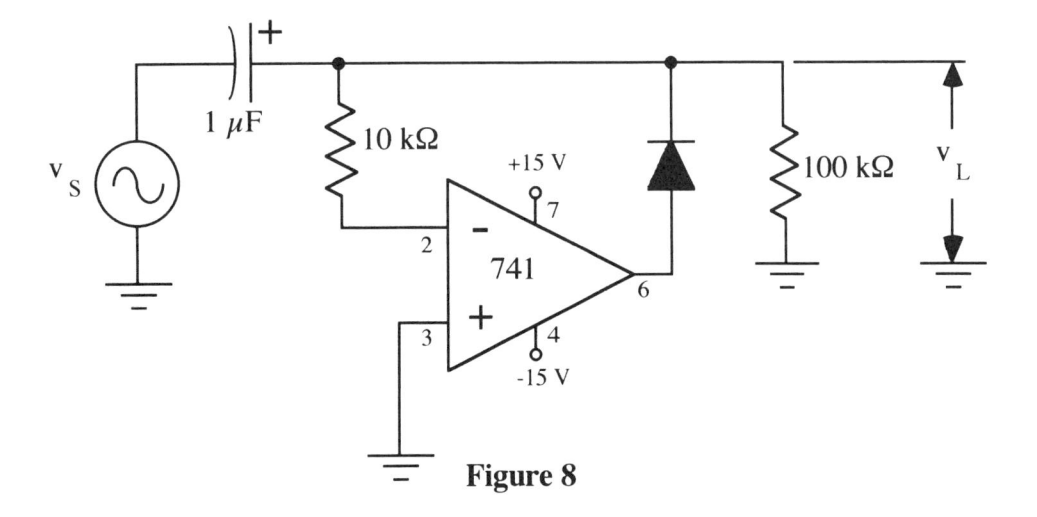

**Figure 8**

12. Repeat procedure step 10 for the circuit of Figure 8.

165

# EXPERIMENT 23 - CLIPPING AND CLAMPING CIRCUITS

## Questions

1. Compare and contrast the sketches obtained from procedure steps 2 and 6. Under what conditions would the active clipping circuit work more effectively than the passive circuit?

2. Repeat question 1 for the sketches obtained from procedure steps 4 and 8.

3. Compare and contrast the sketches obtained from procedure steps 10 and 12. How well did the circuits of Figure 7 and Figure 8 clamp the input voltage when the input was 5 Vp-p? What happened as the input voltage's amplitude was decreased for both circuits?

4. Some amplifiers can be damaged by excessive input voltages. If a particular amplifier's input voltage can be no greater than 3 V, design a protection circuit (active or passive) for the amplifier using the circuits in this experiment as examples.

5. The output of a certain analog-to-digital converter is a number between 0 and 255 when the amplitude of the analog input changes from 0 V to 10 V. Design a circuit (active or passive) that will shift any 10 kHz input voltage so that none of the waveform swings negative. (This shift is required to convert the full analog variation of the input to a digital output.)

## SPICE

To plot a clipping circuit's response, use the .TRAN command with the circuit of Figure 3. The time span should be sufficient to show 2 or 3 cycles of the waveform. Repeat this procedure for the circuit of Figure 7.

# Voltage Regulators 24

## Reference

*Electronic Devices and Circuits, Sixth Edition:* Section 13-2, Voltage Regulation; Section 13-5, Adjustable Integrated Circuit Regulators

## Objectives

1. To demonstrate the three-terminal 7805 5-volt regulator.
2. To measure the load and line regulation of the 7805 regulator.
3. To investigate the adjustable 723 regulator with current limiting.

## Equipment List

1. 7805(LM340-05) fixed 5-volt voltage regulator or equivalent
2. 723 adjustable voltage regulator
3. Variable dc power supply (0–20 V)
4. Resistors: 1-1 kΩ, 2-470 Ω, 1-47 Ω, 1-22 Ω (all 1/4 W); 1-100 Ω, 1-47 Ω, 1-22 Ω (all 1 W); 1-10 Ω (2 W)
5. Capacitor: 1-100 pF
6. Potentiometers: 1-10 kΩ, 2-1 kΩ
7. Digital voltmeter, dc ammeter

## Discussion

The output voltage of an *unregulated* power supply can be expected to change when the load is changed or when the input voltage to the supply changes. A voltage regulator is a device that senses any tendency of the output voltage to change and automatically compensates for that change by increasing or decreasing the output. An *ideal* voltage regulator maintains a

## EXPERIMENT 24 - VOLTAGE REGULATORS

perfectly constant output voltage regardless of how much the load changes or how much the input voltage changes. The output of a practical regulator is never perfectly constant, even though the output variation may be too small to measure. One measure of the ability of a power supply to maintain a constant output voltage when the load is changed is its *output resistance*, $R_O$:

$$R_O = \frac{\Delta V_O}{\Delta I_L} \text{ ohms}$$

where:

$\Delta V_O$ is the change in output voltage that occurs when the change in load current is $\Delta I_L$

Manufacturers' specifications for *load regulation* usually give a "typical" and a "maximum" value for $\Delta V_O$ corresponding to a specified value of $\Delta I_L$. The output resistance of an ideal regulator is zero ohms and that of a good, practical regulator is on the order of milliohms.

The measure of how well a regulator can maintain a constant output voltage when the input voltage changes is called its *line regulation*. Line regulation is often specified as the change in output voltage, $\Delta V_O$, that occurs for a specific change in input voltage, $\Delta V_{in}$, when the load current is constant.

In this experiment, we will investigate two kinds of integrated-circuit voltage regulators: the three-terminal, fixed-voltage regulator and the adjustable regulator. As the name implies, a three-terminal regulator has only three external connections: the unregulated input voltage, the regulated output, and ground. Figure 2 shows these connections to a 7805, three-terminal, 5 V regulator. This regulator is one from the commercially available series designated 78XX, where XX is the *nominal* regulated output voltage. The actual output of the regulator may vary somewhat from its nominal value, among units of the same type.

Figure 3 shows an adjustable regulator circuit using the 723 adjustable voltage regulator. While the external circuitry required to operate this regulator is more complex than it is for a three-terminal regulator, the 723 is a more versatile device and has many additional features, including

# EXPERIMENT 24 - VOLTAGE REGULATORS

adjustable short-circuit protection (current-limiting). The regulated output voltage is adjusted by adjusting the voltage that is connected to pin 5 (labeled +IN). A built-in reference voltage, labeled $V_{ref}$, appears at pin 6 and is divided down to provide the voltage required at +IN. The regulated output (load) voltage is given by:

$$V_L = \left(\frac{R_2}{R_1 + R_2}\right) V_{ref}$$

The nominal value of $V_{ref}$ is +7 Vdc, but its actual value varies somewhat among devices of the same type.

Resistor $R_{SC}$ in Figure 3 is used to provide short-circuit protection by limiting the load current that can flow from the regulator. The maximum load current is approximately:

$$I_L(\max) \approx \frac{0.7\,V}{R_{SC}} \text{ amperes}$$

The 723 regulator has a built-in current limit of 150 mA, even if $R_{SC}$ equals zero.

Figure 1 shows a typical plot of load voltage versus load current for a current-limited regulator. Note that $V_L$ drops off rapidly as $I_L$ approaches its maximum permissible value.

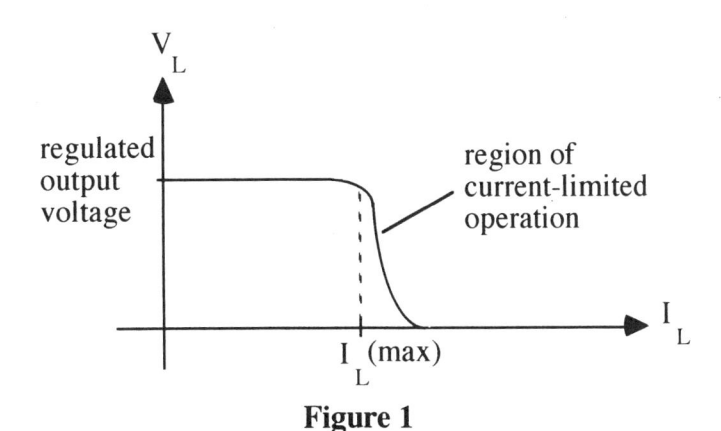

**Figure 1**

# EXPERIMENT 24 - VOLTAGE REGULATORS

## Procedure

1. To demonstrate the 7805 three-terminal fixed-voltage regulator, connect the following circuit:

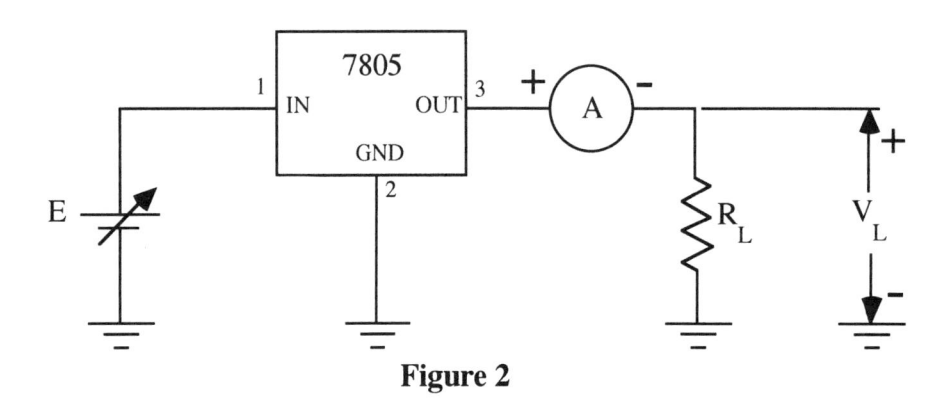

**Figure 2**

2. To determine the load regulation of the 7805 voltage regulator, with E = 10 V, measure the load voltage and current for the load resistances listed in Table 1. Use a digital voltmeter or digital VOM accurate to within a few millivolts dc for all voltage measurements.

3. To determine the line regulation of the 7805 voltage regulator, with $R_L$ = 100 Ω (1 W), adjust the input (line) voltage E to each voltage listed in Table 2. Measure the load voltage and current for each line voltage in Table 2. Use a digital voltmeter or digital VOM accurate to within a few millivolts dc for all voltage measurements.

4. To investigate the 723 adjustable-voltage regulator, connect the circuit in Figure 3.

# EXPERIMENT 24 - VOLTAGE REGULATORS

**Figure 3**

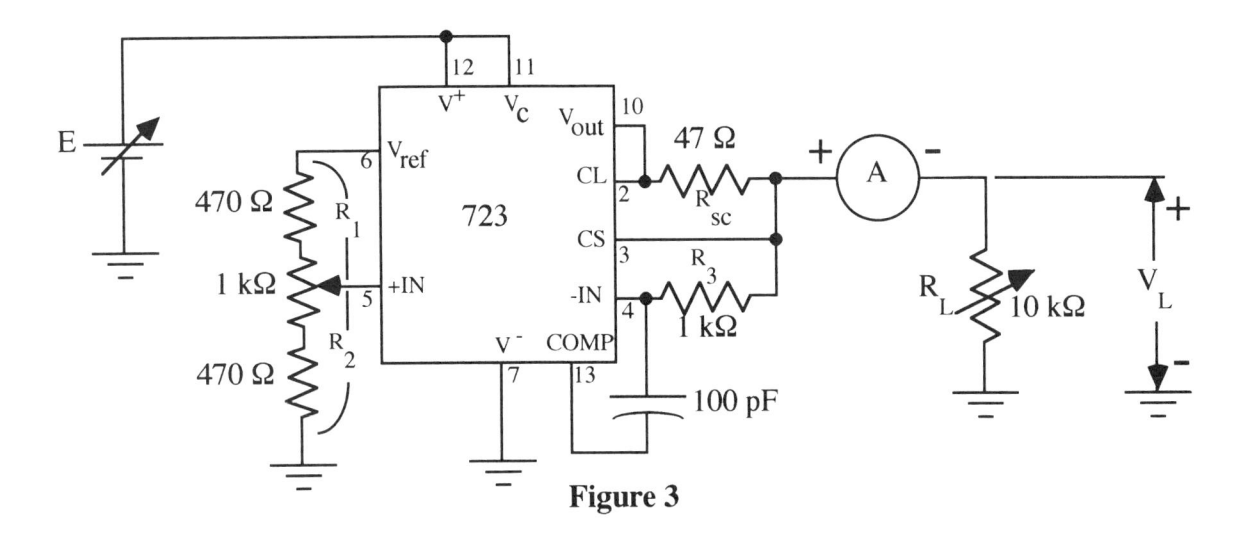

5. With E = 10 V, measure and record the voltage $V_{ref}$ from pin 6 to ground. Momentarily remove the 10 kΩ load potentiometer and measure the minimum and maximum values of the output voltage by adjusting the 1 kΩ potentiometer through its entire resistance range. Then adjust the 1 kΩ potentiometer until the no-load output voltage equals 5 V.

6. Reconnect the 10 kΩ load potentiometer. Now adjust the load potentiometer so that it draws 5 mA from the output of the regulator and measure the load voltage $V_L$. Slowly decrease the load resistance until the load voltage suddenly decreases. Record the current where this occurs.

7. Replace the 47 Ω current-limiting resistor $R_{SC}$ with a 22 Ω resistor and repeat procedure step 6.

8. To measure the maximum short-circuit output current, replace the current-limiting resistor $R_{SC}$ with a short-circuit and replace the 10 kΩ load potentiometer with a 1 kΩ potentiometer. Repeat procedure step 6.

## EXPERIMENT 24 - VOLTAGE REGULATORS

### Questions

1. Using the values in Tables 1 and 2, determine the output resistance and line regulation of the 7805 three-terminal fixed-voltage regulator. Use manufacturer's specifications to compute specified output resistance. Compare specified values of output resistance and line regulation with those determined experimentally.

2. With $R_{SC} = 47\ \Omega$, calculate the theoretical short-circuit current for the circuit in Figure 3. Compare the theoretical value with that measured in procedure step 6.

3. Repeat question 2 for the circuit in Figure 3 with $R_{SC} = 22\ \Omega$.

4. Compare the maximum load current ($R_{SC} = 0\ \Omega$) measured in procedure step 8 with the maximum load current specified by the manufacturer.

5. Using the circuit in Figure 3 as a guide and the measured value of $V_{ref}$, design a voltage regulator with an output voltage of 6 V and a maximum load current of 50 mA.

## Data

### TABLE 1

| $R_L$ (ohms) | $V_L$ (volts) | $I_L$ (amps) |
|---|---|---|
| 100 Ω | | |
| 47 Ω | | |
| 22 Ω | | |
| 10 Ω | | |

### TABLE 2

| E (volts) | $V_2$ (volts) | $I_L$ (amps) |
|---|---|---|
| 10 V | | |
| 12 V | | |
| 15 V | | |
| 20 V | | |

# EXPERIMENT 24 - VOLTAGE REGULATORS

# D/A and A/D Converters 25

## Reference

*Electronic Devices and Circuits, Sixth Edition:* Section 14-1, Overview; Section 14-4, The Switched Current-Source DAC; Section 14–10, The Successive Approximation ADC

## Objectives

1. To demonstrate D/A and A/D converters.
2. To demonstrate the concept of digital sampling and playback.

## Equipment List

1. DAC0800 8-bit digital-to-analog converter
2. ADC0800 8-bit analog-to-digital converter
3. 8-NTE3007 red LED or the equivalent
4. DC power supplies (+10.24 V and -10 V)
5. Analog signal generators (square wave that alternates between 0 V and 10 V at 100 kHz, 6 to 11 Vp-p sine with variable frequency)
6. Resistors: 3-4.7 kΩ, 1-3.9 kΩ, 1-270 Ω
7. Capacitors: 3-10 µF, 2-0.1 µF, 1-0.01 µF (all 25 V)
8. Potentiometers: 1-10 kΩ, 3-1 kΩ
9. VOM
10. Dual-trace oscilloscope

## Discussion

Analog-to-digital and digital-to-analog conversion have become an important part of everyday life. Compact discs store music digitally, and using DACs, convert it back into analog signals for playback. Some answering machines use this technique, called *digital sampling*, to store audio messages in digital media. Many keyboard synthesizers use digitally sampled waveforms to reproduce hi-fi audio sounds like pianos, horns, etc.

# EXPERIMENT 25 - D/A AND A/D CONVERTERS

To convert an analog signal to a digital one means representing the instantaneous voltage level with a binary (digital) word. An 8-bit word contains 8 binary digits or *bits*, each one corresponding to the 1, 2, 4, 8, 16, 32, 64, and 128s place from right to left (00101100, for example, would be 4 + 8 + 32 or 44, and 10110001 would be 1 + 16 + 32 + 128 or 177). The rightmost bit (the 1s place) is referred to as the *least significant* bit (LSB). The leftmost bit (the 128s place) is called the *most significant* bit (MSB). The total possible decimal numbers that can be represented using $n$ bits is $2^n$. Thus, an 8-bit A/D will yield one of $2^8$, or 256, possible 8-bit words, 00000000 (0) to 11111111 (255) corresponding to one of 256 possible voltages at its input. An 8-bit D/A will yield one of 256 possible voltages at its output when supplied with an 8-bit word at its inputs.

The most common type of ADC is the successive-approximation ADC. The technique it uses is a common method used to guess a number in the minimum number of tries. Suppose an 8-bit A/D is used. The input voltage will be converted to a digital number from 0 to 255 (00000000 to 11111111). The A/D *guesses* 128 (10000000), which is one half of the maximum possible. This digital guess is converted to an analog voltage by a DAC. The guess is compared to the input voltage using a comparator. The comparator determines if the guess was high or low. If the guess was too high, the output register is loaded with a "0" in the most significant bit's place and the control circuit guesses 64 (01000000), which is halfway between 0 and 128. If, for example, the guess is low, the output register is loaded with a "1" in the next most significant bit's place. This type of logic is used to guess each bit until the A/D *zooms* in on the correct answer. Then the EOC pin on the chip indicates that the conversion is over.

The DAC used in this experiment uses the *switched current-source* technique. Each of the binary inputs controls an electronic switch connected to a current source. The values of the individual current sources are weighted according to the bit controlling them (i.e., more significant bits control higher-valued current sources and less significant bits control lower-valued current sources). These current sources are summed in an operational amplifier, which converts the sum of the currents to an appropriate voltage.

## Procedure

1. To demonstrate the switched current-source DAC, connect the following circuit:

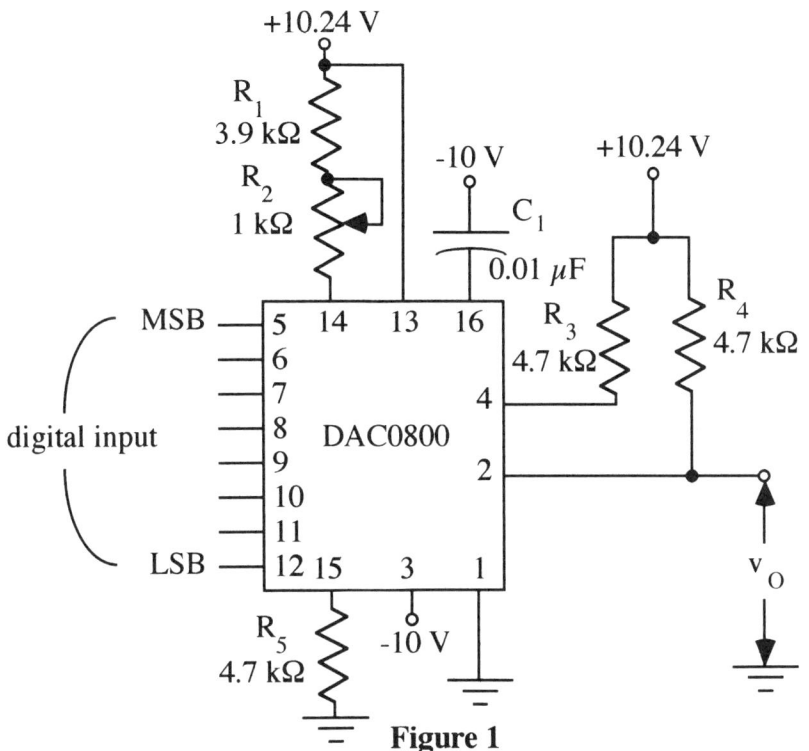

**Figure 1**

2. Using a sensitive VOM to measure $v_O$, ground each of the digital inputs and adjust the 1 kΩ potentiometer $R_1$ for exactly 0 V output.

3. Connect pin 5 to +10.24 V while keeping the other input pins grounded. Measure the output voltage, which will be the interval of output voltage for each 1 bit increment of digital input.

4. Measure and record the output voltage for each of the following 8-bit digital words:

                10100001       01001010
                01101111       11111111

## EXPERIMENT 25 - D/A AND A/D CONVERTERS

5. Without disconnecting the circuit of Figure 1, connect the following circuit in order to investigate the successive-approximation A/D converter. The LEDs will illuminate, indicating a logic-high at that pin:

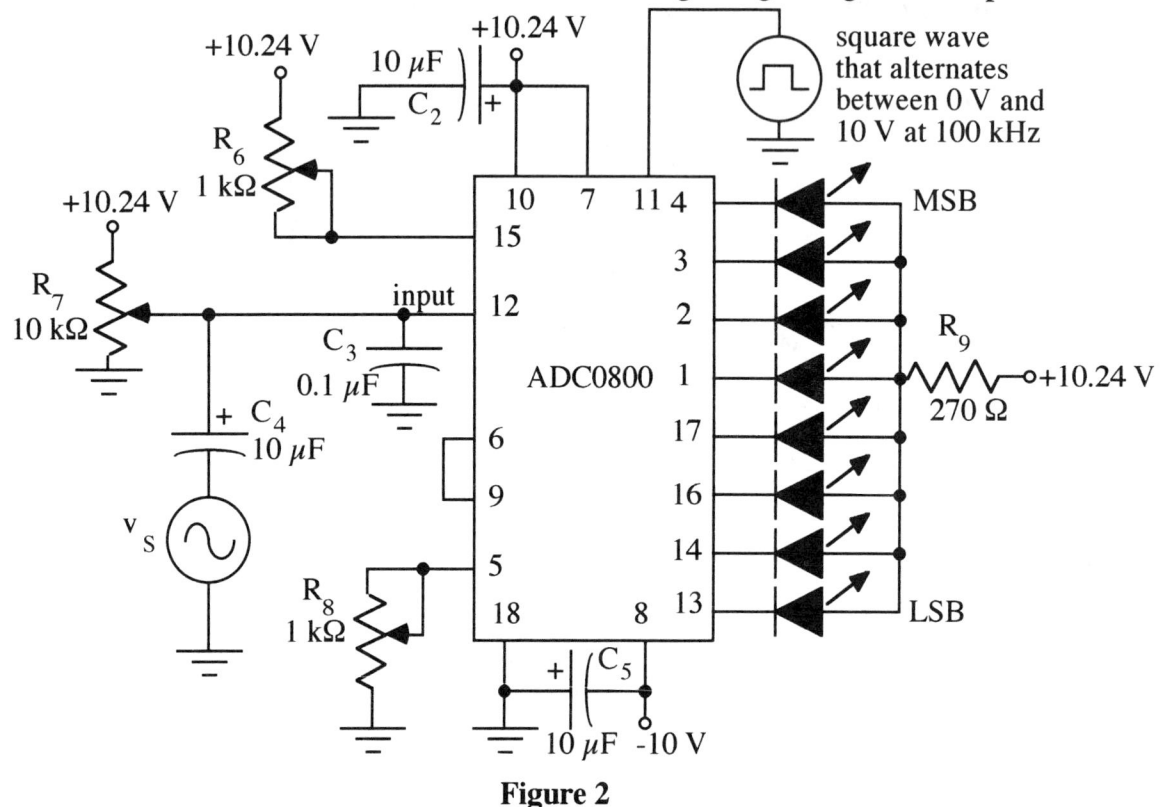

**Figure 2**

6. With $v_S = 0$ V and $R_7$ set for 20 mVrms input, adjust potentiometer $R_8$ until the LSB LED just begins to flicker with all other LEDs off. Then adjust $R_7$ until the input voltage at pin 12 = 10.18 Vrms. Now, adjust $R_6$ until the LSB LED flickers and all other LEDs are on. This creates a 40 mV per bit interval.

7. Adjust $R_7$ for the following input voltages at pin 12 and record the digital word that results:

                40 mV DC      1 VDC
                2.88 VDC    10.24 VDC

8. To demonstrate the concept of digital sampling and playback, connect the previous circuits as shown in Figure 3.

EXPERIMENT 25 - D/A AND A/D CONVERTERS

**Figure 3**

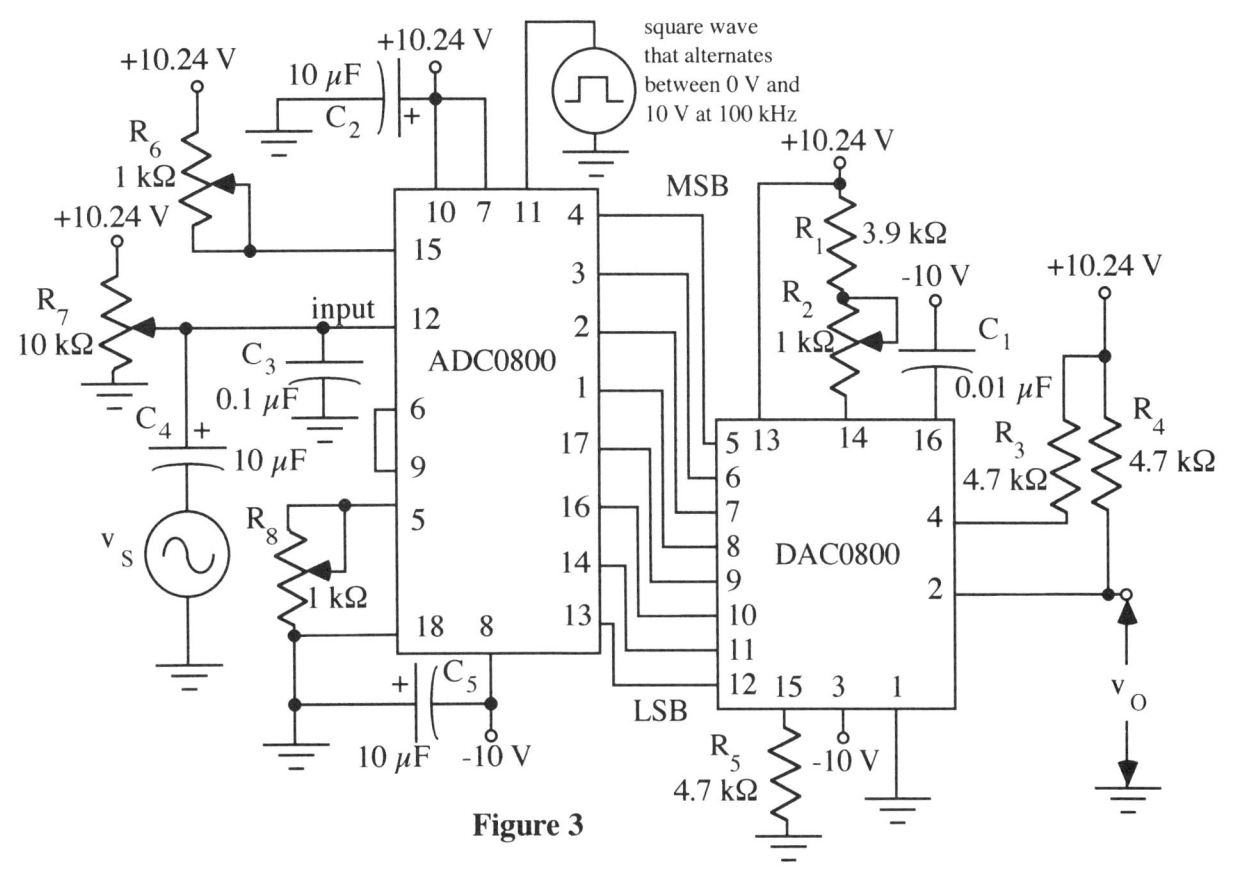

9. With $v_S = 0$ V, adjust $R_7$ for a dc input voltage of 5.12 VDC. Then connect a dual-trace oscilloscope so that $v_O$ and $v_S$ can be viewed simultaneously. Increase $v_S$ to 6 Vp-p at 100 Hz and sketch the output waveform $v_O$.(It may be necessary to adjust the frequency of $v_S$ slightly to stabilize the output waveform.)

10. Change the frequency of $v_S$ to 50 Hz and note the changes in the number of samples per cycle. Repeat at 500 Hz.

11. With $v_S$ again set to a frequency of 100 Hz, slowly increase the amplitude of $v_S$ and note the results in the output waveform $v_O$ when $v_S$ increases above 10 Vp-p. Also, adjust the position of potentiometer $R_7$ and note the effects on the waveform.

12. Add a 0.1 $\mu$F capacitor across the output (between pin 2 of the DAC and ground) and note the change in the output voltage.

# EXPERIMENT 25 - D/A AND A/D CONVERTERS

## Questions

1. For each of the 8-bit digital words in procedure step 4, calculate the theoretical one based on the 1-bit interval of output voltage measured in procedure step 3. Compare these to the measured values from procedure step 4.

2. Using 10 mV as the output voltage interval per bit, calculate the output voltage resulting from each of the following 10-bit digital words:

    1001001100     0000011001
    1111111110     0000000110

3. Using 40 mV per bit as in procedure step 6, calculate the theoretical digital word resulting from each of the input voltages from procedure step 7. Compare these to measured results.

4. Using 25 mV as the input voltage interval per bit, calculate the resulting 10-bit digital word resulting from the following input voltages:

    24.1 V        10.625 V
    0.375 V       1 V

5. In procedure steps 9 and 10, how did changing the frequency of the input waveform $v_S$ change the number of samples? Why? In procedure step 11, what effect did increasing the amplitude of $v_S$ have on the output waveform $v_O$? Explain.

6. What is the purpose for adjusting the potentiometer $R_7$ for 5.12 VDC in Figure 3? What happened when it was adjusted in procedure step 11?

7. What happened to the output waveform when the capacitor was added in procedure step 12?

# SCRs and TRIACs 26

## Reference

*Electronic Devices and Circuits, Sixth Edition:* Section 15-1, Four-Layer Devices

## Objectives

1. To investigate the breakover characteristics of an SCR.
2. To demonstrate half-wave power control using an SCR.
3. To demonstrate full-wave power control using a TRIAC with a DIAC trigger.

## Equipment List

1. NTE 5437 SCR or the equivalent
2. NTE 5608 TRIAC or the equivalent
3. NTE 6406 DIAC or the equivalent
4. Variable dc power supply (0–30 V)
5. Analog signal generator (5 Vpk sine at 1 kHz, 50 Vpk sine at 60 Hz)
6. Resistors: 1-100 kΩ, 1-1 kΩ (2 W), 1-270 Ω
7. Capacitor: 1-0.1 µF (25 V)
8. Potentiometers: 1-500 kΩ, 1-100 kΩ
9. VOM
10. Dual-trace oscilloscope

## Discussion

As the name implies, a silicon controlled rectifier (SCR) is a rectifier because it conducts current in one direction only, but the conducting mode is *controlled* by current supplied to a third terminal, called the gate. For

# EXPERIMENT 26 - SCRs AND TRIACs

any specific value of anode-to-cathode voltage, $V_{AK}$, a particular value of gate current is required to "trigger," or "fire," the SCR into conduction. Once the SCR has been fired, it will remain in its conducting, or ON, state indefinitely, unless the current through it is reduced below a certain *holding current*. If the current is reduced below the holding current, the SCR reverts to its nonconducting, or OFF, state. Figure 1 shows a typical set of characteristic curves for an SCR. The values labeled $V_{BR}$ along the horizontal axis are the *breakover* voltages at which the SCR is triggered into conduction. Note that $V_{BR}$ decreases as gate current increases. The value of holding current, $I_H$, required to sustain conduction can also be seen to decrease with increasing gate current. The $I_G = 0$ curve shows that the SCR can be triggered into conduction and has a specific value of holding current when the gate is open.

**Figure 1**

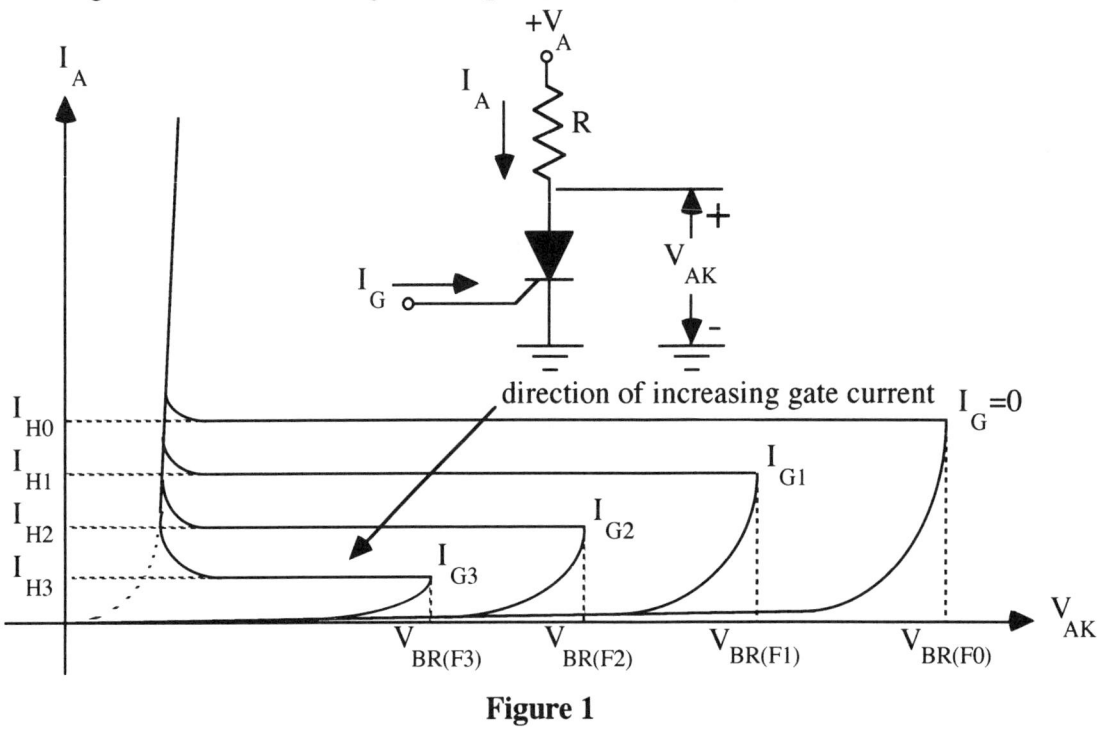

Figure 5 shows a popular application of an SCR as a half-wave power controller. Note that the input voltage, $v_S$, is applied to the anode of the SCR and to the gate of the SCR through an adjustable resistance. By adjusting the resistance, the amount of gate current that flows at any positive value of $v_S$ can be controlled. When the resistance in series with the gate is small, a relatively small value of $v_S$ will trigger the SCR ON. In that case, current will flow in the load during a majority of every positive half-cycle of input, and the average power in the load will be large. Notice that the SCR reverts to its nonconducting state during every negative half-cycle of input. When the resistance is large, a large value of $v_S$ will be required to trigger the SCR ON. In that case, current will flow in the load during a smaller interval of each positive half-cycle, and the average load power will be reduced. The angle $\emptyset_f$ at which the SCR triggers ON is called the *firing angle*, and its value can be adjusted from 0° to near 90°. See Figure 2.

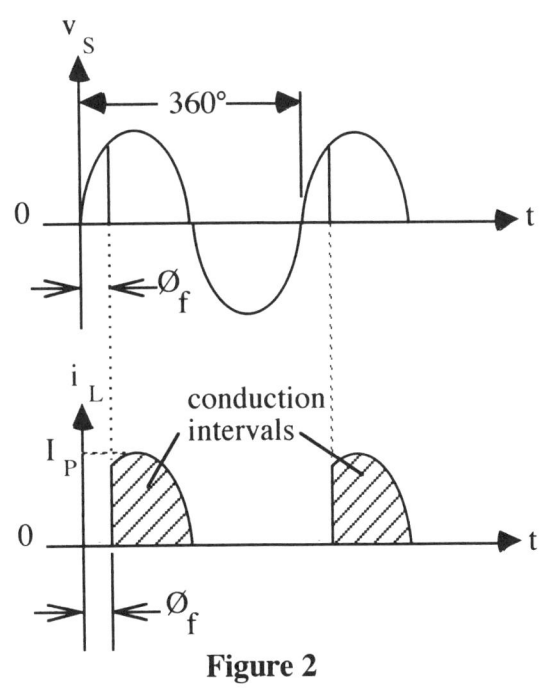

**Figure 2**

The rms current in the load of the half-wave power controller is given by

$$I(rms) = \frac{I_P}{2}\sqrt{\left(1 - \frac{\emptyset_f}{180°}\right) + \frac{\sin 2\emptyset f}{2\pi}}$$

where:
$\emptyset_f$ is in degrees

A TRIAC is similar to two parallel SCRs having a single gate terminal and arranged so that one conducts positive current and the other conducts

# EXPERIMENT 26 - SCRs AND TRIACs

negative current. Modern TRIACs are designed so that current flowing into the gate triggers one SCR-equivalent and current flowing out of the gate triggers the other. A DIAC is a TRIAC with no gate terminal. If the voltage across a DIAC is made sufficiently large, it will breakover (conduct) until the current through it falls below the holding current. If the voltage across the DIAC is made sufficiently large in the reverse direction, it will break over and conduct in the reverse direction.

Figure 6 shows a full-wave power controller using a DIAC and a TRIAC. During the positive half-cycle of $v_S$, the capacitor charges until the breakover voltage of the DIAC is reached. At that time, the DIAC conducts a pulse of current into the gate of the TRIAC, which triggers the TRIAC into its ON state. Current then flows in the load until $v_S$ drops to near zero. During the negative half-cycle of $v_S$, the capacitor charges negatively until the DIAC breaks over in the reverse direction. The current pulse that flows out of the gate of the TRIAC triggers the TRIAC into conduction and current flows in the reverse direction through the load. The adjustable resistance controls the rate at which the capacitor charges and therefore controls the firing angle, $\emptyset_f$. Figure 3 shows the waveform of the load current in the full-wave power controller.

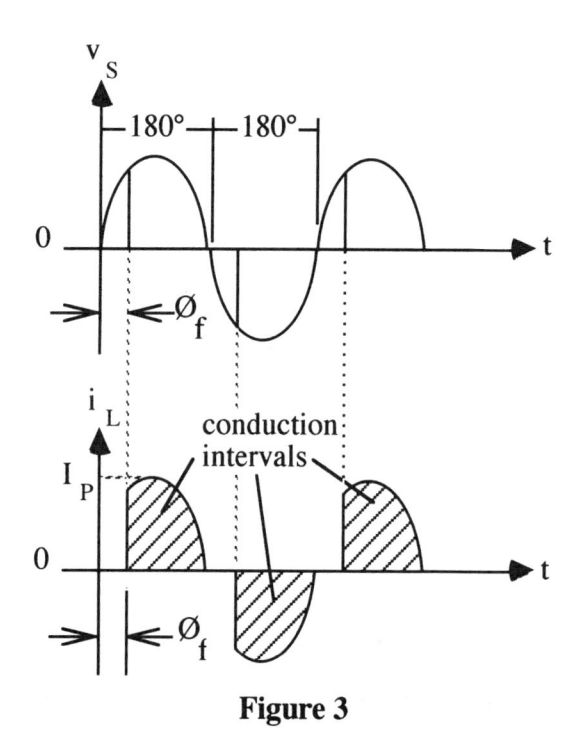

**Figure 3**

The rms current in the load of the full-wave power controller is

$$I(rms) = \frac{I_P}{\sqrt{2}}\sqrt{\left(1 - \frac{\varnothing_f}{180°}\right) + \frac{\sin 2\varnothing_f}{2\pi}}$$

where:
$\varnothing_f$ is in degrees

The *minimum* firing angle that can be realized in the full-wave power controller is

$$\varnothing_f(min) = \sin^{-1}\left(\frac{V_{BR}}{V_P}\right)$$

where:
$V_{BR}$ is the breakover voltage of the DIAC
$V_P$ is the peak value of $v_S$

EXPERIMENT 26 - SCRs AND TRIACs

## Procedure

1. To investigate the breakover characteristics of an SCR, connect the circuit in Figure 4. The adjustable voltage source E should be set to 0 V before power is turned on.

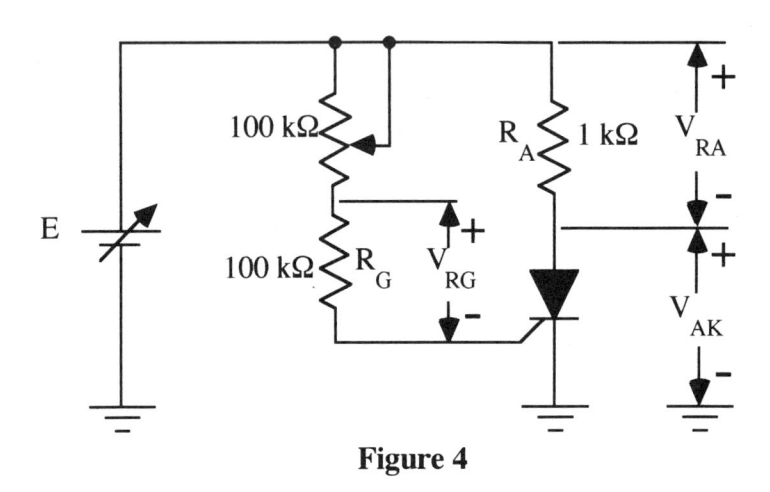

**Figure 4**

2. Set the 100 kΩ potentiometer for maximum resistance. Connect a dc voltmeter to measure the voltage $V_{AK}$ across the SCR. Now gradually increase E until $V_{AK}$ suddenly drops to about 0.7 V, indicating that the SCR has "fired" (been triggered into conduction). Then disconnect the 100 kΩ resistor, leaving the gate of the SCR open. Verify that the SCR remains in its ON, or conducting, state with zero gate current flowing.

3. Connect a dc voltmeter across $R_A$ to measure $V_{RA}$. Gradually decrease E, while closely observing $V_{RA}$, until $V_{RA}$ suddenly drops, indicating that the SCR has reverted to its OFF state. Record the value of $V_{RA}$ just before the SCR turns off. The holding current with the gate open, $I_{H0}$, is this value of $V_{RA}$ divided by $R_A$.

4. Reconnect the 100 kΩ resistor, set the 100 kΩ potentiometer for maximum resistance, and set E to 0 V. Connect a dc voltmeter to measure $V_{AK}$. Gradually increase E until $V_{AK}$ suddenly drops to about 0.7 V. Record the value of $V_{AK}$ just before that drop in voltage. Without

# EXPERIMENT 26 - SCRs AND TRIACs

increasing E any further, measure $V_{RA}$ and $V_{RG}$. These values can be used to determine the holding current and gate current corresponding to the breakover voltage just observed. Repeat this procedure with the potentiometer set for minimum resistance.

5. To demonstrate the use of an SCR in power control, connect the half-wave power controller in Figure 5.

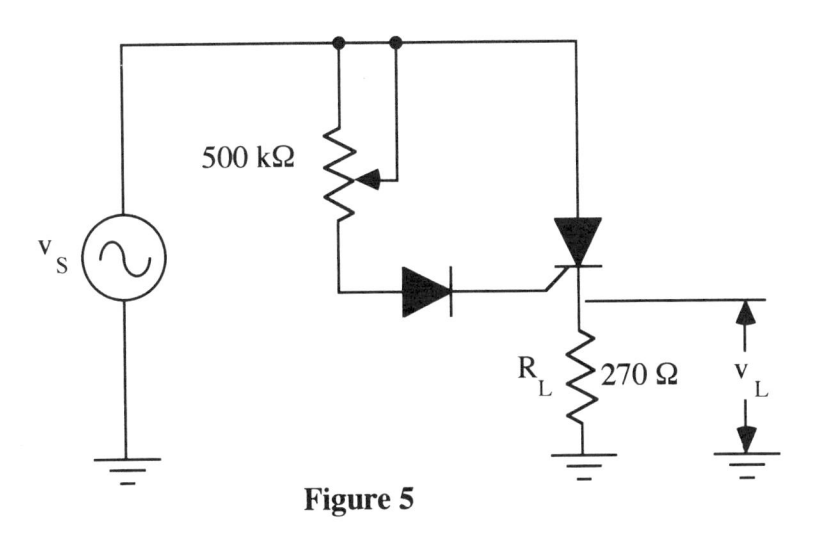

**Figure 5**

6. Connect a dual-trace oscilloscope so that both $v_L$ and $v_S$ can be observed simultaneously. With $v_S$ = 5 Vpk at 1 kHz, adjust the potentiometer until the firing angle is as close as possible to 0° (making $v_L$ resemble a half-wave rectified waveform). Sketch the input voltage $v_S$ and the output voltage $v_L$. Be certain to record the peak value of $v_L$. Also record the point in time at which the SCR is triggered ON, so the actual firing angle can be determined. Observe the effect on the waveform of $v_L$ as the potentiometer is adjusted through its range.

7. Carefully adjust the potentiometer until $v_L$ has a firing angle of close to 90°. Sketch the input voltage $v_S$ and the output voltage $v_L$. Be certain to record the peak value of $v_L$ and the point in time where the SCR is triggered ON.

## EXPERIMENT 26 - SCRs AND TRIACs

8. To demonstrate the use of a TRIAC for power control, connect the full-wave power controller in Figure 6.

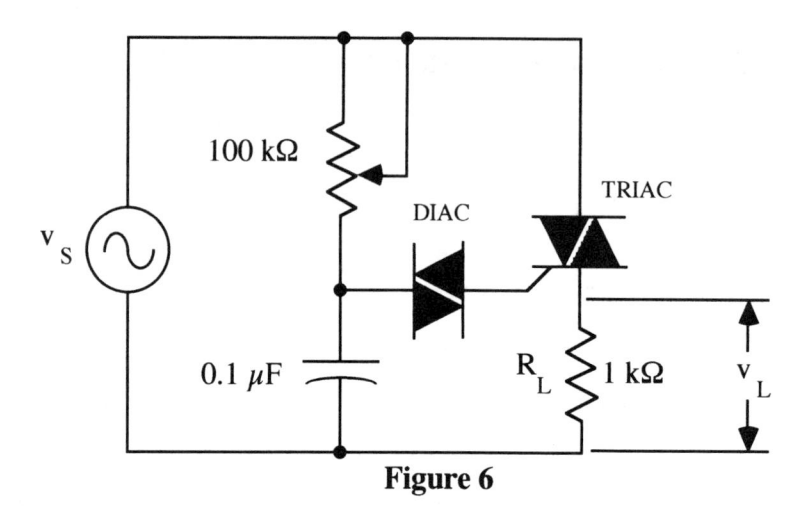

**Figure 6**

9. It will be necessary to adjust $v_S$ to obtain at least 50 V peak at 60 Hz. If the signal generator cannot develop this voltage, use a step-down transformer connected to 120 V ac, 60 Hz power and observe the WARNING notes in step 1 of Experiment 2. Connect a dual-trace oscilloscope so that $v_L$ and $v_S$ can be observed simultaneously. Adjust the potentiometer through its range and note the effect on the waveform of $v_L$.

10. Now adjust the potentiometer until the waveform of $v_L$ has the smallest firing angle possible. Sketch the input voltage $v_S$ and the load voltage $v_L$. Be certain to note the peak value of $v_L$ and the point in time where the TRIAC triggers ON. Also record the value of $v_S$ at which the TRIAC triggers ON. This value is the breakover voltage $V_{BR}$ of the DIAC.

11. Adjust the potentiometer until the $v_L$ waveform has the greatest firing angle possible. Sketch the input voltage $v_S$ and the load voltage $v_L$. Be certain to note the peak value of $v_L$ and the point in time where the TRIAC triggers ON.

# EXPERIMENT 26 - SCRs AND TRIACs

## Questions

1. How did you know that the SCR remained in its ON state when the gate circuit was opened in procedure step 2?

2. What is the value of the holding current for the SCR when the gate is open?

3. Calculate the gate current that was required to trigger the SCR ON in each case in procedure step 4. What is the breakover voltage for each value of gate current? What is the holding current (approximately)?

4. Calculate the rms load current in the half-wave power controller when the firing angle was set to its minimum value in procedure step 6. (Use the peak value of $v_L$ to determine the peak value of $I_L$.) Calculate the average power delivered to the load ($P_{AVG} = I^2(rms)R_L$).

5. Repeat question 4 using the data obtained in procedure step 7 for the maximum firing angle.

6. Using the time measurement obtained in procedure step 10, determine the minimum firing angle observed in the full-wave power controller. Also calculate the minimum firing angle using the breakover voltage of the DIAC (see discussion), and compare that value with the angle observed.

7. Calculate the rms load current and the average power delivered to the load when the TRIAC is operated at its minimum firing angle.

8. Determine the maximum firing angle of the full-wave power controller and calculate the rms load current and the average load power under that condition. Explain why the power is smaller or greater than that calculated in question 7.

# EXPERIMENT 26 - SCRs AND TRIACs

# LEDs and Optocouplers 27

## Reference

*Electronic Devices and Circuits, Sixth Edition:* Section 15-2, Optoelectronic Devices

## Objectives

1. To investigate the forward-biased I-V characteristic of an LED.
2. To design an LED driver circuit.
3. To measure the current transfer ratio (CTR) of an optocoupler.

## Equipment List

1. 4N25 optocoupler or the equivalent
2. 2N2222 silicon transistor or the equivalent
3. NTE 3007 red LED or the equivalent
4. DC power supplies (5 V and variable)
5. Analog signal generator (square wave that alternates between 0 V and 5 V at 1 Hz)
6. Resistors: 1-1 k$\Omega$, 2-100 $\Omega$
7. VOM

## Discussion

A conventional diode liberates energy in the form of heat when electrical current flows through it. A light-emitting diode (LED) is a specially constructed semiconductor diode that also liberates light energy when current flows through it. Materials used in the construction of LEDs include gallium phosphide (GaP) and gallium arsenide phosphide (GaAsP). In this experiment, we will investigate an LED that emits *visible* light,

## EXPERIMENT 27 - LEDs AND OPTOCOUPLERS

making it useful in the construction of visual displays. Infrared emitting diodes (IREDs), constructed from gallium arsenide (GaAs), do not emit visible light but are useful in applications such as optocouplers.

The forward-biased characteristic of an LED is similar to that of a conventional diode because the forward voltage drop becomes essentially constant when sufficient current flows through it. However, the voltage drop is considerably greater than that of a conventional germanium or silicon diode. Depending on the type of LED, the forward drop may range from about 1.5 V to 3 V.

LEDs are often used as output displays in low-power circuits that are incapable of supplying the current necessary to illuminate the LED. In those applications, an LED *driver* circuit is required. Figure 2 shows a typical single-transistor driver for an LED. The NPN transistor is operated like a transistor switch or inverter (Experiment 6), and provides the current gain (ß) necessary to illuminate the LED when a positive voltage is applied to the base. The following equations are used to design a driver for use with a particular LED:

$$R_B = \frac{\beta(V_{HI} - 0.7)}{I_D}$$

$$R_C = \frac{V_{CC} - V_D}{I_D}$$

where:
- $V_D$ and $I_D$ are the voltage across and current through, respectively, the LED when it is illuminated
- $V_{HI}$ is the positive voltage applied to the base of the transistor
- ß is the current gain of the transistor

An *optocoupler* is a light-emitting diode (often an IRED) fabricated in one package with a photosensitive device such as a phototransistor. When a phototransistor is exposed to light, it can conduct current from collector-to-emitter in the same way that a conventional transistor conducts when it is supplied with base current. Figure 3 shows an optocoupler consisting of an LED that illuminates an NPN phototransistor. When the current supplied to the LED is sufficient to illuminate it, the transistor is activated

### EXPERIMENT 27 - LEDs AND OPTOCOUPLERS

and draws collector current from the external supply. An important specification for the optocoupler is its *current transfer ratio* (CTR), defined as:

$$\text{CTR} = \frac{I_C}{I_D}$$

where:

$I_C$ is the collector current that flows in the phototransistor when $I_D$ flows in the LED. The CTR of a given device is not constant, but varies with the value of $I_D$

Unlike the circuit shown in Figure 3, where the LED and the transistor are both driven by the same 5 V source, an optocoupler is most often used to electrically *isolate* one circuit (the LED side) from another (the phototransistor side). In fact, optocouplers are often called *optoisolators*. Good electrical isolation is possible because the circuits can be coupled through light energy only.

## Procedure

1. Complete the procedures of Appendix A to measure the ß of the transistor used in this experiment.

2. To determine the forward-biased characteristic of the LED, connect the following circuit:

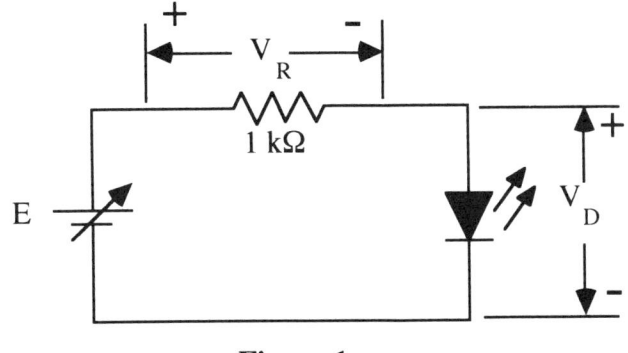

**Figure 1**

# EXPERIMENT 27 - LEDs AND OPTOCOUPLERS

3. Adjust the voltage source E so that $V_D$ equals each of the values in Table 1. Measure the voltage $V_R$ across the current-limiting resistor at each value of $V_D$. By adjusting E, determine and record the values of $V_D$ and $V_R$ at which the LED first becomes fully illuminated.

4. Using the measurements made in procedure step 3, calculate the forward-biasing current through the LED at the point where the LED first became fully illuminated. Knowing the voltage across and current through the LED necessary to achieve illumination, design an LED driver circuit in the configuration shown in Figure 2. The ß of the transistor is the measured value obtained from procedure step 1. Use the closest 5% resistors that are less than the calculated values of $R_B$ and $R_C$. The signal source, $v_S$, in Figure 2 is a 0 to 5 V square wave with a frequency of 1 Hz. Connect the designed circuit and test for correct operation: The LED should flash on and off once each second.

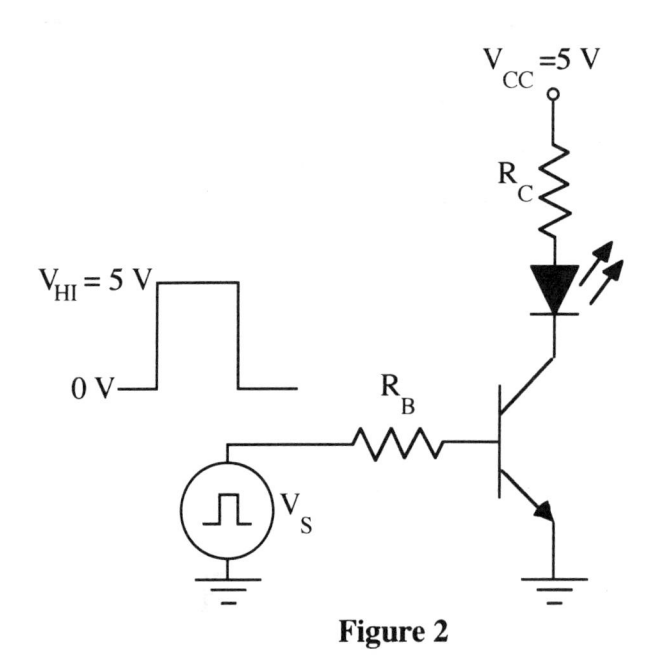

**Figure 2**

# EXPERIMENT 27 - LEDs AND OPTOCOUPLERS

5. To measure the current transfer ratio (CTR) of the optocoupler, connect the circuit in Figure 3.

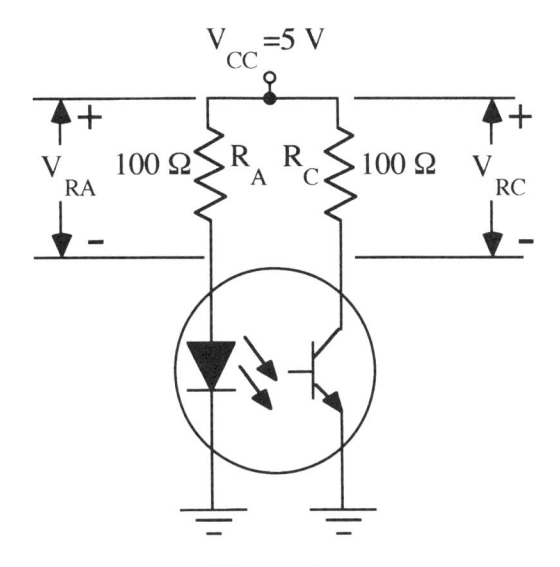

**Figure 3**

6. In the circuit of Figure 3, measure $V_{RA}$ and $V_{RC}$. The LED's anode current is $V_{RA}/R_A$ and the transistor's collector current is $V_{RC}/R_C$. The ratio of collector current to anode current is the current transfer ratio.

7. Increase the 5 V supply to 7.5 V and repeat procedure step 6.

# EXPERIMENT 27 - LEDs AND OPTOCOUPLERS

## Questions

1. Using the data from procedure step 3 and Table 1, plot the forward-biased I-V characteristic of the LED. Indicate the point on the characteristic where the LED first became fully illuminated.

2. Show the calculations used to design the LED driver circuit in procedure step 4. Did the circuit work as expected? Redesign the LED driver circuit for a 10 V supply and an input voltage that alternates between 7.5 V and ground (0 V). Why should the resistors used be the closest 5% values that are *less* than the calculated values?

3. Calculate the values of the CTR of the optocoupler using the measurements made in procedure steps 6 and 7. Based on your results, does the CTR increase or decrease with the value of LED current?

4. Give examples of circuits where the isolation quality of an optocoupler (optoisolator) would be desired.

# EXPERIMENT 27 - LEDs AND OPTOCOUPLERS

## Data

### TABLE 1

| $V_D$ (volts) | $V_R$ (volts) | $I_D = V_R/R$ |
|---|---|---|
| 0.5 V | | |
| 1 V | | |
| 1.5 V | | |
| 1.6 V | | |
| 1.65 V | | |

# EXPERIMENT 27 - LEDs AND OPTOCOUPLERS

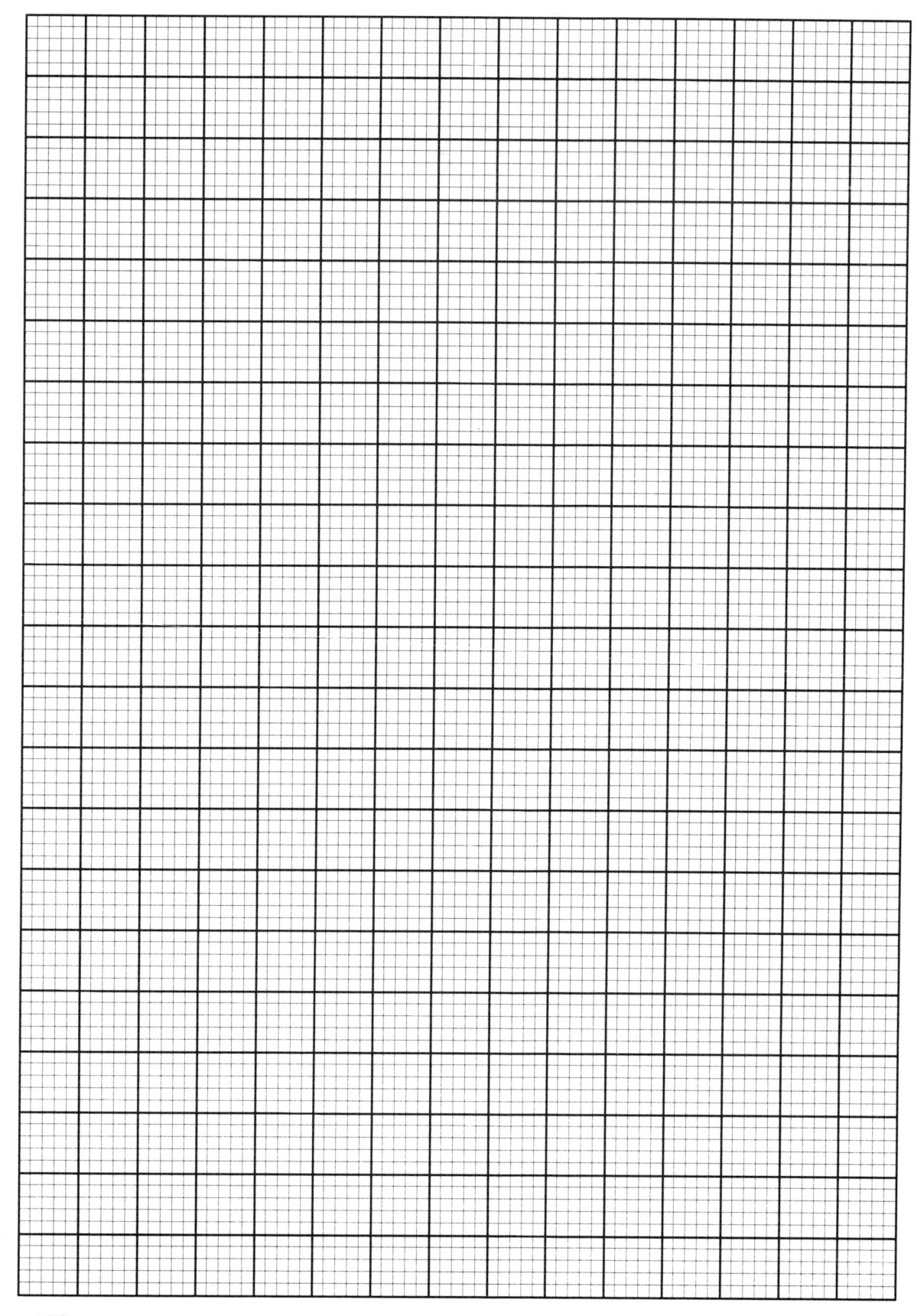

# UJTs and PUTs 28

## Reference

*Electronic Devices and Circuits, Sixth Edition:* Section 15-3, Unijunction Transistors

## Objectives

1. To determine the values of $V_P$, $V_V$, and $\eta$ for a unijunction transistor.
2. To demonstrate a relaxation oscillator using a unijunction transistor.
3. To demonstrate a relaxation oscillator using a programmable unijunction transistor.

## Equipment List

1. 2N4871 (NTE 6410) unijunction transistor
2. 2N6028 (NTE 6402) programmable unijunction transistor
3. DC power supplies (15 V and variable)
4. Resistors: 1-39 kΩ, 1-15 kΩ, 1-680 Ω, 1-270 Ω, 1-100 Ω, 1-47 Ω
5. Capacitors: 1-0.1 µF, 1-0.01 µF
6. Voltmeter and dc milliammeter
7. Dual-trace oscilloscope

## Discussion

A unijunction transistor (UJT) contains just one PN junction and therefore operates quite differently from a bipolar junction transistor. A typical UJT is constructed from a bar of lightly doped N material in which is embedded a rod of heavily doped P material called the emitter. The two

# EXPERIMENT 28 - UJTs AND PUTs

ends of the N-type bar are called base 1 and base 2. Figure 1(a) shows the schematic symbol for a UJT and identifies the three terminals. When the emitter is open and a voltage is applied across the two bases, the emitter-to-ground voltage is $V_1 = V_{BB} R_{B1} / R_{BB}$, where $V_{BB}$ is the applied voltage, $R_{B1}$ is the resistance of the bar between emitter and ground, and $R_{BB}$ is the total resistance between the bases. See Figure 1(b). The resistance ratio is called the *intrinsic standoff ratio*, $\eta$:

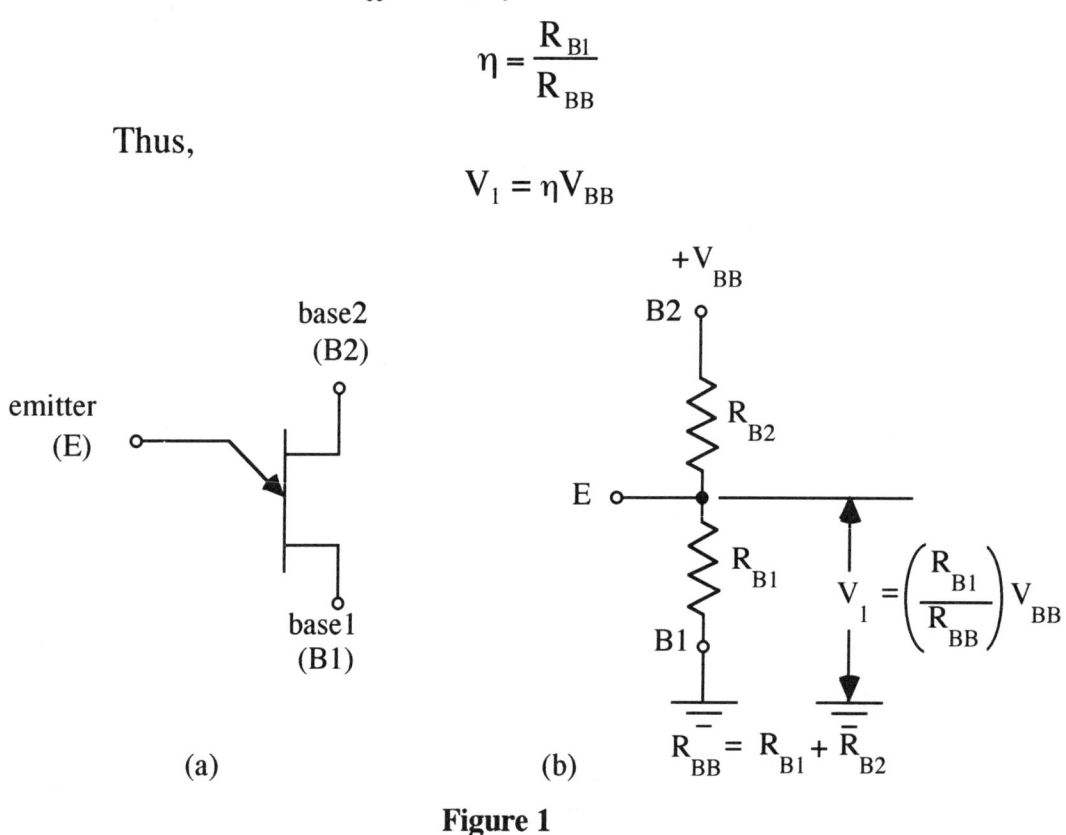

$$\eta = \frac{R_{B1}}{R_{BB}}$$

Thus,

$$V_1 = \eta V_{BB}$$

**Figure 1**

In order for current to flow in the emitter, the emitter voltage, $V_E$, must be raised to a large enough value to overcome the PN junction drop (about 0.6 V) and the emitter-to-ground voltage $V_1$. This value of $V_E$ is called the *peak voltage*, $V_P$, of the UJT:

$$V_P = \eta V_{BB} + 0.6$$

As the emitter voltage approaches $V_P$, a small amount of current begins to flow into the region between the emitter and base 1. The additional charge carriers in this region increase the conductivity of the region. The increase in conductivity (i.e., the reduction of resistance $R_{B1}$) permits additional current to flow, which further increases the conductivity, which permits more current to flow, and so forth. As a result of this regenerative action, there is a sudden and dramatic increase in current accompanied by a decrease in voltage. The UJT is said to have been triggered ON, because it can then conduct heavily between the two bases. Figure 2 shows a typical characteristic curve and identifies the *peak* and *valley* points of the characteristic. Note that the UJT is cutoff until $V_E$ reaches $V_P$. It then switches through a negative resistance region (increasing I for decreasing V), and behaves like a conventional diode as $V_E$ increases further into the saturation region. If the emitter current is allowed to fall below $I_V$, the UJT reverts to its OFF state.

**Figure 2**

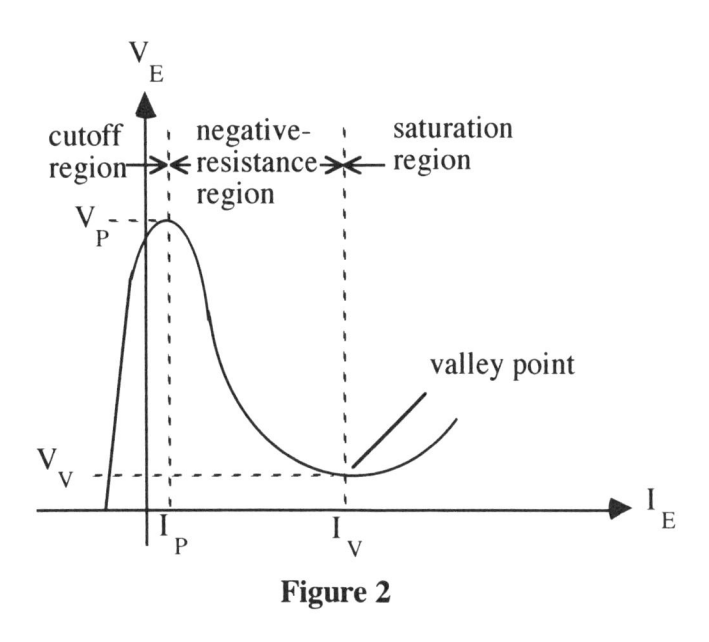

Figure 5 shows an application of a UJT in a *relaxation oscillator*. The capacitor charges through $R_E$ until the voltage reaches $V_P$. At that time, the UJT is triggered ON and a pulse of current flows through $R_L$. The capacitor discharges quickly, and when its voltage drops to $V_V$, the UJT reverts to its OFF state, provided $R_E$ is large enough to keep the emitter current below $I_V$. The capacitor then recharges and the cycle repeats itself. The waveform of the voltage across $R_L$ is not sinusoidal, but is a series of

# EXPERIMENT 28 - UJTs AND PUTs

pulses that are useful in synchronization and trigger circuits. Figure 3 shows typical waveforms in the relaxation oscillator.

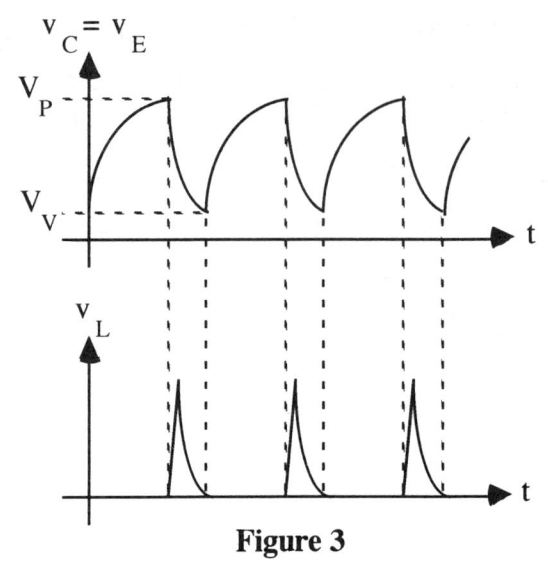

**Figure 3**

The period of the waveform produced by the relaxation oscillator is:

$$T = (R_E C) \ln\left(\frac{V_{BB} - V_V}{V_{BB} - V_P}\right) \text{ sec.}$$

If $V_{BB} \gg V_V$ and $\eta V_{BB} \gg V_D$, then the period can be approximated by:

$$T \approx (R_E C) \ln\left(\frac{1}{1-\eta}\right) \text{ sec.}$$

A programmable UJT (PUT) is not a UJT at all, but is a four-layer device like an SCR. It is called a PUT because its characteristic curve and its applications are similar to those of a UJT. Figure 6 shows a circuit containing a PUT and identifies the anode (A), cathode (K), and gate (G) terminals. When the anode is made about 0.7 V more positive than the gate, the device regeneratively switches ON and conducts heavily from anode to cathode. The PUT is "programmed" by the value of voltage connected to its gate: the larger the gate voltage, the larger the anode voltage necessary to trigger the PUT into conduction. The device is usually programmed by connecting a voltage divider across the gate terminal, like the $R_1$-$R_2$ divider shown in Figure 6. The intrinsic standoff ratio $\eta$ for the PUT is then defined by:

$$\eta = \frac{R_2}{R_1 + R_2}$$

The characteristic curve of the PUT is like that of the UJT shown in Figure 2. The value of $V_P$, where the PUT switches ON, is given by

$$V_P = V_G + V_D = \eta V_{BB} + V_D$$

where:
$$V_D \approx 0.7 \text{ V}$$

The circuit in Figure 6 is a PUT relaxation oscillator that operates like the UJT relaxation oscillator. When the capacitor charges to $V_P$, the PUT triggers ON, a pulse of current flows in $R_L$, and the capacitor discharges. When the capacitor voltage falls below $V_V$, the PUT reverts to its OFF state and the cycle starts over. The period of the oscillation is approximately:

$$T \approx (R_A C) \ln\left(\frac{1}{1-\eta}\right) \text{ sec.}$$

## Procedure

1. To determine the values for $V_P$ and $\eta$ of the unijunction transistor, connect the following circuit:

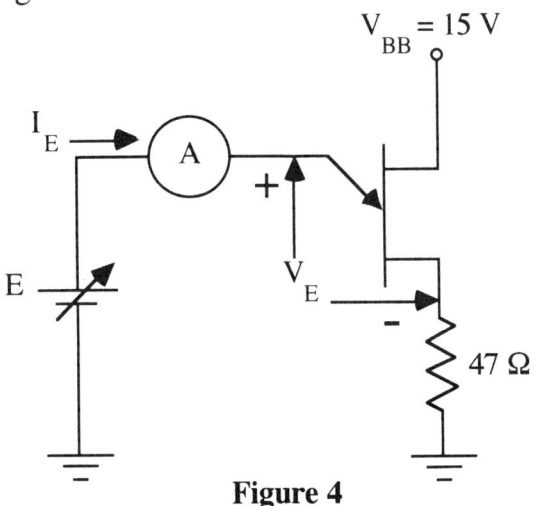

**Figure 4**

# EXPERIMENT 28 - UJTs AND PUTs

2. With E = 0 V, slowly increase E until there is a large increase in emitter current, $I_E$. Measure and record the emitter voltage, $V_E$ (equals $V_P$), when this occurs. This value can be used to determine the $\eta$ of the unijunction transistor.

3. To demonstrate the use of a unijunction transistor in a relaxation oscillator, connect the following circuit:

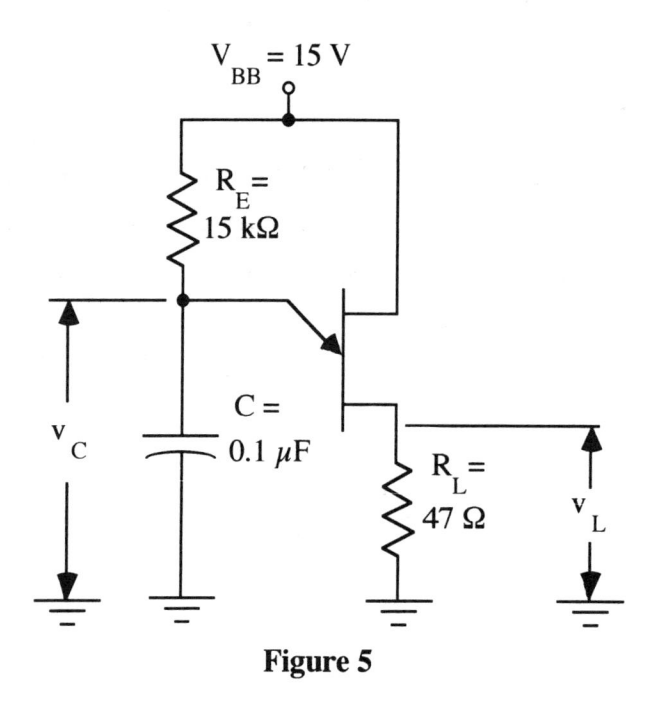

**Figure 5**

4. Connect a dual-trace oscilloscope so that $v_C$ and $v_L$ can be observed simultaneously. Measure and record the period of the output waveform $v_L$. Sketch the waveforms of $v_L$ and $v_C$. With the oscilloscope connected for dc input coupling, measure and record the minimum and maximum values of $v_C$.

5. Replace the 0.1 $\mu$F capacitor with a 0.01 $\mu$F capacitor and repeat procedure step 4.

# EXPERIMENT 28 - UJTs AND PUTs

6. To demonstrate the use of a programmable unijunction transistor in a relaxation oscillator, connect the circuit in Figure 6. Measure the exact values of resistors $R_A$, $R_1$, and $R_2$ used. If possible, also measure the exact value of C.

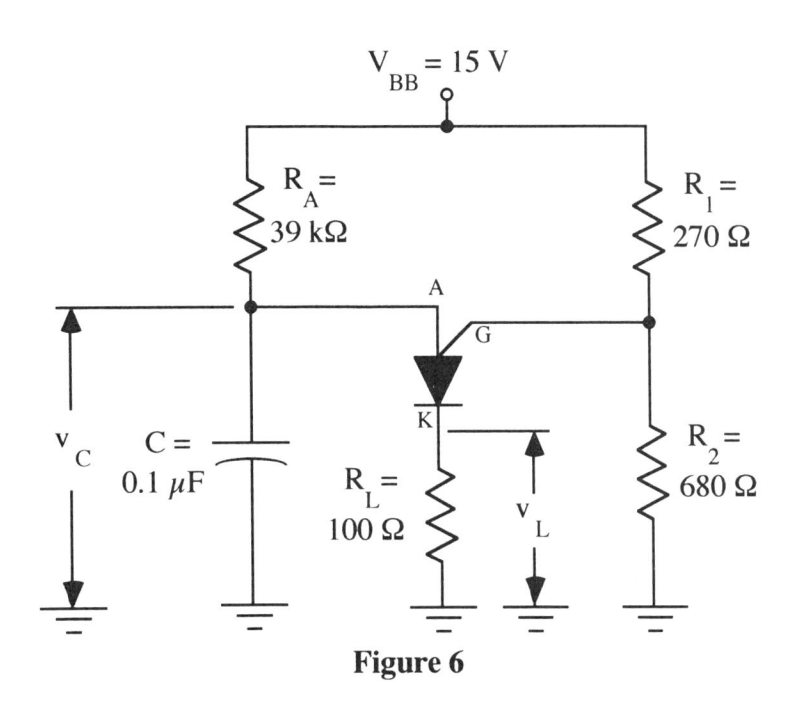

**Figure 6**

7. Connect a dual-trace oscilloscope so that $v_C$ and $v_L$ can be observed simultaneously. Measure and record the period of the output waveform $v_L$. Sketch the waveforms of $v_L$ and $v_C$.

8. Replace the 0.1 $\mu$F capacitor with a 0.01 $\mu$F capacitor and repeat procedure step 7.

# EXPERIMENT 28 - UJTs AND PUTs

## Questions

1. Using the measurement obtained in procedure step 2, calculate the $\eta$ for the unijunction transistor. Assume $v_D = 0.6$ V.

2. Based on your measurement of $v_C$ in procedure step 4, what are the values of $V_P$ and $V_V$ for the UJT? Compare the value of $V_P$ obtained this way with the value of $V_P$ obtained in procedure step 2.

3. Using the values of $V_P$ and $V_V$ from question 2, calculate the theoretical period and frequency of the relaxation oscillator in Figure 5. Compare the calculated frequency with that determined from the period measurement in procedure step 4.

4. Using the value of $\eta$ obtained in question 1, calculate the *approximate* theoretical period and frequency of the oscillator. Compare with the frequency determined from the period measurement in procedure step 4.

5. Repeat questions 2, 3, and 4 using the data obtained in procedure step 5.

6. Calculate the $\eta$ for the programmable unijunction transistor in the circuit shown in Figure 6.

7. Using the calculated value for $\eta$ obtained in question 6, calculate the theoretical frequency of the relaxation oscillator in Figure 6. Repeat this calculation for the circuit when $C = 0.01$ $\mu$F. Compare these theoretical calculations with frequencies based on the measured values of the periods obtained in procedure steps 7 and 8.

# Class-A Power Amplifiers 29

## Reference

*Electronic Devices and Circuits, Sixth Edition:* Section 16-1, Definitions, Applications, and Types of Power Amplifiers; Section 16-4, Amplifier Classes and Efficiency

## Objectives

1. To determine the efficiency of a series-fed class-A power amplifier.
2. To determine the proper bias point of a capacitor-coupled class-A power amplifier for maximum voltage swing.
3. To determine the efficiency $\eta$ of a capacitor-coupled class-A amplifier.

## Equipment List

1. 2N2222 silicon transistor or the equivalent
2. DC power supply (15 V)
3. Analog signal generator (variable sine wave at 1 kHz)
4. Resistors: 1-10 k$\Omega$, 1-1 k$\Omega$, 1-680 $\Omega$
5. Capacitors: 2-10 $\mu$F (25 V)
6. Potentiometer: 1-500 k$\Omega$
7. Dual-trace oscilloscope
8. VOM

## Discussion

Power amplifiers are used to deliver a large amount of power to a load. Typically, voltage amplifiers are cascaded together to amplify the

# EXPERIMENT 29 - CLASS-A POWER AMPLIFIERS

input signal, and the power amplifier will be the last stage of amplification. Heavy-duty transistors are used in power amplifiers, because in order to deliver a large amount of power, the transistor must be able to dissipate a large amount of heat. In this experiment, power levels will be small so that conventional transistors can be used.

Class-A power amplifiers are amplifiers that are biased in the active region. Under normal operation, the transistor will never saturate or cut off. The amplifiers studied thus far have been class-A voltage amplifiers and class-A current amplifiers.

The ratio of load power delivered to power drawn from the dc supply is called the efficiency, $\eta$, of an amplifier. In many cases, it is more important to have the highest efficiency possible than to deliver the most power to the load. The efficiency, $\eta$, can be calculated using the following equations:

$$\eta = \frac{P_L}{P_S} = \frac{\text{average signal power delivered to load}}{\text{average power drawn from dc source}}$$

where:
$$P_S = V_{CC} I_Q$$

and:
$$P_L = \frac{V_{L(peak)}^2}{2R_L} = \frac{V_{L(p-p)}^2}{8R_L}$$

$I_Q$ is the quiescent collector current
$V_{L(peak)}$ is the peak value of a sinusoidal load voltage
$V_{L(p-p)}$ is the peak-to-peak value of a sinusoidal load voltage

The two types of class-A power amplifiers investigated in this experiment are the series-fed amplifier shown in Figure 1 and the capacitor-coupled amplifier shown in Figure 2.

# EXPERIMENT 29 - CLASS-A POWER AMPLIFIERS

The load in the series-fed amplifier in Figure 1 is the collector resistor. In this case, maximum output swing is possible when the collector voltage equals $V_{CC}/2$. The maximum possible efficiency, $\eta$, of the series-fed amplifier is 0.25. Maximum efficiency occurs when the amplifier is driven for maximum possible output swing without distortion, i.e., $V_{CC}$ volts, peak-to-peak.

The load resistor in the capacitor-coupled amplifier shown in Figure 2 is capacitor-coupled to the collector of the transistor. In this case, maximum output swing occurs when the collector is biased in the center of the *ac* load line. If the value of the collector resistor is 1.414 times that of the load resistor, the efficiency, $\eta$, is maximized. With this value of $R_C$, the maximum efficiency, $\eta$, for the capacitor-coupled amplifier is only 0.0858, when the output swing is the maximum possible without distortion.

## Procedure

1. To investigate the efficiency of a series-fed class-A power amplifier, connect the following circuit:

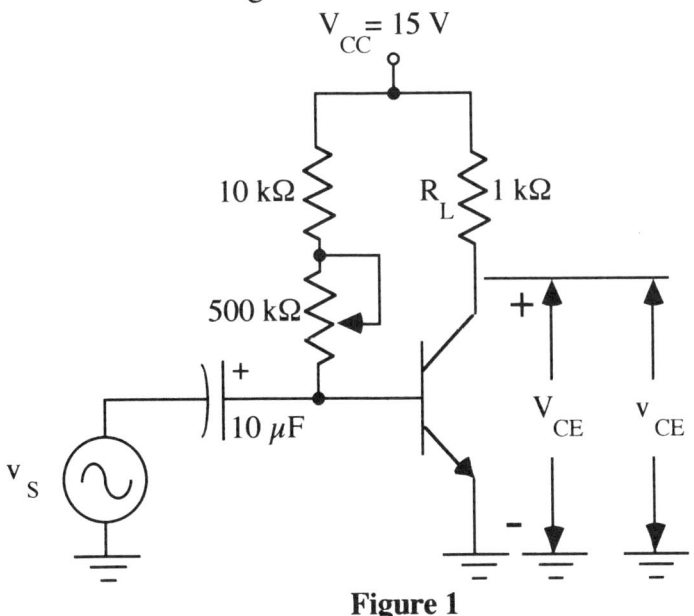

**Figure 1**

2. For maximum voltage swing of a series-fed class-A amplifier, the collector must be biased at $V_{CC}/2$ volts. Therefore, with $v_S = 0$ V, adjust the 500 kΩ potentiometer until the dc voltage $V_{CE}$ is equal to 7.5 V.

209

# EXPERIMENT 29 - CLASS-A POWER AMPLIFIERS

3. With $v_S$ set at about 1 kHz, increase the amplitude of $v_S$ until the ac collector voltage $v_{CE}$ is just at the onset of clipping (but not clipped). Measure and record the peak-to-peak value of $v_{CE}$ at this point.

4. To investigate the biasing and efficiency of a capacitor-coupled class-A amplifier, connect the following circuit:

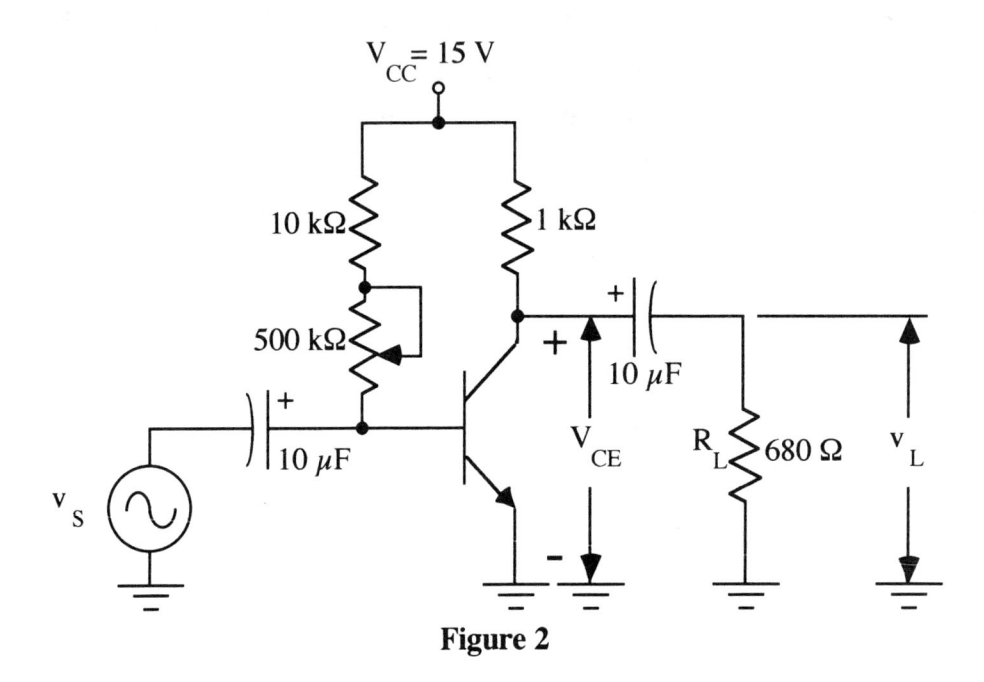

**Figure 2**

5. Recall that for maximum output swing of a capacitor-coupled common-emitter amplifier, the collector must be biased in the center of the ac load line. Calculate the dc collector voltage that will yield the maximum possible output swing.

$$\text{Hint: } I_Q = \frac{V_{CC}}{R_C + r_L} \text{ where } r_L = R_C \| R_L$$

6. With $v_S = 0$ V, adjust the 500 k$\Omega$ potentiometer to obtain the dc collector voltage calculated in procedure step 5.

7. With $v_S$ set at about 1 kHz, increase the amplitude of $v_S$ until the load voltage $v_L$ is just at the onset of clipping (but not clipped). Measure and record the peak-to-peak value of $v_L$ at this point.

# EXPERIMENT 29 - CLASS-A POWER AMPLIFIERS

## Questions

1. Calculate the average power drawn from the dc supply for the series-fed class-A power amplifier of Figure 1 using the voltage measurements obtained in procedure step 2. Calculate the average signal power delivered to the load of the series-fed class-A power amplifier of Figure 1 using the measurements obtained in procedure step 3.

2. Using the results of question 1, calculate the efficiency, $\eta$, of the series-fed class-A power amplifier of Figure 1. Compare the calculated value for $\eta$ with the maximum possible value of 0.25. Explain any difference in these values.

3. Show the calculations used to determine the dc collector voltage necessary for maximum output swing for the capacitor-coupled class-A power amplifier of Figure 2.

4. Calculate the average power drawn from the dc supply for the capacitor-coupled class-A power amplifier of Figure 2 using the voltage measurements obtained in procedure steps 5 and 6. Calculate the average signal power delivered to the load of the capacitor-coupled class-A power amplifier of Figure 2 using the measurements obtained in procedure step 7.

5. Using the results of question 4, calculate the efficiency, $\eta$, of the capacitor-coupled class-A power amplifier of Figure 2. Compare the calculated value for, $\eta$, with the maximum possible value of 0.0858. Explain any difference in these values.

# EXPERIMENT 29 - CLASS-A POWER AMPLIFIERS

# Push-Pull Amplifiers 30

## Reference

*Electronic Devices and Circuits, Sixth Edition:* Section 16-5, Push-Pull Amplifier Principles; Section 16-8, Distortion in Push-Pull Amplifiers; Section 16-9, Transformerless Push-Pull Amplifiers

## Objectives

1. To demonstrate the push-pull class-B power amplifier.
2. To demonstrate the use of a push-pull class-AB power amplifier to reduce crossover distortion.
3. To demonstrate the complementary push-pull power amplifier.

## Equipment List

1. 2-2N2222 silicon transistors or the equivalent
2. 2N2907 (PNP) silicon transistor or the equivalent
3. DC power supply (15 V)
4. Analog signal generator (variable sine wave at 1 kHz)
5. Resistors: 1-22 kΩ, 2-1 kΩ, 2-10 Ω (0.5 W), 1-8 Ω (0.5 W)
6. Capacitors: 1-100 μF, 2-10 μF (all 25 V)
7. Speaker: 1-8 Ω (0.5 W)
8. Dual-trace oscilloscope
9. Transformers: Triad T-32X driver (1500 ΩCT : 600 ΩCT), Triad TY-48X output (100 ΩCT : 16/8/4 Ω)
10. VOM

## Discussion

A transistor is said to be operated *class-B* when it conducts only during positive half-cycles or only during negative half-cycles of a sine

# EXPERIMENT 30 - PUSH-PULL AMPLIFIERS

wave input. When two transistors are connected so that one conducts only positive current through the load and the other conducts only negative current through the load, the arrangement is called a class-B *push-pull* amplifier. Figure 1 shows one way to construct such an amplifier. Transformer $T_1$, called a *driver* transformer, is used to generate out-of-phase signals to drive transistors $Q_1$ and $Q_2$. Thus, when the base of $Q_1$ is positive, the base of $Q_2$ is negative, so $Q_1$ conducts while $Q_2$ is cutoff. Similarly, $Q_2$ conducts when its base is positive and $Q_1$ is cutoff. The current produced by either transistor flows through the primary of *output* transformer $T_2$ and is coupled to the load by the secondary winding. In this way, both positive and negative current flow in the load, even though only one transistor is conducting at any instant of time. The advantage of the push-pull amplifier in comparison to a class-A amplifier is that it is much more efficient, because there is virtually no power dissipation in a transistor during the time it is cutoff.

One disadvantage of the push-pull amplifier in Figure 1 is that it creates *crossover distortion* in the output. Crossover distortion can be observed as a flattening of a sinusoidal waveform in the regions of the waveform near zero (at the crossovers), and is caused by the nonlinearity of the base-to-emitter junction of each transistor when the base-to-emitter voltage is less than about 0.7 V. To reduce crossover distortion, each base-to-emitter junction can be slightly forward-biased, using a circuit like that shown in Figure 2. The dc voltage divider in this circuit supplies a small forward-biasing voltage to each base. The 10 Ω resistors connected to each emitter further reduce distortion by introducing negative feedback. This amplifier is less efficient than the class-B amplifier because neither transistor cuts off completely. Operation in this manner is called *class-AB*.

Figure 3 shows how a push-pull amplifier can be constructed without using a driver or an output transformer. Note the complementary (NPN and PNP) transistors, $Q_1$ and $Q_2$. When $v_S$ is positive, NPN transistor $Q_1$ conducts and PNP transistor $Q_2$ is cutoff. When $v_S$ is negative, $Q_1$ is cutoff and $Q_2$ conducts. For optimum operation, all components must be closely matched, in which case the dc voltage at point A is $V_{CC}/2$. Coupling capacitor $C_C$ prevents the dc voltage from appearing in the load and eliminates the need for an output transformer. The coupling capacitor affects the low-frequency response of the amplifier. The lower cutoff frequency due to $C_C$ is:

$$f_1(C_C) = \frac{1}{2\pi(R_L + R_E)C_C}$$

## Procedure

1. To demonstrate the transformer-coupled class-B push-pull power amplifier, connect the circuit in Figure 1.

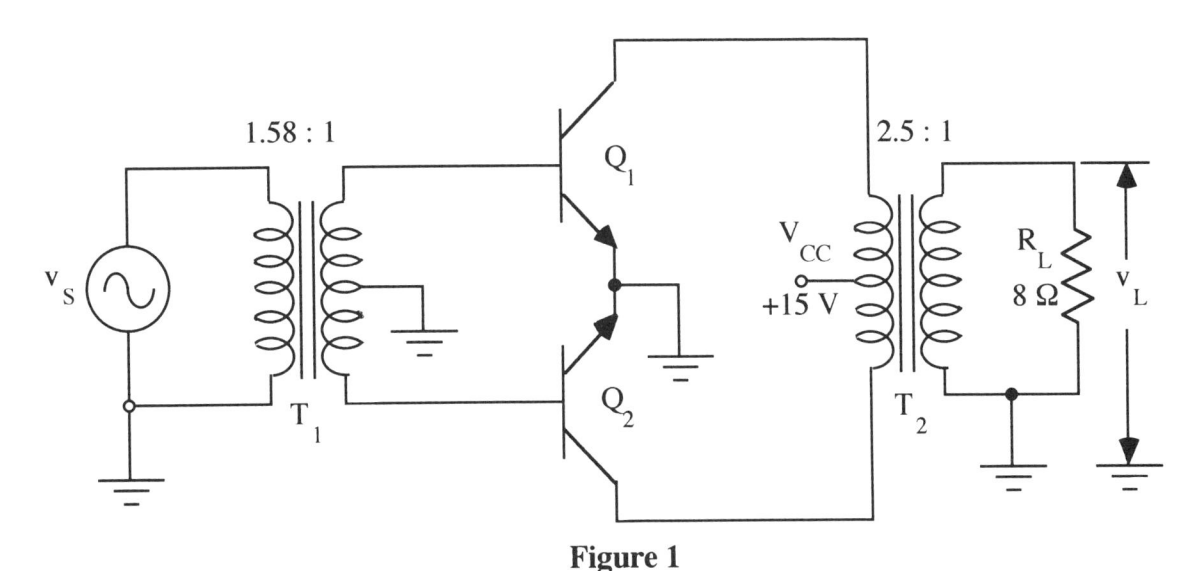

**Figure 1**

2. With $v_S$ = 6 Vp-p at 1 kHz, connect a dual-trace oscilloscope so that $v_S$ and $v_L$ can be observed simultaneously. Sketch the output voltage $v_L$ and the input voltage $v_S$. Note carefully the appearance of the output voltage in the vicinity of the crossovers.

3. Replace the 8 Ω load resistor with an 8 Ω speaker. Note the *quality* of the tone (pleasant, harsh, clear, distorted, etc.). Now increase or decrease the amplitude and frequency of the input signal $v_S$. Note how the *volume* (how loud the tone is) and *pitch* (how high or low the tone is) of the sound changes with changes in input amplitude and frequency.

# EXPERIMENT 30 - PUSH-PULL AMPLIFIERS

4. To demonstrate the reduction of crossover distortion by adding a dc-bias to the class-B amplifier, connect the class-AB amplifier in Figure 2.

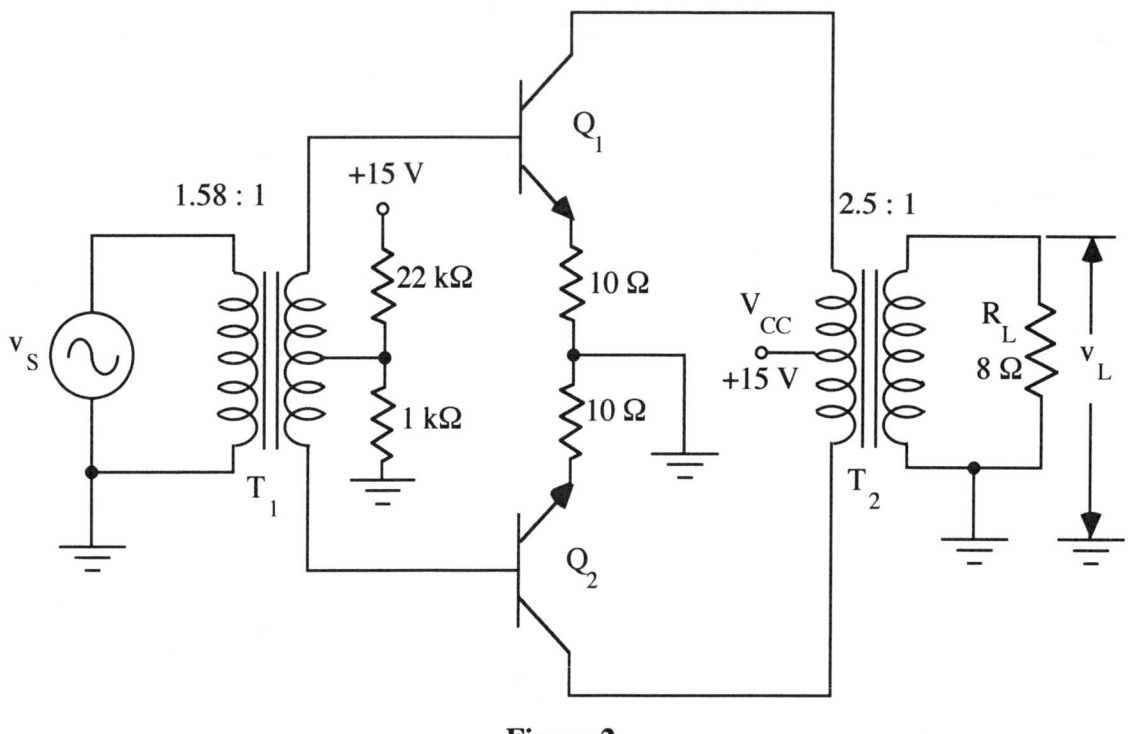

**Figure 2**

5. With $v_S$ = 6 Vp-p at 1 kHz, connect a dual-trace oscilloscope so that $v_S$ and $v_L$ can be observed simultaneously. Sketch the output voltage $v_L$ and the input voltage $v_S$.

6. Replace the 8 Ω load resistor with an 8 Ω speaker. Note any difference in the quality of the tone compared to the sound from the class-B amplifier noted in procedure step 3.

7. To demonstrate the capacitor-coupled, complementary push-pull class-AB power amplifier, connect the circuit in Figure 3.

# EXPERIMENT 30 - PUSH-PULL AMPLIFIERS

**Figure 3**

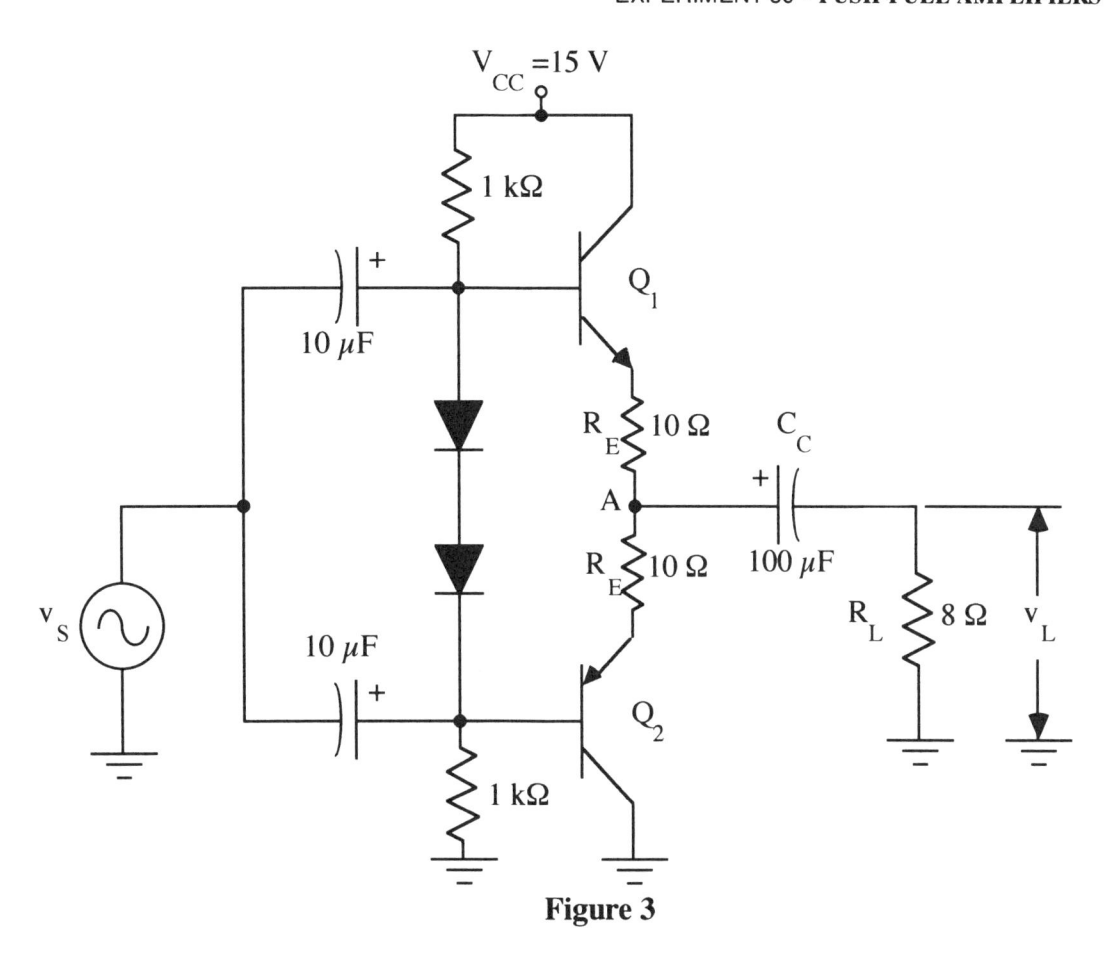

8. With $v_S$ = 3 Vp-p at 1 kHz, connect a dual-trace oscilloscope so that $v_S$ and $v_L$ can be observed simultaneously. Sketch the output voltage $v_L$ and the input voltage $v_S$. Also sketch the voltage at point A in the circuit, with the oscilloscope set for dc input coupling. Note and record the dc level in the waveform at this point.

9. Decrease the frequency of the signal source, $v_S$, until the output voltage, $v_L$, equals 0.707 times the output voltage measured in procedure step 8. Measure and record this frequency, the lower cutoff frequency due to $C_C$, $f_1(C_C)$.

# EXPERIMENT 30 - PUSH-PULL AMPLIFIERS

## Questions

1. Using the sketches obtained in procedure steps 2 and 5, calculate the average load power for the class-B and class-AB power amplifiers. Describe the differences in the quality of the sounds observed in procedure steps 3 and 6. Was there a decrease in load power when the dc-bias circuitry (class-AB) was added? Using these results, discuss the advantages and disadvantages of class-B and class-AB power amplifiers.

2. How did the volume and the pitch of the sound from the speaker vary with changes in input signal amplitude and frequency, as observed in procedure step 3? Explain.

3. Using the sketch obtained in procedure step 8, calculate the average load power for the class-AB complementary, push-pull amplifier of Figure 3. What could cause the positive and negative amplitudes of the output waveform to be slightly different?

4. Calculate the theoretical lower cutoff frequency, $f_1(C_C)$, due to the output coupling capacitor in the circuit of Figure 3. Compare this theoretical frequency to the frequency measured in procedure step 9. If the power amplifier in Figure 3 had to be operated over the entire audio frequency range (20 Hz to 20 kHz), what new value would the output coupling capacitor have to be?

# The BJT Current Mirror 31

## Reference

*Electronic Devices and Circuits, Sixth Edition:* Section 17-3, The Current Source/Sink; Section 17-4, The Current Mirror

## Objectives

1. To demonstrate the use of a BJT as a current source.
2. To construct a BJT current mirror.

## Equipment List

1. 3-2N2222 silicon transistors or an equivalent transistor array
2. 2N2907(PNP) silicon transistor or the equivalent
3. Variable dc power supply (0–5 V)
4. DC power supplies (15 V, 5 V)
5. Resistors: 1-1.5 MΩ, 1-4.7 kΩ, 1-1 kΩ, 1-470 Ω
6. VOM

## Discussion

One of the most important applications of BJTs in analog circuits is as a source or sink of current for other circuits. The terms *source* and *sink* refer to whether the current is provided to or drawn through the load circuit. The reason current sources are so important in IC design is because it is much easier to build transistors than resistors. Therefore, it is more efficient to bias transistor circuits with current sources rather than with resistive dividers, etc.

# EXPERIMENT 31 - THE BJT CURRENT MIRROR

The two fundamental building blocks used in this arrangement are the transistor current source shown in Figure 2 and the current mirror system used for distributing that current among several stages of transistor circuitry.

The current source uses a bias voltage on its base to provide enough current to place the transistor in its active region. The collector current will then be constant for most loads. Rather than a resistor, the load is normally another transistor in a gain stage, diode, differential amplifier, or other configuration.

The current mirror approach shown in Figure 3 is used to distribute current to several stages instead of building separate current sources for each stage. It uses a transistor connected as a diode to set up the base currents for the other loads. Assuming the transistors have matched values of $V_{BE}$, it can be shown that the current for the load resistor $R_{C2}$ can be calculated using the following equation:

$$I_{C2} = \frac{\beta_2}{\beta_1} \times I_{C1}$$

where:
$I_{C2}$ = current through load resistor $R_{C2}$
$\beta_2$ = beta of $Q_2$
$\beta_1$ = beta of $Q_1$
$I_{C1}$ = current sourced by $Q_4$

This same calculation can be used to determine the current through each of the remaining loads, such as $Q_3$, in this example. It should be noted that temperature variation plays an important part because the value of a transistor's $V_{BE}$ varies with temperature. However, the temperature of transistors within an integrated circuit will typically track very well, since they are physically close together, and they are also usually matched, i.e., they have the same value for ß. A transistor array IC can be used in this experiment to minimize the ß variations and the temperature variations.

# EXPERIMENT 31 - THE BJT CURRENT MIRROR

## Procedure

1. Complete the procedures of Appendix A to measure the ß of the three NPN transistors. The following circuit can be used to measure the ß of the PNP transistor:

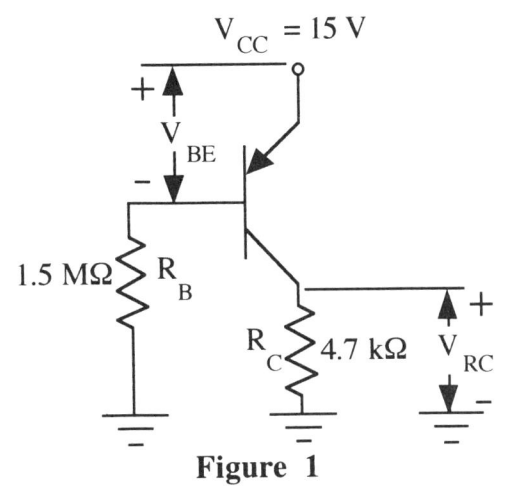

**Figure 1**

2. After measuring the values of $V_{RC}$ and $V_{BE}$, the ß of the PNP transistor can be determined using the following equation:

$$\beta = \frac{(V_{RC})(R_B)}{(R_C)(V_{CC} - V_{BE})}$$

3. To demonstrate the use of a BJT as a current source, connect the following circuit:

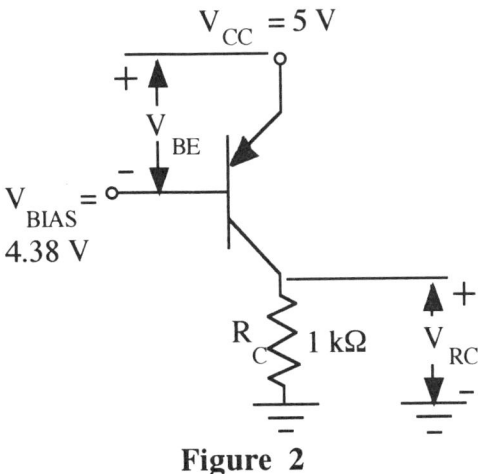

**Figure 2**

## EXPERIMENT 31 - THE BJT CURRENT MIRROR

4. After adjusting $V_{BIAS}$ to 4.38 V, measure and record $V_{BE}$ and $V_{RC}$. Note that the transistor's temperature can affect the measurements, so wait until the voltage stabilizes.

5. Now replace the 1 kΩ resistor in Figure 2 with the current mirror circuit in Figure 3 using either NPN transistors or a transistor array IC:

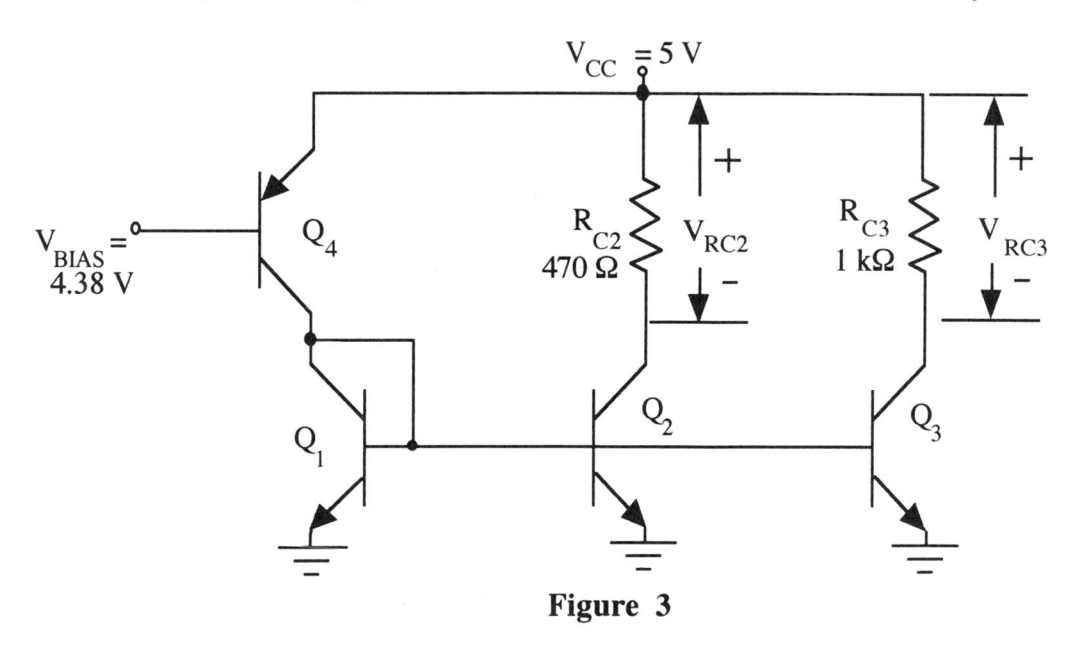

**Figure 3**

6. Measure and record the voltages $V_{RC2}$ and $V_{RC3}$. These can be used to determine the currents $I_{C2}$ and $I_{C3}$.

## Questions

1. Using the measurements made in Appendix A and procedure steps 1 and 2, calculate the ß for the four transistors.

2. Using the measurements made in procedure step 4, determine the current that the current source delivers, $I_C$.

3. Calculate the currents $I_{C2}$ and $I_{C3}$ in Figure 3 based on the results of questions 1 and 2. Compare these to the currents calculated using Ohm's law in procedure step 6.

# Differential Amplifier 32

## Reference

*Electronic Devices and Circuits, Sixth Edition:* Section 17-6, Differential Amplifiers

## Objectives

1. To investigate the differential amplifier in the difference- and common-mode configurations.
2. To determine the common-mode rejection ratio (CMRR).

## Equipment List

1. 3-2N2222 silicon transistors or the equivalent
2. DC power supplies (±15 V)
3. Analog signal generator (0–1 Vpk sine at 1 kHz)
4. Resistors: 1-100 kΩ, 1-15 kΩ, 2-10 kΩ, 1-1 kΩ (5% tolerance!)
5. Potentiometer: 200 Ω or less
6. Dual-trace oscilloscope
7. DVM

## Discussion

Operational amplifiers are the most widely used electronic devices for *linear* (nondigital) applications. The input stage to an *op-amp* is a differential amplifier. Most differential amplifiers are constructed as *integrated circuits,* but to facilitate experimentation, we will investigate a discrete version of the same circuit.

Differential amplifiers can be operated in either of two manners: the input signals can be different, or the input signals can be identical. If the input signals are different, the amplifier is said to be operating in its

# EXPERIMENT 32 - DIFFERENTIAL AMPLIFIER

*difference-mode*. In this configuration, the output voltage will be proportional to the difference in the two input signals. If the input signals are the same, or the inputs are tied together, the amplifier is said to be operating in its *common-mode*.

Figure 1 shows a differential amplifier with small external emitter resistors designed to compensate for any differences in the values of $r_e$ of the two transistors.

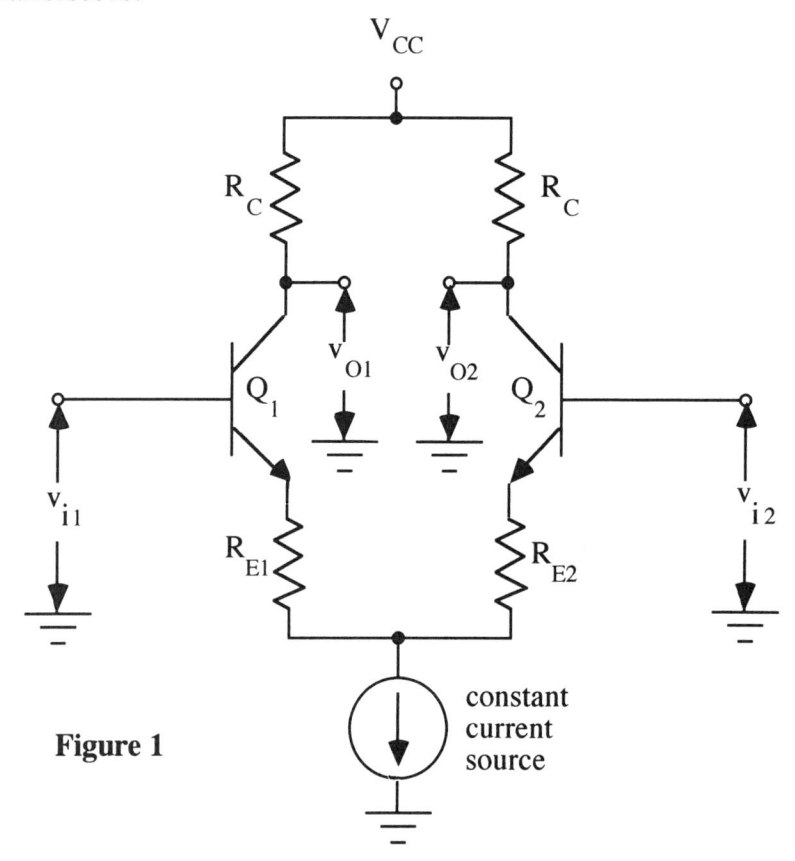

**Figure 1**

The single- and double-ended difference-mode gains of the ideal differential amplifier are:

$$\text{single-ended } A_V = \frac{v_{O1}}{v_{i1} - v_{i2}} = \frac{-R_C}{r_{e1} + R_{E1} + r_{e2} + R_{E2}}$$

$$\text{double-ended } A_V = \frac{v_{O1} - v_{O2}}{v_{i1} - v_{i2}} = \frac{-2 R_C}{r_{e1} + R_{E1} + r_{e2} + R_{E2}}$$

## EXPERIMENT 32 - DIFFERENTIAL AMPLIFIER

The differential input resistance is:

$$r_{id} = \beta(r_{e1} + R_{E1} + r_{e2} + R_{E2})$$

where:
$r_{id}$ is the total ac resistance between the input terminals

The following equations apply to operation of the differential amplifier in its common-mode—when the two input signals are equal in magnitude and phase:

$$\text{single-ended } A_v = \frac{v_{O1}}{v_{i1}} = \frac{v_{O1}}{v_{i2}}$$

$$\text{double-ended } A_v = \frac{v_{O1} - v_{O2}}{v_{i1}} = \frac{v_{O1} - v_{O2}}{v_{i2}}$$

The most important benefit of the differential amplifier in common-mode operation is the elimination of noise present at both inputs. Ideally, any noise voltage present at both inputs is cancelled out by the phase inversion of the two sides of the amplifier. The common-mode rejection ratio (CMRR) is a ratio of signal gain to noise gain—that is, how well the amplifier amplifies the wanted signal and cancels the unwanted noise. The *single-ended* CMRR is a ratio of the single-ended difference-mode voltage gain to the single-ended common-mode voltage gain. The double-ended CMRR is a ratio of the double-ended difference-mode voltage gain to the double-ended common-mode voltage gain. Typically, the CMRR is extremely high (75 to 100 dB is not uncommon).

$$CMRR_{(dB)} = 20 \log \left| \frac{A_d}{A_{cm}} \right|$$

where:
$A_d$ is the difference-mode voltage gain
$A_{cm}$ is the common-mode voltage gain

# EXPERIMENT 32 - DIFFERENTIAL AMPLIFIER

## Procedure

1. To *match* two transistors, complete the procedures in Appendix A. Apply the procedures in Appendix A until two transistors are found with very similar values of ß (within 10 or 15).

2. Using the matched transistors for $Q_1$ and $Q_2$, connect the differential amplifier circuit in Figure 2. Make sure that the two 10 kΩ resistors connected to the differential amplifier's collectors are closely matched also (no more than 5% deviation). Also measure the maximum resistance of the potentiometer (across its outer terminals).

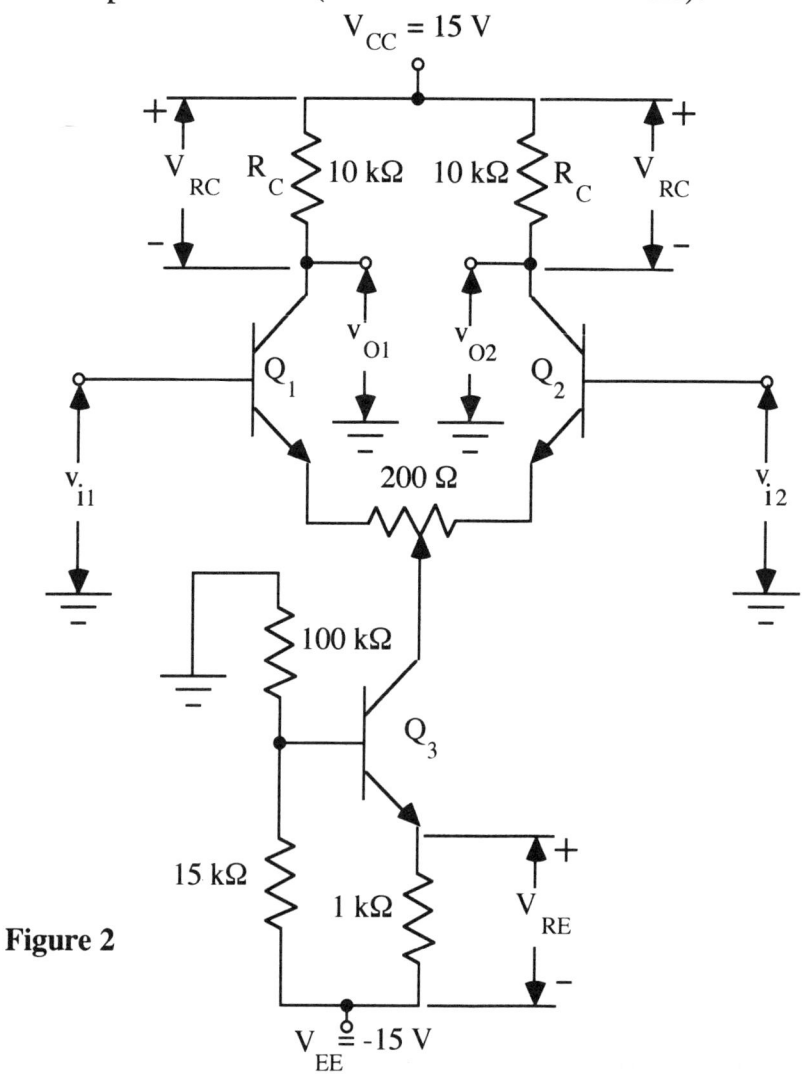

**Figure 2**

# EXPERIMENT 32 - DIFFERENTIAL AMPLIFIER

3. With $v_{i1}$ and $v_{i2}$ set to 0 V (grounded), connect a digital voltmeter between the outputs $v_{O1}$ and $v_{O2}$ so it will read dc volts. Now adjust the 200 Ω potentiometer until the voltmeter reads 0 V dc. This procedure is called *balancing* the differential amplifier.

4. To determine the quiescent currents in the circuit, measure the dc voltage $V_{RC}$ across each collector resistor and the voltage $V_{RE}$ across the emitter resistor of $Q_3$.

5. Set $v_{i1}$ to 50 mVpk at 1 kHz and ground $v_{i2}$. Measure the ac voltage from the center tap of the potentiometer to ground. Connect a dual-trace oscilloscope to observe and measure the single-ended output voltages $v_{O1}$ and $v_{O2}$ with respect to ground. If the oscilloscope has a difference-mode setting, also measure the output difference voltage ($v_{O1} - v_{O2}$). In each case note the phase relation with the input.

6. Set $v_{i2}$ to 50 mVpk at 1 kHz and ground $v_{i1}$. Repeat the measurements of procedure step 5.

7. Using a single function generator, set both $v_{i1}$ and $v_{i2}$ to 1 Vpk at 1 kHz. Repeat the measurements of procedure step 5. The inputs may have to be increased above 1 Vpk if the amplifier has an extremely small common-mode voltage gain because the output voltage may otherwise be too small to measure.

# EXPERIMENT 32 - DIFFERENTIAL AMPLIFIER

## Questions

1. Using the dc voltage measurements made in procedure step 4, determine the collector currents in each of the three transistors. Use these values to calculate the internal emitter resistances, $r_{e1}$ and $r_{e2}$, of $Q_1$ and $Q_2$, respectively.

2. Using the results of question 1 and the maximum resistance of the potentiometer (which equals $R_{E1} + R_{E2}$), calculate the difference-mode single-ended voltage gain with $v_{i1}$ set to 50 mVpk at 1 kHz and $v_{i2}$ set to 0 V. Also calculate the differential voltage gain (or double-ended voltage gain) using the same inputs. Compare these with the measured values obtained in procedure step 5.

3. Calculate the value of $r_{id}$ using the results of question 1 and the value for ß as determined from Appendix A.

4. Using the results of procedure step 7, calculate the differential common-mode gain and calculate the CMRR in dB.

5. What is the purpose of the common-emitter stage, which has the differential amplifier in its collector circuit?

# CMOS Logic 33

## Reference

*Electronic Devices and Circuits, Sixth Edition:* Section 18-2, Transistor-Level Implementation of CMOS Combinational Logic Circuits; Section 18-3, A Design Procedure for Creating CMOS Combinational Logic Circuits

## Objectives

1. To demonstrate the use of MOSFETs in combinational logic circuits.
2. To build NAND and AND gates using a CD4007 IC.

## Equipment List

1. 1-CD4007 dual complementary pair plus inverter IC
2. DC power supply (5 V)
3. DVM

## Discussion

Modern digital VLSI (very large scale integration) ICs utilize a mixture of analog and digital technologies. Usually, an analog signal is processed, converted to digital, then further processed in the digital domain. Many times the final stages may be used to convert this signal back to an analog signal. With this mix of technologies, it is helpful to understand the design criteria and device limitations involved.

CMOS (complementary MOSFET) designs are the most commonly used in VLSI chips found in microprocessor, communications, and signal-processing ICs. Their inherent benefits include high-speed operation, low

# EXPERIMENT 33 - CMOS LOGIC

power supply requirements, and ease of implementation at the transistor level.

Combinational logic, such as NAND/AND, and OR/NOR gates are standard building blocks used in VLSI circuits. The CD4007 transistor array IC contains two complementary pairs of MOSFETs and a complementary pair inverter. It can be used to implement various gate configurations for the purposes of designing VLSI circuits and demonstrating the use of complementary pairs of MOSFETs in combinational logic circuits.

## Procedure

1. To investigate the use of the CD4007 in constructing combinational logic circuits, connect the following circuit: (note that the gates are already tied together internally in the IC)

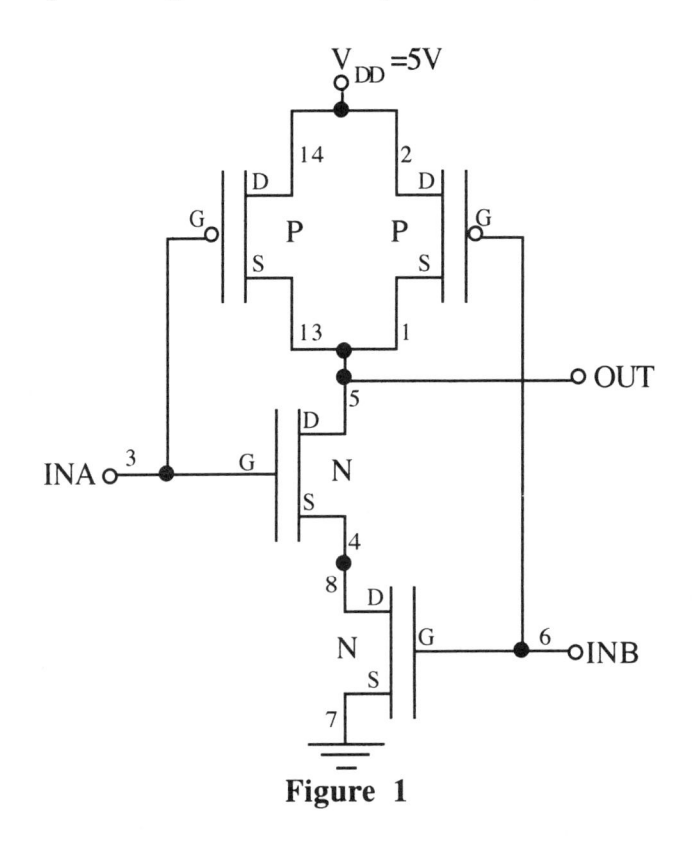

**Figure 1**

EXPERIMENT 33 - CMOS LOGIC

2. Measure and record the voltage OUT for each value of INA and INB in the following truth table for the circuit of Figure 1:

| INA | INB | OUT |
|-----|-----|-----|
| 0 V | 0 V |     |
| 0 V | 5 V |     |
| 5 V | 0 V |     |
| 5 V | 5 V |     |

3. Now add the inverter section of the IC to the output as shown in Figure 2. (Note that the gates are tied together internally as is the connection of the P-channel's source to the N-channel's drain.)

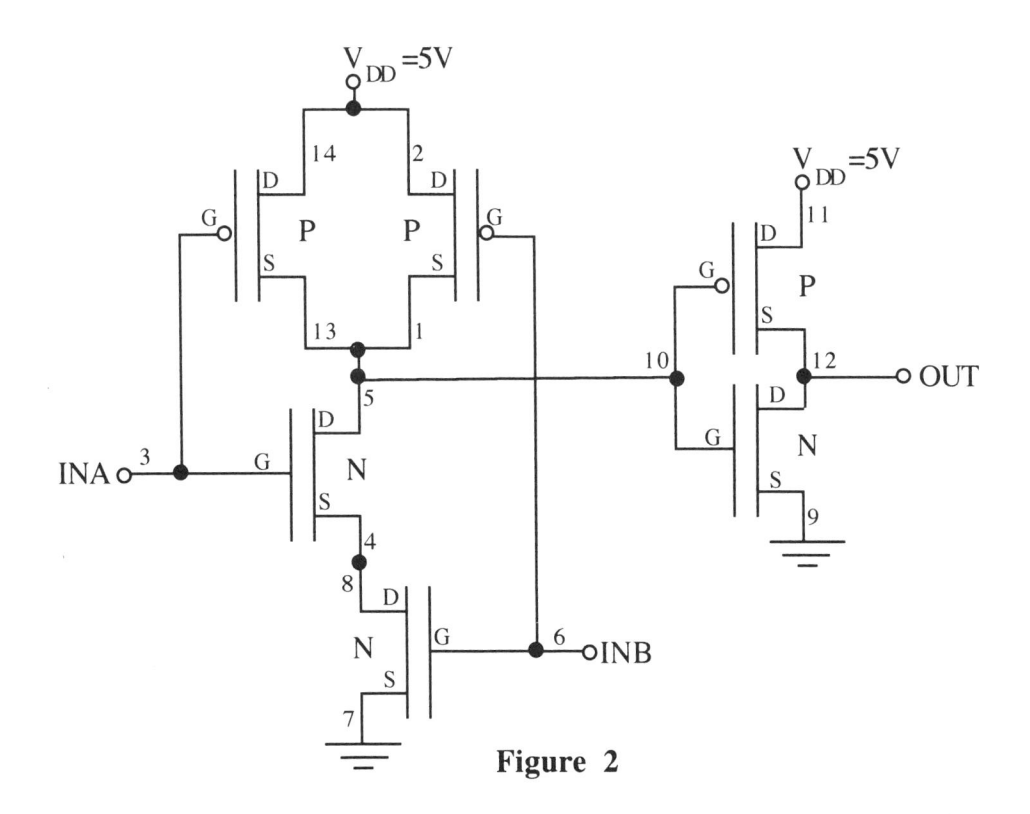

**Figure 2**

231

# EXPERIMENT 33 - CMOS LOGIC

4. Measure and record the voltage OUT for each value of INA and INB in the following truth table for the circuit in Figure 2:

| INA | INB | OUT |
|-----|-----|-----|
| 0 V | 0 V |     |
| 0 V | 5 V |     |
| 5 V | 0 V |     |
| 5 V | 5 V |     |

5. With INB set to 5 V, use a potentiometer connected as a voltage divider to experiment with varying the INA voltage lower than 5 V to see how this changes the resulting output voltage OUT. Measure the voltage where the output results change or become unpredictable.

## Questions

1. What combinational logic operation was implemented in the circuit of Figure 1?

2. What combinational logic operation was implemented in Figure 2 by adding the inverter circuit?

3. How low could the INA voltage be adjusted without changing the output voltage OUT? What does this mean about the noise immunity of CMOS ICs?

# β Measurement   A

## Objective

This appendix can be used to measure the ß of a bipolar junction transistor for use in the experiments in this manual.

## Equipment List

1. 2N2222 silicon transistor or the equivalent
2. DC power supply (15 V)
3. Resistors: 1-1.5 MΩ, 1-4.7 kΩ
4. VOM

## Procedure

1. In order to determine the ß of the transistor, connect the following circuit (after measuring resistors):

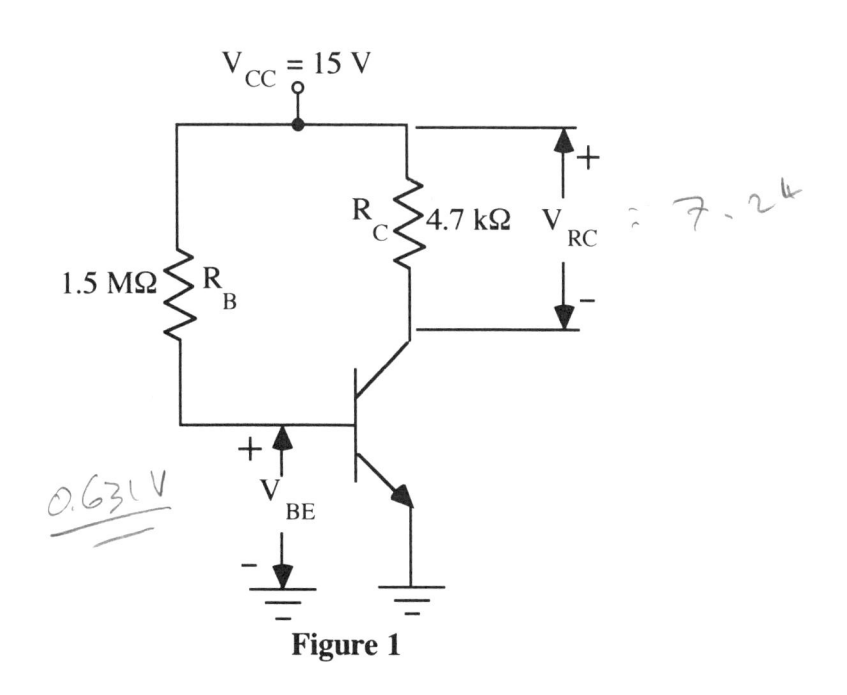

**Figure 1**

$V_{CC} = 15$ V, $R_B = 1.5$ MΩ, $R_C = 4.7$ kΩ, $V_{RC} = 7.24$, $V_{BE} = 0.631$ V

# APPENDIX A - ß MEASUREMENT

2. Measure the voltage across the collector resistor $V_{RC}$ and the base-to-emitter voltage $V_{BE}$.

## Calculations

Using measured values for resistance and the measurements made in procedure step 2, calculate the ß of the transistor using the following equation:

$$\beta = \frac{(V_{RC})(R_B)}{(R_C)(V_{CC} - V_{BE})} = \frac{(7.24)(1.5M)}{(4.7K)(15 - 0.631)}$$

$$\beta = 160.8$$

Use this value of ß when making calculations in the experiments.

# JFET Measurements  B

## Objective

This appendix can be used to measure the values of $I_{DSS}$ and $V_P$ of a JFET for use in the experiments in this manual.

## Equipment List

1. 2N5459 silicon N-channel JFET or the equivalent
2. DC power supplies (15 V and variable)
3. Resistor: 1-1 kΩ
4. VOM

## Procedure

1. In order to determine the values of $I_{DSS}$ and $V_P$ of the JFET, connect the following circuit (after measuring resistor):

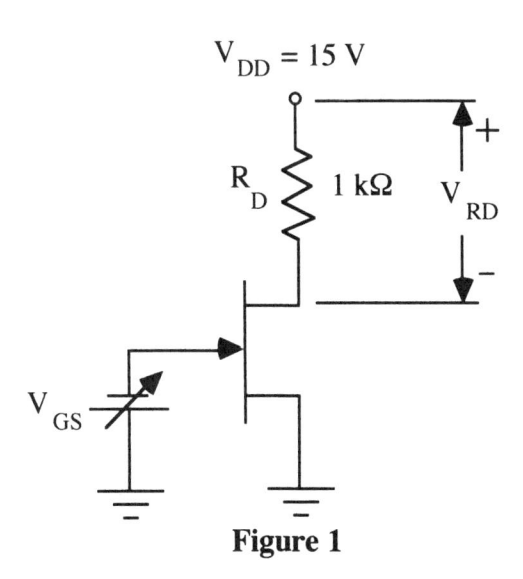

**Figure 1**

## APPENDIX B - JFET MEASUREMENTS

2. With $V_{GS} = 0$ V, measure and record the voltage $V_{RD}$ across the drain resistor. Then $I_{DSS} = V_{RD}/R_D$. = 8 V

$= \dfrac{8}{1k} = 8\mu A$

3. Slowly increase $V_{GS}$ (more negative) until $V_{RD} = 0$ V. This is the point where $I_D = 0$ A. The value of $V_{GS}$ where $I_D = 0$ A is $V_P$.

3.339 Volts

$I_D = 0.5 \beta (V_{GS} - V_T)^2$

# SPICE C

## Introduction

SPICE is a circuit simulation program available on various mainframe and microcomputer systems. It uses input files consisting of *statements* describing the circuit components, and *commands* or *control statements* that describe the functions to be performed on the circuit. The following is a brief summary of some input file statements and commands necessary for completion of the experiments in this book. For a more comprehensive explanation, see Bogart, Rico and Beasley, *Electronic Devices and Circuits, Sixth Edition*, Prentice Hall Publishing, 2003.

## Statements

The first step to setting up a SPICE input file is to number all nodes in the circuit, as shown in the example circuit of Figure 1. The order is unimportant, as long as one node is labeled 0. It is good practice to label ground as node 0 to simplify locating ground in the statement list.

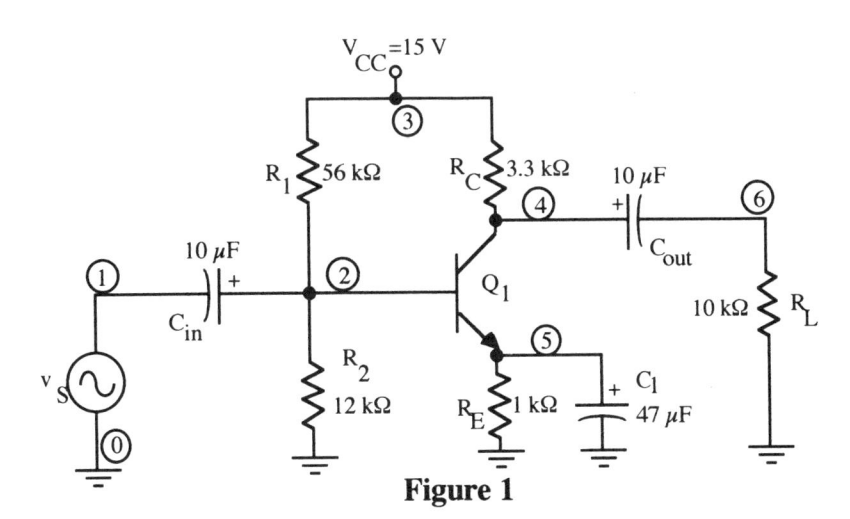

**Figure 1**

The table on the following page uses SPICE statements and commands to demonstrate functions necessary to complete SPICE exercises in this book.

237

APPENDIX C - SPICE

| Example | Description |
| --- | --- |
| BIFET CASCODE | Title |
| VCC 3 0 DC 15 | $V_{CC}$ is a 15 V dc supply between node 3 and gnd. |
| R1 3 2 56K | $R_1$ is a 56 kΩ resistor between nodes 2 and 3. |
| CIN 2 1 10U | $C_{in}$ is a 10 μF capacitor between nodes 2 and 1. |
| R2 2 0 12K | $R_2$ is a 12 kΩ resistor between node 2 and gnd. |
| RC 4 3 3.3K | $R_C$ is a 3.3 kΩ resistor between nodes 4 and 3. |
| RE 5 0 1K | $R_E$ is a 1 kΩ resistor between node 5 and gnd. |
| RL 6 0 10K | $R_L$ is a 10 kΩ resistor between node 6 and gnd. |
| C1 5 0 47U | $C_1$ is a 47 μF capacitor between node 5 and gnd. |
| COUT 4 6 10U | $C_{OUT}$ is a 10 μF capacitor between nodes 4 and 6. |
| Q1 4 2 5 TYPE1 | $Q_1$ is a transistor using the model TYPE1, its C, B, and E terminals are connected to 4, 2, and 5. |
| VS 1 0 AC 1 SIN(0 0.1 5K) | $V_S$ is a source between node 1 and gnd. During .AC analysis it has an amplitude of 1 volt, & during .TRAN analysis it has an amplitude of 0.1 volt at 5 kilahertz with a 0 V dc offset. |
| .MODEL TYPE1 NPN BF=150 | This models the transistor TYPE1 using NPN and BF, which is the beta of the transistor. |
| .AC DEC 10 40 18K | Does frequency response (spectrum analyzer) from 40 Hz to 18 kHz with 10 steps per decade. |
| .TRAN 20US 10MS | Does transient analysis (O'scope) from t = 0 to 10 msecs. using 20 μsec steps or increments. |
| .PRINT AC V(6) V(1) | Prints the calculated values for node 6 and node 1 for each of the increments defined by the .AC statement. |
| .PLOT TRAN V(6) V(1) | Plots the calculated values for node 6 and node 1 for each of the increments defined by the .TRAN statement. |
| .END | Always the last statement. |

The following are other statements needed to complete the SPICE exercises:

| Example | Description |
| --- | --- |
| .DC V1 -5 5 .1 | Does a dc sweep. The supply $V_1$ is swept from −5 V to 5 V in 0.1 V increments. |
| D1 1 2 DIODE1 | D1 is a diode modeled by DIODE1 with anode connected to node 1 and cathode to node 2. |
| .MODEL DIODE1 D BV=12 | This models the diode DIODE1, which is a 12 V zener diode since its breakdown voltage is only 12 V. |
| J1 3 5 6 FET2 | $J_1$ is a JFET modeled by FET2 with drain, gate, and source connected to nodes 3, 5, and 6, respectively. |
| .MODEL FET2 NJF VTO=-5 BETA = 0.5M | This models the JFET FET2, which is an N-channel (PJF is a P-channel) with $V_P = -5$ (always labeled as negative) and beta = 0.5E-6. Beta = $I_{DSS}/(V_P^2)$. |
| X1 3 4 5 OPAMP | This is a subcircuit defined below. The inverting input, noninverting input, and output are connected to nodes 3, 4, and 5, respectively. |
| .SUBCKT OPAMP 1 2 3 | This is a subcircuit defining an op-amp. |
| RIN 1 2 1E12 | $R_{in}$ is the input resistance of the op-amp. |
| EOP 2 3 1 2 1E9 | This is the op-amp with open-loop gain = 1E9. |
| .ENDS OPAMP | Always the last statement of a subcircuit. |

# Signal Generator Divider    D

## Objective

This appendix can be used to reduce the signal level of a signal generator that has a limited output selection, for use in the experiments in this manual. It will preserve the output impedance while reducing the signal level about 20 dB.

## Equipment List

1. Signal generator
2. Resistors: 1-1.5 MΩ, 1-4.7 kΩ
3. Dual-trace oscilloscope

## Procedure

1. To reduce the output signal of a signal generator by 10 (–20 dB) connect the following circuit: (Use values from Table 1 for $R_1$ and $R_2$.)

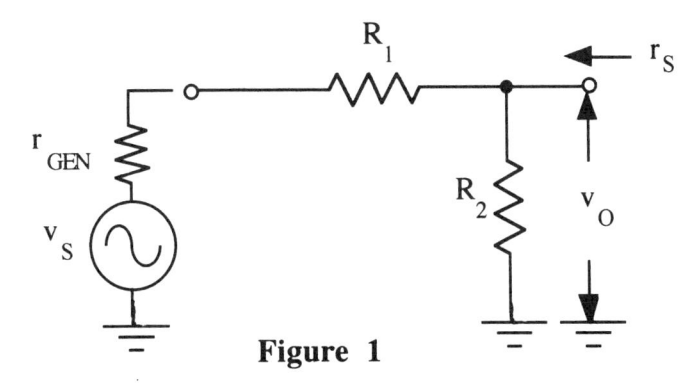

**Figure 1**

| $r_{GEN}$ | $R_1$ | $R_2$ |
|---|---|---|
| 50 Ω | 470 Ω | 56 Ω |
| 75 Ω | 680 Ω | 82 Ω |
| 100 Ω | 1 kΩ | 120 Ω |
| 600 Ω | 5.6 kΩ | 680 Ω |

**TABLE 1**

## APPENDIX D - SIGNAL GENERATOR DIVIDER

2. To verify the operation of the voltage divider, set $v_S = 1$ Vp-p and measure the voltage $v_O$ across the collector resistor $R_2$. It should measure $\approx 100$ mVp-p.

3. To verify the output resistance, $r_S$, of the voltage-divided circuit, connect a 1 k$\Omega$ to 10 k$\Omega$ potentiometer (rheostat) across $R_2$. Adjust the resistance until the voltage across it is 0.05 Vp-p. The resistance of the rheostat then equals the system's $r_S$.

## Calculations

The output voltage $v_O$ in Figure 1 can be calculated by:

$$v_O = v_S \left( \frac{R_2}{R_{GEN} + R_1 + R_2} \right)$$

The output resistance $r_S$ in Figure 1 can be calculated by:

$$r_S = R_2 \| (R_1 + R_{GEN})$$

If the generator's internal resistance can't be found in Table 1, values can be determined by:

$$R_1 \approx R_{GEN} \times 1.1$$

$$R_2 \approx R_{GEN} \times 9$$

# Component Pin-Outs

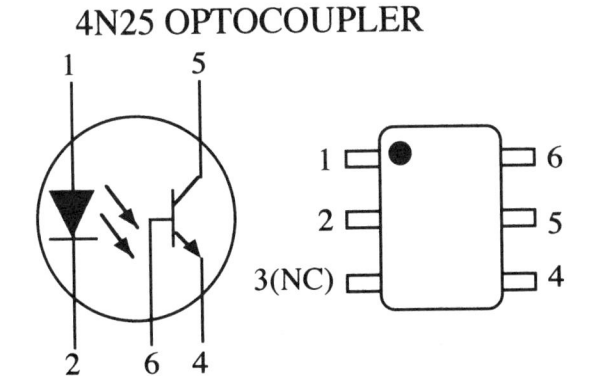

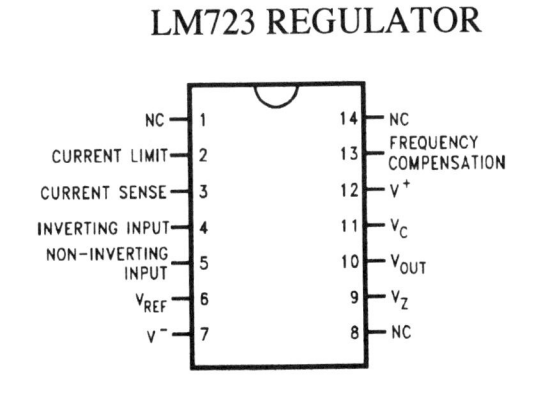

**E**

### 7805 (LM340-05)

Output
GND
Input

### 1N4004 Diode / 1N4736 Zener

Cathode    Anode

### NTE 5437 SCR

Gate
Anode
Cathode

A
G
C

### NTE 6410 UJT

B1 E B2

E
B2
B1

### NTE 5608 TRIAC

Gate
MT1
MT2

MT2
G
MT1

### NTE 6402 PUT

A G K

A
G
K

### 4N25 OPTOCOUPLER

1   5
2
3 (NC)

1   6
2   5
    4

### LM723 REGULATOR

| Pin | Signal | Pin | Signal |
|---|---|---|---|
| 1 | NC | 14 | NC |
| 2 | CURRENT LIMIT | 13 | FREQUENCY COMPENSATION |
| 3 | CURRENT SENSE | 12 | $V^+$ |
| 4 | INVERTING INPUT | 11 | $V_C$ |
| 5 | NON-INVERTING INPUT | 10 | $V_{OUT}$ |
| 6 | $V_{REF}$ | 9 | $V_Z$ |
| 7 | $V^-$ | 8 | NC |

241

## P2N2222 NPN TRANSISTOR

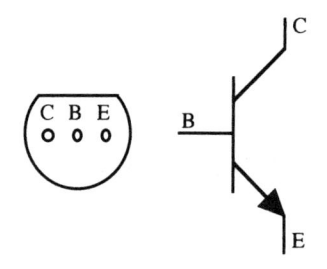

## P2N2907 PNP TRANSISTOR

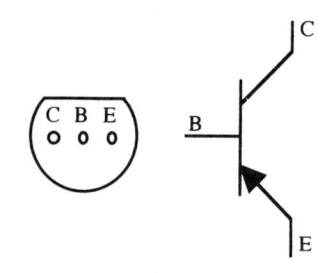

## 2N5459 N-Channel JFET

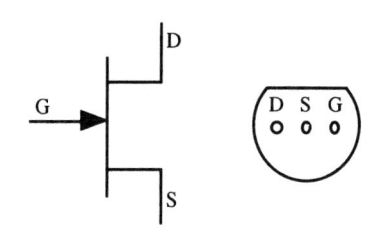

## 2N4351 N-Channel MOSFET

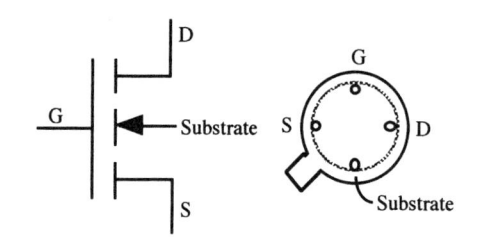

## LM741 (DIP package)

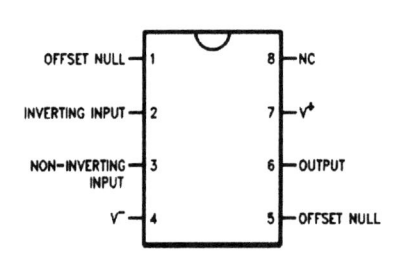

## CD4007 (DIP package)

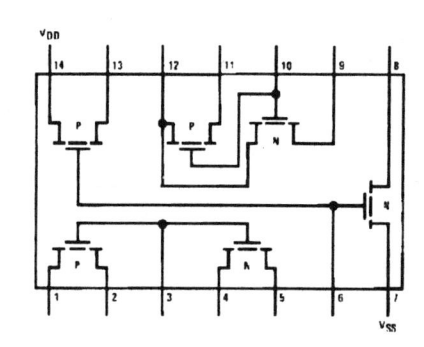

## DAC 0800 (DIP package)

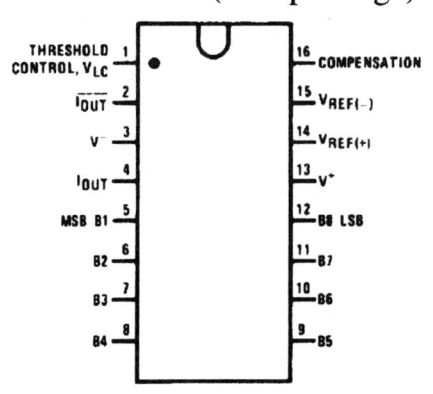

## ADC 0800 (DIP package)

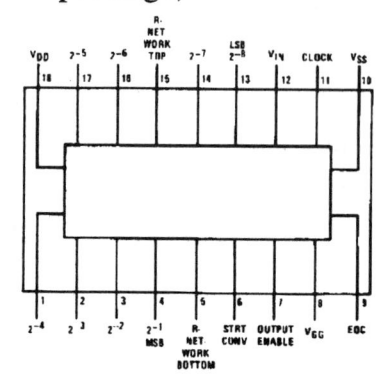